OPERATION
DOLBY

THE EX-COPPER WHO WAS FRAMED AND THROWN IN JAIL FOR PLAYING IT STRAIGHT

CONSTANTINE BULLER

OPERATION
DOLBY

THE EX-COPPER WHO WAS FRAMED AND THROWN IN JAIL FOR PLAYING IT STRAIGHT

MEMOIRS

Cirencester

Published by Memoirs

MEMOIRS
PUBLISHING

25 Market Place, Cirencester, Gloucestershire, GL7 2NX
info@memoirsbooks.co.uk www.memoirspublishing.com

Printed in England

OPERATION DOLBY

"The price good men pay for indifference to public affairs is to be ruled by evil men."

Plato

"This story is true. Protocol imposed on the writer has protected the identity of the guilty. It is only reasonable therefore that the names of the innocent should be offered the same protection in the constant battle against the principalities, powers and rulers of this world, where they remain concealed. Where truth battles against falsehood, love against hate and good against evil in the realms of the world, the flesh, the devil and his evil spirits."

Constantine Buller

CONTENTS

INTRODUCTION

▪ ▪ ▪ ▪ ▪ ▪ ▪ ▪

My grandfather, Richard Alexander Buller, was the eldest child from his father's first marriage; he had thirteen brothers and sisters of mixed Irish and Scottish descent. The family lived in a small village called Ballynakelly, Dungannon, in Northern Ireland. Richard lied about his age and joined the British Army to become a boy soldier and see the world.

While serving as a military policeman, Richard was stationed in Greece just after the Second World War. He met and quickly married a petite dark-haired local girl called Coralie Georgiades, whose father, Constantine, taught languages and mathematics at the American Farm School in Thessalonica. His wife, Marika, taught embroidery to the female students.

As fate would have it, Richard's chance meeting and subsequent marriage to Coralie instigated his union with a family whose heritage could be traced back to a Sultan in the Ottoman Dynasty. The Georgiades family occupied a prestigious and all-encompassing position as chefs to the Sultan and the entire Ottoman Royal Family (III).

The outbreak of World War I found Turkey lined up with the Central Powers (Ref: Smyrna 1922: The Destruction of a City).

Although Turkish troops succeeded against the Allies in the Gallipoli campaign (1915), Arabia rose against Turkish rule, and British forces occupied (1917) Baghdad and Jerusalem. In 1918, Turkish resistance collapsed in Asia and Europe. An armistice was concluded in October and the Ottoman Empire came to an end. The Treaty of Sèvres confirmed its dissolution. In 1922, with the victory of the Turkish nationalists, who had refused to accept the peace terms, the Sultan was overthrown and Turkish persecution began to remove the Greeks and Christianity from Turkey. On 29 October 1923 Turkey was declared a republic and modern Turkey's history began.

The Greeks were repelling the Turkish invasion and showing compassion to all their Turkish prisoners of war, but they were ordered by the Allied forces to stop fighting and lay down their arms on the order of General Bristol, under the threat that they would become the enemy of the allied forces and would be attacked.

The Greeks and Italians had been promised Smyrna for their part in joining and fighting with the Allied forces during the First World War, but what they had not been told was that the Allies, together with the Americans, had betrayed them and had also promised Smyrna to the Turks in a clandestine agreement for oil. As a result of this situation the Turks were allowed to butcher the Greeks in their homes and on the streets and Smyrna was destroyed. A small Muslim region in Smyrna was left untouched and the Turks, having claimed a victory, rebuilt the area and gave it a new name, Izmir.

Constantine and Marika Georgiades were two of the fortunate evacuees who had fled Constantinople and had journeyed through to the Smyrna region. They were lucky enough to board a Japanese ship anchored in the harbour. The captain, seeing the plight of the Greeks, ordered the cargo to be dumped overboard and rescued as many souls as they could, literally pulling men, women and children out of the water. The ship sailed on to Thessalonica. Those Greeks who were unfortunate enough to swim out to the British ships were given a completely different experience. On the orders of General Bristol the evacuees were pushed back into the sea and left to drown. Those who were able to swim ashore were mercilessly butchered by the Turks.

At the end of their careers, Constantine and Marikas Georgiades retired to the United States of America. They died in Montana on 22nd December 1979 and 3rd August 1993 respectively.

Richard and Coralie Buller had five children, each born in a different country. This book focuses on one of those children, named Constantine after his grandfather. Constantine has an elder brother, Richard, named after his father and born in Egypt; an older sister called Coralia, named after her mother and born in Northern Ireland; a younger brother John, born in Bath, and a younger sister, Sophie, was born in Malta.

Constantine received his education predominantly in western English-speaking schools. Because of his unusual name and dark complexion he suffered consistent bullying at school from children and teachers alike. As a result of this he was moved continually from school to school. After having attended twelve junior schools Constantine finally settled into a small village school in Alresford, near Colchester in Essex. To the amazement of his teachers, Constantine was the only boy to pass the Eleven Plus examination, together with one girl in his year. The headmistress took it upon herself to advise Constantine's mother to send him to Brightlingsea Secondary Modern School. The boy was devastated to hear this news. His heart had been set on going to Colchester Royal Grammar School, where he could be with his elder brother, Richard.

Constantine stood and listened in the hall of the family bungalow while the Headmistress talked to his mother. "It will help to firm him up a bit. You know, he's a bit too softly spoken and weak" she said.

After hearing his mother agree to this request, Constantine switched himself off emotionally and academically and resolved not to work. When he arrived at the new school the bullying continued, unchecked by the staff. Constantine was singled out and attacked by the older boys at every opportunity during break times, having his head pushed down toilets, which were then flushed. As he was made to wear shorts for the first year with his elder brother's old purple jacket, the older boys whipped his legs with sticks, punched, kicked and spat on him during break and called him filthy names.

Unable to retaliate, Constantine memorised the faces of his attackers and waited patiently for the opportunity to take revenge on every one of them, mercilessly. He quickly learned that the one thing a bully hated most of all was the sight of his own blood, so he made sure that he spilled as much of it as he could in the playground. The other children soon learned to give him a wide berth. As a result of this he was again labelled a troublemaker.

Constantine's father, being an Irish Protestant, insisted that all the children attend St Peter's Church in Alresford, where Constantine was invited to sing in the choir. Constantine had been baptised in the Greek Orthodox Church of St. George, Valletta, Malta when he was five years old. When he asked his father to explain the difference between the Orthodox Church and the Protestant Church, his father said "They're the same thing, you stupid bastard! They run along together. Don't you know anything?" Constantine never asked again. He continued to receive his 2s 6d wage for attending all the services, for his work in the choir and for being the soloist.

As an apparent sign of mutual respect of faiths within this 'parallel' Christian understanding between both parents, on the fourth Sunday of every month the family attended the Orthodox Monastery of St John the Baptist in Tolleshunt Knights. It was here that Constantine came to meet Archmandrite Sophrony, a well known monastic in the Eastern Orthodox Church who had come from Mount Athos to retire and compile the writings of Saint Silouan.

Archmandrite Sophrony was born on September 23, 1896 of Orthodox parents in Russia. He began a career as an artist, first in his homeland, and after the Revolution he went to Paris. Here the aspirations of his heart moved him to seek a life in Christ. He first enrolled in the newly-opened Paris Orthodox Theological Institute; the formal study of theology, however, did not satisfy his internal longing, and he soon set off for the Holy Mountain, where men strive not for thirty-fold, or sixty-fold, but one hundred-fold for the deification which is possible in the here and now.

Constantine left school in Brightlingsea and joined Essex Police on 8th February 1973 after serving three years as a police cadet. Here he met his first wife, Sarah, who was also a serving police officer. On their first date, which happened to be his 20th birthday, Sarah conceived their first child. In an attempt to save the child, Constantine quickly proposed marriage, and the wedding was hastily arranged by her parents for Saturday 22nd November 1975. However, to Constantine's horror, Sarah insisted on aborting their first child before the wedding. Her reason was "It's my body and I will do what I want to do with it. I'm not going down the aisle with a lump under my wedding dress and that's final!"

Constantine, much to his regret, allowed the wedding to continue and he married Sarah in St James Anglican Church, West Tilbury as planned. Before the service he was violently sick in the graveyard. Looking up for help from his best man, he was told "It's too late to pull out now!"

There followed five bumpy years of marriage, during which Constantine and Sarah transferred forces and joined the Metropolitan Police. Sarah quickly became very popular and was immediately recruited on to the CID, where she worked extremely long hours which frequently kept her away from home overnight.

Constantine was recruited on to the Crime Squad, where he sometimes worked alongside the Flying Squad on large and complex cases. During this time he saw his Detective Inspector suspended for taking bribes over fraudulent insurance claims which were agreed with victims of burglaries, drugs being planted on innocent victims returning home from working in London, stealing cash from criminals during their arrest, handling stolen property from burglaries and committing burglaries. He would have preferred to have stayed at Tilbury and was quite horrified at how unprofessional the working practices of the squads in the

Met were. Consequently he became very disillusioned with the police.

In 1978 the couple bought their first house and left the police force, securing higher-paid civilian work. They went on to have two children in quick succession, Michael and Luke.

Constantine started his new job as a Free Trade Manager for a national brewery on 7th December 1979. All appeared to be going well at work, but his family life with Sarah was becoming unbearable. In January 1981, while on a management course in Tamworth, Constantine met Janet in a local pub. Janet was with a group of friends and Constantine joined their gathering. The two immediately struck up a friendship which turned into a night of passion; they took themselves to a local hotel and spent the night together. It was the first time Constantine had betrayed Sarah in this way, and his inner frustration at Sarah's constant physical rejection left him with absolutely no feelings of regret. Janet and Constantine took what they needed from their dalliance and agreed never to meet again. That night of passion was to remain their secret.

When Constantine returned home from Tamworth, as fate would have it, Sarah announced angrily that she was pregnant with his third child and the baby was expected in September. Janet and Constantine were true to their word and never contacted each other again. They went on living their own separate lives, putting aside their frenzied night of passion.

CHAPTER ONE

■ ■ ■ ■ ■ ■ ■ ■

JUDGEMENT DAY

My father thought nothing of knocking back twelve pints of Ben Truman on his way home from work. He had to agree with me that we couldn't think of a better job than mine; a beer taster for a reputable brewery. I have to admit that I shared many of my father's inherent characteristics, which over the years had goaded my anger, leading me to feel much shame and regret for all the hurtful things I have done in my life.

Although working for the brewery had its benefits, it also opened the door to opportunity, which inevitably allowed me to take advantage of situations where I could satisfy my inner passions as they presented themselves to me. One day I used this flexibility to arrange my working hours to take Sarah shopping and to concentrate on trying to improve my relationship with her. I wanted to try to forge a new beginning for our broken marriage with a focus on our third son, Peter, to spend more time with Michael and Luke and for us to bond together more as a family.

It had been a distinctly cold and dry morning and the afternoon appeared to be turning out to be much the same. I had planned my day well and made the Poacher's Pocket Coaching House in Burlescombe my last call of the day. The owner, John, was a good man, tall, well built and with a completely bald head and an enormous grin. From my limited knowledge of John, his great passion in life was cricket. He wore his Somerset County Cricket Club tie with such deep pride that one might have suspected he wore it with his pyjamas when he finally retired to bed instead of the Club House.

I looked as if I might be John's twin brother, although I was slightly taller, heavier in build and "bald on top with a bit of hair around the sides" as Michael frequently described my hairstyle. At first glance John reminded me of an older version of the great swimmer Duncan Goodhew MBE. Duncan was my sporting hero, but my achievements in athletics as Essex shot and discus champion for three consecutive years and being in the winning team in numerous national swimming and lifesaving competitions were insignificant in comparison to Duncan's success.

He knew the licensing trade well and always kept our products in perfect condition, particularly the Ushers Pale Ale on draught. I put that quality, in part, down to the fact that his pub was within easy reach of my house, which always gave me a good excuse to call in on my way home from the depot in Taunton.

As I came in through the front entrance I met Pat, John's wife, a well-educated petite woman with short jet-black hair. She was clearing away dishes from the lunchtime session. She smiled and waved me through to the cellar.

"John's trying to fix one of the coolers in the cellar" she said with a knowing nod and a warm, mischievous smile.

"Thanks Pat. All right to go straight through?" I pointed in the direction of the cellar and hesitated momentarily, waiting for a response. Pat was trying to wipe off a knob of butter from one of the heavy oak tables with her index finger. She smeared what she could on to a pile of dirty plates piled high with serviette, coffee pots and knives and forks, leaving the finger-stained glasses behind. Her face fell as she returned to the job in hand, lost in her own Cinderella dreams of happier days. Pat suddenly noticed my hesitation, raised her weary puckered brow and said: "Go straight through, he'll be pleased to see you."

I opened the heavily-insulated door and peered into the cellar. As soon as John saw me he stretched his back to its full height, grinned and reached out for my hand, abandoning the job at hand. "What about a drink, Con?" he asked.

I gave him a disappointed smile and said "Not today, John. I'm on a mission."

We left the cellar and walked down the narrow passage to a small bar, reminiscent of the helm of a tall ship, cosseted between the restaurant and the main bar and with a panoramic view through the bay window on to the old coaching route where modern wheeled vessels now rumble on past on a more determined passage along the A38 between Wellington and Waterloo Cross. The pub creaked like an old ship. It was decorated throughout with timbered walls and timber panelling and was full of charm, warmth and character.

All my business clients called me 'Con' and not 'Costa', as this allowed me and my family to make a distinction between family and friends and work. It had always been 'Con' for work and Costa for family and friends. It seemed to make sense, because when a pub had run out of beer at 11.30 pm and the client tried to call me at home to try to get me to drop a barrel off at short notice, Sarah would immediately know if it was to do with work if they asked for 'Con' and she would invariably say I was out. Calling a brewery representative at that time of night to say you had run out of beer was definitely taking liberties!

The change in my name for work stemmed from when I

joined the police in 1973 and was posted to my first station, an old converted house with large sash windows and a faded front door which was used as a urinal by seamen returning to their ships after staggering back from the Seamen's Mission, the Apostleship of the Sea, Stella Maris at 66 Dock Road. The yard at the rear was only big enough to park three Mini panda cars.

One of my colleagues, Mick, asked "What's your name?"

"Costa" I told him. The station felt cosy, so I assumed, in my naivety, that they would call me by that name.

Mick looked very uncertain and thought for a moment. Then he asked "What sort of name is that?"

"It's Greek and that's what my family call me. My full name is quite long so it makes it easier to pronounce."

Mick hadn't finished. He went on holding this dumb twisted expression and said "So what's your proper name then?" and he waited for my response.

Still trying to be polite, I said: "Oh, I see, my full name? Oh that's Constantine."

Mick appeared to be really struggling to understand this new information and spluttered out: "Concertina?"

I said "No, Constantine."

Mick replied indignantly: "What sort of name is that?"

"It's my name!" I snapped.

Mick appeared to have worked out a solution. He announced: "From now on your name is Con. It sounds more manly that Concertina. But to start with we are going to call you the Sprog and you'll be getting all the shit jobs that come in. When we get someone else in to take your place you can move up in position."

So from that day onwards, the police station lost its cosy feeling and I began to use Con for work. It makes a good divide between work and my personal life and I have got used to it now.

Back to John. I usually had a drink with him, so I had to explain.

"Listen, John, I'm off to Taunton in a few minutes with the family, so I'll have a drink with you next time I'm in. Is that OK?"

John opened his arms, put his left hand on my shoulder and shook my right hand in a warm and familiar manner "No problem, Con. I expect we'll see you again soon."

It was unusual to finish my calls for the day without having an alcoholic drink and I was pleased to go home without the smell of alcohol on my breath as I left to drive the short distance home. I bade John and Pat farewell and climbed into the car and drove back to the house.

Uffculme was the small Devonshire village where I lived with my wife Sarah, a five foot four, freckle-faced, stern looking, blunt, self elected and outspoken fashion, personality and design guru. She had straight, frustrated shoulder-length red hair with a classic bang cut fairly straight above her eyebrows; She always insisted on any reference to its colour as auburn. Sarah knew exactly what she wanted and inevitably got her own way. (Bitch! I hated her. Why did she have to kill our first unborn baby?) How she achieved this mystified me.

Michael, the eldest of our sons at nearly four, was tall for his age, slim and with a mop of blonde straight hair. You could dress him in the morning and at bedtime his clothes still looked fresh and clean. Luke, on the other hand, who had turned one the previous April, was a cheeky little chap and the opposite in outward appearance to Michael. It didn't matter what you put him in, he would need to be changed again after fifteen minutes, even on a good day. His hair was a lighter blond than Michael's and for some strange reason he hated new shoes and clothes, preferring to wear his brothers hand-me-downs, even though there was no need to do so. Peter, although he was only a few weeks old, had all the hallmarks of being the same temperament as Michael, quiet, good and clean.

They were really excited to see me. As I entered the house I heard Michael shout "Daddy!" and he ran into my arms for a cuddle. I swept him off his feet and said "Hello son. Have you been a good boy for Mummy?" I immediately realised that this was a silly question because Michael was always such a good little boy. Michael was beaming. "Yeah!" he replied.

I turned to look at Luke, who was standing with both arms extended, his little fingers trying to reach out to touch me. "Hello Luke. Don't you look smart in your new coat?" I bent down and lifted him off the ground too. Now I was holding them both in my arms for a cuddle. "Come on lads, we're going shopping!"

I lowered them on to the floor and turned to pick up Peter, who was asleep in his carrycot. We all walked out to the family car. I opened the back hatch and gently placed Peter inside. Sarah helped the two boys climb into the rear seats and belted them in.

We drove out of the village and headed north up the M5 towards Taunton. Our shopping trip was under way and it wasn't long before we drove into the car park in the old market place.

Sarah opened the front passenger door and said "They'll be fine for ten minutes."

I had hoped that she was joking, but from the look on her face I could see that this was not the case. "You can't just leave three children in a car, Sarah!" I said in surprise.

Sarah responded immediately, giving me one of her "I am not amused" glares. "They'll be fine. We won't be long. Come on! We could have been there and back by now if it wasn't for your dithering."

I could feel an uncomfortable moment approaching which normally brought on an argument over parental responsibility, so I tried to compromise as usual. "I'll wait in the car with the boys and you can go to Debenhams on your own" I said.

Sarah's mood turned ugly and her face reflected her displeasure at my remark "You just can't be bothered, can you?" she snapped.

I was trying to remain composed in an attempt to keep her from blasting off in a temper in front of the children. So I tried to reason with her. "I can't leave three children alone in a car and go shopping, Sarah. My conscience and sense of responsibility to the boys just won't let me do that."

Sarah was adamant that she wanted me to go with her to Debenhams, which was only about three hundred metres away, but it meant leaving the children strapped in their car seats and the baby in the back of the car. The reason for this was quite simple. I had discovered that she had run up a bill on her storecard for £1,400. I had had to go to see my bank manager, for the third time, about rolling it over yet again into our mortgage, and he had suggested that this time I should destroy her storecard. So I had cut up her Debenhams card and now, if she wanted to buy something, she would need to use cash.

If only I had realised the effect this would have had on her spending, I would have done it years ago. Give Sarah a store card with a £1,600 credit limit and before you can spit at the wall she would be up to it. But give Sarah cash, dirty filthy lucre, and she would be crushed. It somehow paralysed her appetite to spend money. I suppose it was the reality of physically seeing it in her hand that made it real. I was fascinated. This change in character was truly incredible and I was determined to use it to my full advantage. Having me with her somehow eased this burden as it gave her some sort of comfort when the money had been spent.

Not that this was necessary. In my opinion it was easier to purchase a stain remover to remove a mark from a piece of furniture that was less than a year old than to go out and buy a new three-piece suite, only telling me when I found it in the lounge when I came home from work!

I remembered challenging Sarah about it. "Where's the old suite gone?" I asked.

"Oh, I meant to tell you. I ordered this one last week and Sue has got the old one. She really needed hers replacing too."

"But it was less than a year old!"

"Yes I know, but it had that awful stain on it. This one has got a sprung edge and the floral pattern looks so much better. What do you think?"

"I think it should go back!"

Now Sarah raised her voice. "Here we go again. What's the matter with you?" She grabbed her handbag from the floor of the car, looked across at me and gave me a hard glare. "Why do you have to make things so bloody difficult?"

"Calm down, Sarah. There's no need to do this in front of the children. We left Peter in the car before. Remember? You insisted on leaving him alone and look how upset he was when we got back. He was screaming his head off. He was distraught!"

Sarah climbed out of the car and snapped back "You're such a bloody drama queen! He was hungry, that's all. They've all been fed!"

It felt as if Sarah was trying to provoke some sort of display of emotion or even anger from me in response to her behaviour, but like her passion in the bedroom, she had always managed to remain uninterested and at the same time, resolute. Sarah found this particularly annoying and hard to deal with, as I found her lack of interest in me. Her sudden loss of temper had often led to violent outbursts which had been so severe that she had kicked in the door panel in the lounge on two separate occasions. So I lowered my voice.

"Sarah, we had abandoned him in the car for too long and he

was terrified. You could tell by the look on his little face!"

Sarah snapped back "Just hungry, that's all! They'll be fine for a few minutes. Michael can keep an eye on the others." She turned to face Michael, who was sitting directly behind her. "Won't you Michael?" But poor Michael was bemused by what was going on.

"Sarah, how can you expect a three-year-old boy to look after his one-year-old brother and a baby?" I retorted.

"You're a bloody drama queen!" she shouted back. She started to close the car door.

"It's neglect, Sarah. I'm not prepared to take that risk. Go on your own. Did you remember to bring the money I gave you this morning?"

"Yes! What the hell am I going to buy for two hundred and fifty pounds?"

"You'll find something."

"OK. I won't be long." She marched off in the direction of her favourite store.

"Cow!" I muttered. "Bye then, darling!" I said sarcastically. She ignored my comment, so I raised my voice to make sure she could hear me and answered for her "Bye then, Costa." No response, so I called out "You can take Michael and Luke with you if you want to."

I wasn't making a very good job of relationship building and it made me feel a sort of justification for betraying her earlier in the year. I could feel the cold dry air gushing in through the open window and looked around the car park to see if anyone was listening to me rattling on and making a complete idiot of myself. The car park was full of cars but devoid of people.

Sarah turned momentarily and snapped back in anger "You love them so much, you look after them! I won't be long."

I thought for a moment. I couldn't stand being in the house

with her. I had been able to once, but not any more. Not on my own. So after having called on pubs all day with work, once I put the boys to bed, I would end up walking into the village on my own to sit at a bar with a group of total strangers and listen to them bleat on about absolutely nothing of any significance, rather than sit in the house with Sarah.

Michael and Luke always loved my stories, so I turned to them with a big silly grin on my face and said "OK lads, what's that I can hear? Bleep, bleep!" I raised my hand as if I was answering a telephone "Commander Daddy here. What's happened? Oh. Really? OK. A helicopter's crashed into the sea? Where? There are dangerous sharks in the water! We'll be straight over!"

Michael and Luke looked at me wide-eyed "What's happened Daddy?" Luke looked across at his brother and then back to me for a response.

"Can we get there in time? Will we save the crew? This is a job for Major Michael, Captain Luke and Commander Daddy!" I immediately began to brief the rescue team in an accent with American overtones. "Our mission is to rescue the crew of a helicopter that has crashed into shark-infested waters. Are we going to accept the mission, men?"

Michael and Luke's response was instant. "Yeah!" they shouted, and big grins came over both their faces.

I thought for a moment and said "What shall we do now, men? Shall we launch the rescue mission?"

There was a unanimous cheer. "Yeah, Daddy!"

"That's Commander Daddy to you" I said and they both grinned. "OK, what vehicle are you going in Major Michael?" Michael thought carefully for a moment and I felt compelled to offer him some constructive advice, as Commanders tend to do to their three-year-old sons. "What do you think? Helicopter?

Speed boat? Jet? A tank wouldn't be a good idea, it's water and you know how heavy tanks are. Water? Sharks? Now I don't really know what's best."

"Daddy! I know! Helicopter!" Michael had raised his arms above his head in excitement.

"Get your helicopter ready then Major Michael, and that's an order!"

Following the chain of command, I now turned to Luke. "OK Captain Luke, what vehicle are you going to choose?"

Luke looked puzzled. "My name's not Captain" he moaned. "My name's Luke! I want to be me in the story!"

"It is you, son. You're in the army and your rank is Captain and you are in the story. That's why you are called Captain Luke."

Luke fell silent while he worked out what I had just said, trying to think what to say next. He looked around the car in panic, so I thought I should come up with some suggestions.

"Well, how about a submarine?"

Luke's response was instant. "Yeah! Sunbarine!"

As I launched into the story I became aware of people filing past the car and smiling as they heard the boys laughing and giggling. Throughout all of this excitement Peter slept quietly on in the back of the car.

During the forty five minutes Sarah was gone I checked on Peter three times. I jumped out of the car and opened the back hatch and stuck my nose into his carry cot, then gave him a kiss and let him sleep on. Any parent knows that there's a very special warmth and smell with their child, especially a newborn baby, that gives you that assurance that your baby is truly a part of you. Michael and Luke had been really good babies and Peter was no different. He never whinged or cried for no good reason. I have to admit that he was perfect in my eyes. All my boys are.

"Mummy's coming boys!" I said. I climbed out of the car, opened the back and placed Sarah's small bag of shopping carefully next to the carrycot. Then I squeezed the hatch shut quietly again. I climbed back into the car and said "You didn't get much."

She thought for a moment. "I don't know what it is, it was just so much easier when I had the card. I saw something and tried it on, but when I went to buy it I changed my mind."

"Why?" I said.

"I don't know. I just saw all that money and didn't want to let it go."

I started the engine and said "Oh".

Within a few minutes we were heading down the M5 towards Exeter and the boys were now singing away happily together in the back of the car. Sarah's mood could swing like the pendulum on a grandfather clock, and now she appeared to be in a slightly better frame of mind. "Thank God for retail therapy and for my bank manager's advice" I thought. So I tried to retain her lighter disposition, knowing that she wanted some non essential shopping from Tiverton.

Sarah glanced across at me and said "Why the smug look?"

"No reason Sarah, I was thinking about the story I was telling the boys just before you came back to the car." I wasn't - I was thinking about her chopped up store card.

As I drove down the M5 towards Exeter I had no idea that what was about to happen would change my life forever. If I were a time traveller I would, without hesitation, immediately transport myself back in time to that dreadful day, shut all the doors and windows, hide in the house and wait for it to pass. But alas, I am not a time traveller. In my ignorance and through a lack of any divine revelation whatsoever, I carried on compromising and pandering to the whims of Sarah, my poor judgement and fate.

CHAPTER ONE

Of all the days I could have chosen to go shopping I chose Yom Kippur. It is often considered to be the holiest day in the Jewish calendar and the Day of Atonement, but that meant nothing to me. I am not a Jew but Sarah's father was, or so I have often reasoned with myself, trying to blame him for what was about to happen. He, of all people, should have given me a warning that this is considered the day when God decides the fate of each human being. Even though we couldn't tolerate each other, Daniel, being a lapsed Jew, at least owed me some consideration. He might have said something - I don't know, I probably wasn't listening to anything he said anyway, mainly because I thought I had everything under my personal control.

As we approached our exit from the M5, I looked across at Sarah and said.

"Right?" I thought for a moment and then went on. "I mean, is it right or left at junction 27?"

Sarah was looking through a Dulux colour chart, trying to decide what colour to paint the dining room. She looked up momentarily and said "I should get the rest of the shopping really."

"So it's over to Norman's then?" I said.

Sarah seemed rather distracted as she looked through the various colours "I suppose so" she said.

"What about Peter's feed?" I quickly glanced at the chart and made a note of where her index finger was resting – barley. My next job.

Sarah glanced at her watch and squinted as she calculated Peter's next feed. "He should be OK for another half an hour" she said.

The thought of painting the house again agitated me. I could guarantee that as soon as I had finished painting the last wall, after going through the whole interior and exterior of the house,

Sarah would be looking at paint charts again. I had never met anyone before who had to paint the whole house, inside and out, every year. So I couldn't resist saying "Breastfeeding would have been so much easier".

I immediately regretted this inappropriate and hurtful remark, aimed at her decision to bottle-feed Peter, as she had now done for all three boys.

Sarah's response was electric. "Let's not go there again! I'm just not interested, so leave it alone! Anyway it's too late now."

An eerie silence fell on us for a moment. Sarah seemed to be really irritated by my remark. "Why do you have to keep going on and on about breast feeding?" she said. You keep going over old ground and we've moved on now."

There was a long silence.

I made a mental note to leave a two-foot strip unpainted next time I went through the house. That would mean it wasn't quite finished, so it would be left to go beyond the magic twelve months before the next overhaul.

"You've moved on, you mean." I couldn't resist the opportunity to have the last word again on the subject of breastfeeding.

As I approached the slip road at junction 27 I double-checked with Sarah in case she had decided to change her plan to go to Norman's again, which happened quite frequently.

"Right then?"

"Yes!" Sarah snapped.

"So that's right then?" I was pushing back a wall of anger that was raging inside of me and trying to give the appearance of calm. Not an easy task for me.

"Yes, it's right. Stop mucking around and just drive will you!"

"Yes, Mein FÜHRER!" Sarah hated me using that

expression, which only made me want to use it more frequently in situations such as these.

Sarah did not speak again on our way into town. She got out of the car in silence and I waited with the children.

I turned around to look at their questioning eyes.

"OK boys, how about another story?" There clearly wasn't a need to ask a second time as the response was unanimous: "Yeah!"

Peter had been seen by Julie the midwife that morning and he'd received a glowing report. "Peter is a healthy little boy" she had said. I kept opening the back of the car to check on him and stuck my nose into his carrycot in between stories. I took a deep whiff of that familiar baby smell. I love it! You can tell a lot from the smell of a child and I could always tell if the children were sickening with something just by their smell. Peter smelt good.

"He's asleep" I assured myself.

I have never stopped questioning myself about that. Did I miss something? My unconscious mind keeps beating me up with feelings of guilt. That niggling doubt still kills me inside to this very day. When I revisit the scene in my mind, even with all the constant reasoning, I still keep coming up with the same answer: "He was fine. I checked him!"

A few moments later Sarah emerged from Norman's and climbed into the passenger side of the car while I placed the shopping around the carrycot and returned the trolley. Then we made our way home. Michael and Luke were still on a high from their story and they were singing nursery rhymes in the back of the car as Peter slept on.

As the car approached the house I spoke quietly "Quieten down now, boys, we don't want to wake Peter. He's due a feed."

How is it that babies and small children always seem to wake up when the car stops or when it goes quiet? I was trying to think ahead.

"OK Dad." More giggles.

I swung the car gently on to the drive and Sarah got out with the two boys and quietly scampered into the house. I opened the back of the car and gently lifted out the carry cot.

"Strange" I thought. Suddenly fear began to race through my body. There was normally a bit of bounce.

"Nah" I thought and walked towards the front door. But as I entered I felt my chest tightening. My whole body was gripped in panic. I pushed the half open door back against the wall and lifted the carry cot up.

There was something wrong with Peter's colour. I felt my legs go weak.

"Sarah, quick!" I shouted. She ran from the kitchen and into the small narrow hall and stared at me in panic.

"No!" she screamed. As a former policewoman, she immediately sensed that something terrible had happened.

"Go next door and call an ambulance" I barked. '"Now!"

Sarah ran out of the front door behind me screaming hysterically. I had to make a conscious effort to steady my legs. To protect the boys from what was happening, I ran up the stairs to the main bedroom. I lifted Peter out of his cot and immediately checked his vital signs. Nothing.

"Come on Peter, don't die on me for God's sake!" I gasped, checking again. No breath, no heartbeat. I checked his throat for blockages and then started mouth-to-nose resuscitation. "Not too hard, he's only a baby" I thought as I cradled him in my arm. I was trying to remember all that I had been taught when I was doing my training for my life-saving competitions. I needed to remember quickly what I had to do.

I checked his colour. 'It's coming back' I thought and then

called out "Peter, hang in there son!"

I opened his eyes to check his pupils, then carried on. I could hear the sound of sirens in the distance. Suddenly the crew walked into the bedroom.

I looked across at them in desperation, calling out in panic "His colour's back, but there's no heartbeat and he won't breath on his own!"

The crew glanced at each other and the taller of the two said "I'm Dave, I'm a paramedic. Can I take a look at your son?"

I quickly and carefully passed Peter over to him and Dave checked Peter's breathing and searched for a pulse. His response was very quick. "You're wasting your time. Peter's gone."

I was flabbergasted. "Gone? How do you know that?"

Dave replied. "Trust me, he's gone. You're welcome to carry on until the doctor arrives if you want to. He's on his way, he'll be here in a minute."

The other paramedic, who was in his forties with a rosy complexion and rather rotund, said "You look like you know what you're doing, why don't you just carry on?"

"I'm an ex-copper."

He nodded and said "Ah, right. Do you want to carry on?"

I reached out to Dave and said "Is that OK?"

Dave, looking very sympathetic, passed Peter back to me. "Yes, of course it is."

I immediately restarted mouth-to-nose resuscitation and gentle heart massage. The next thing I can remember was Dave chipping in.

"The doctor's here."

Dr Pike gathered Peter into his arms, placed him quickly on to the bed and began his examination. He tugged at the studs on Peter's little white Babygro and in a moment he reported "He's gone, I'm afraid."

I was desperate "Are you sure? Can I carry on?" I wanted to reach out to help my son and I was prepared to accept any odds. I searched their faces for some hope of recovery. "It might work? He might respond in a minute?"

Dr Pike was adamant. "Peter's gone. You're going to have to accept that. He's passed on." He called out the time of death and the crew made a note on their report sheet. Dr Pike looked at me sympathetically and said "Have you got a towel?"

I went to the airing cupboard in a daze and took out a large white bath towel. I opened it up and wrapped Peter in it gently, then passed him back to the doctor.

"Good night Peter, my little boy" I said. I kissed him and stood motionless in the room as they started to leave. I felt absolutely numb and would have gladly swapped places with Peter.

Dr Pike said "I'll make sure Peter is properly looked after for you." Then he carried my son's lifeless body out of the house.

It was only then that it really hit me. I fell on to my knees and started shaking uncontrollably. "Why? Why take my little boy away from me?" It was so hard to accept this loss and I was so angry with myself. I looked heavenwards in shame, wanting an explanation or some kind of response, but there was nothing, absolutely nothing.

Later that evening a policewoman arrived, telling us she needed statements from us about what had happened. I was still in shock and was unable to speak or compose myself, let alone make a statement. I remained silent, riddled with guilt.

"That's OK, I understand." Sarah said. She seemed remarkably detached and composed. Thirty five minutes later, the officer was gone.

In the evening, Geoffrey, our tall, thin, undernourished Anglican priest, arrived. He tapped on the door and Sarah let him in. He seemed reluctant to sit in a chair for some reason, feeling more comfortable parking his bum on the edge of our bow window, which I thought was rather strange and made me feel uneasy.

"I received a call from a neighbour and they told me what had happened" he said. "I thought I should come to see if there was anything that I could do to help."

I was still really struggling with my guilt and grief, and all I could think of saying was "Yes, there is actually. You're a man of God aren't you? Tell me, you know, just explain it simply, what did we do wrong?"

In my heart I felt I had selfishly betrayed all my family and it was really all my fault. But perhaps Geoffrey could see the truth.

Geoffrey seemed a little surprised. He answered softly "Nothing. It just happens like that."

I was confused and needed to know more. "How can God give us someone so special as Peter and then take him away again? We've only had him for a few weeks. Why? Tell me why?" The guilt was bearing down on me like a giant press.

Geoffrey was full of compassion. "God gathers up his little lambs when He chooses and he has taken yours" he said.

Sarah remained quiet, but I crashed on. "Is that all you can say? Is that it? Is that all you can come up with?" I was furious. Though I knew it was my fault, I wanted and needed to blame someone else, anyone, anyone else but me.

Geoffrey was looking even more uncomfortable now. He moved position slightly and I assumed he had lost the feeling in one of his legs.

"Yes, God took your son. He can take any of us at any time."

I'd had enough of all this God talk. I wanted to let Geoffrey know how I felt. So I went on "I'm sorry, but I can't accept this right now. If there is a God and He is all knowing and all loving, He would surely have some compassion on us as a family and our poor baby."

I was overwhelmed with anger and guilt was consuming me, sweeping in from all sides. I was in despair and began to shake uncontrollably. It was easier to reject God in these circumstances, because I couldn't cope with my guilt and grief, let alone help Sarah or Michael and Luke with theirs, although Sarah appeared to be able to remain calm and detached from all of what was going on. As Geoffrey was leaving I spoke again.

"Reverend? Sorry, Geoffrey. Can I ask a favour?" The priest remained composed and respectful even through my ranting. He stopped in his tracks.

"Of course. What is it?"

"Peter hasn't been baptised. Can you find out where they have taken him and go and see him and give him a blessing for me?"

He smiled warmly "Of course I will. Consider it done."

I started sobbing uncontrollably and the priest left us in our grief. He walked down our small drive, climbed into his grey Peugeot estate and disappeared from sight.

The following evening I was in Michael's room telling him and Luke a story when Sarah stuck her head around the door.

"I'm off. See you later. Night night boys. Be good for Daddy won't you?" I was quite surprised to see Sarah in her tracksuit so soon after Peter's death and I tried to comprehend her intentions. Was she going for a walk? Perhaps she needed some space? Air, maybe?

I asked her where she was going. She quickly responded in a matter of fact way, "Badminton of course."

I was trying to think if she had a match to play that compelled her to go out as she played in a local league. So I asked her "Who are you playing?"

She smiled with a broad grin and said "Just the usual crowd."

Yes, I thought, the usual professional crowd of lechers who can give you the attention you crave. I was trying to conceal the anger I had started to feel at what appeared to be her careless attitude towards our loss. It appeared to me from what she had told me previously, that all they were really interested in was trying to get into her knickers. It hadn't taken her long to feel the need to get back into that crowd, I thought.

Her straight shoulder-length auburn hair was loosely tied back by a large bronze clip and she looked as though she had spent hours applying her makeup. She smelt clean and was smothered in perfume, which reminded me of how she looked when we had first met.

"Oh, OK" I said, but secretly I was thinking "This is unbelievable!"

"See you later. Say goodnight to Mummy, boys" I said. The boys responded in a habitual way to my direction and were clearly oblivious to my concerns for Sarah's unsympathetic and carefree attitude. Michael and Luke spoke at the same time. "Goodnight Mummy."

Sarah turned on her heels and trotted down the stairs and I heard the front door close behind her. How could she just carry on?

Michael looked concerned as he spoke. "Dad?"

"Yes, Michael, what is it?"

"Why did Peter have to die?" he said tearfully.

This was a good question, and it pierced me like a sword. I wanted answers to it myself. How was I going to explain my betrayal and the death of Peter to my own son? I had to think quickly.

"He fell asleep, Michael. He just fell asleep and he's gone up to heaven to be with Jesus. He'll look after him for us from now on."

Michael wanted to know more. "Why couldn't Jesus let us look after him?"

"I don't know why son, I really don't. It was just Peter's time to go."

I could sense Michael's mind trying to work out the mystery of death.

"Can we go there now too, Daddy?"

"Not yet, son. It's not our time yet. We have to wait here for now. Do you miss Peter a lot?"

Michael's eyes welled up to overflowing and Luke looked anxiously at his elder brother, then stared into my eyes looking for reassurance. I wrapped my arms around them both and said "I do as well. It really hurts inside, doesn't it?" His little head nodded in agreement against my chest.

"He's not very far away you know" I went on. "He's only in the next room and if we pray he can hear us." I reached out with my hand "Just here. We can't see you, can we Peter, but we know you're there. Shall we ask God to look after little Peter for us? Shall we do that now?" I felt another nod against me. "OK, let's close our eyes and think about all the worries and pain that we have for Peter and pray. In the name of the Father, And of the Son, And of the Holy Spirit…" I couldn't say any more, I was stuck and in my mind I heard a quiet voice say 'Hypocrite!' I was struck dumb for a moment.

"I can't speak or pray any more words to You right now" I thought. "Why did you take our little baby from us?"

I thought back to my management course and then

22

remembered Peter as I struggled to speak and we held on to each other tightly. Michael and Luke waited in silence for me to continue. "Please help little Peter and look after him for us. Amen."

The following day I received a telephone call from Dr Pike. "I'm calling about Peter."

I was desperate to hear his news. "Have you got the result of the post mortem?" I enquired.

"Yes. Peter died of kidney failure."

I was shocked "Not cot death?"

Dr Pike continued "It was kidney failure. I'm sorry. Did you notice anything unusual?"

"Nothing. Absolutely nothing."

Dr Pike tried to reassure me. "There was nothing you could have done. Sorry. You can pop into the surgery if you want to talk and of course you have the funeral to organise."

Having no further questions for the doctor I said "Thank you" and put the telephone down. It was only then that I realised that I had to prepare for Peter's funeral. There were so many questions I needed to have answered.

I reached for the telephone directory and rang the first funeral director I could find in Cullompton. A very kindly gentleman introduced himself over the telephone. I could barely speak and he waited patiently for my reply.

"How do I bury my son?" I said in a rather pathetic and weak voice and then I waited helplessly for his reply.

His voice reassured me as he spoke. Nothing was too much trouble. His voice was soothing and was just what I needed at that time.

"I will collect Peter for you from the hospital and bring him here to our Chapel of Rest" he said. "You are very welcome to come in and see him if you want to. Don't worry, I will take good care of him for you and if there is anything you need just let me know. My name is Oliver."

CHAPTER TWO

■ ■ ■ ■ ■ ■ ■ ■

THE LITTLE WHITE COFFIN

I don't remember whose idea it was to have a cremation. Geoffrey offered to organise a small family burial for Peter's ashes in a small flower bed in the church garden.

The arrival of a huge black hearse outside the family home signalled Peter's arrival. I could see his tiny white coffin through the glass-panelled sides and a cold shudder went through my whole being. My heart felt as if it had been smashed into a thousand pieces and I was crippled with guilt and grief.

"How can any man bury his own son?" I asked myself. "My tiny baby, all alone. I'm so sorry, Son. As a dad I'm worthless. Pathetic!" and I moved slowly to the front door.

Somehow we managed to walk through our pain and out of the house. We were so close to each other as we walked, it was as if we were leaning against each other for support.

The procession of vehicles followed Peter to the crematorium and we were guided into our seats at the front of a small chapel, wrapped together in grief. There was no feeling of comfort, just loss as we looked over to Peter's little coffin all alone. I asked myself "How can I celebrate your little life? How can I talk of the little time I spent with you? You were only here for a moment and then you were gone. I can't sing. I can't read. I can't comfort anyone. I can't breathe".

I was still in deep shock, shivering, emotionally destitute, crippled with guilt. I watched his little coffin as it disappeared behind the screen and my heart cried out. "Peter, you've left me! How can I bear this pain?" Through my tears I glanced across at Sarah, who sat staring in silence, emotionless, with a resolute, stony glare.

After the service we waited outside in silence for Peter's ashes as the cold air struck at our tear-filled eyes. Then everyone seemed to melt away. We were driven back to the small church in the village, where we had watched Michael and Luke thrive. We walked into the churchyard through a type of lychgate. The lawns were well cut and the old gravestones reminded me of the finality of death.

Geoffrey had prepared a small piece of ground in a border outside the porch for little Peter's ashes and we said a few prayers for him. Then I gently poured Peter's ashes into the small hole in the flower bed. I wondered "How can I bury my son? How can I abandon You here into the depths of the earth? To what fate? I do not know. How dare I just stand here drenched in my own guilt and self pity and pull the earth over you with my hands? Hypocrite! Traitor!"

Geoffrey spoke quietly to us both. "You can plant a small bush here for Peter if you would like."

I nodded and said "Thank you Geoffrey". Then our small, shattered family sat on a bench in silence, gathering our thoughts and memories of Peter. I felt I didn't deserve compassion for what I had done. I did not deserve pity for my betrayal. I wanted the earth to open up and devour me.

Sarah's cold voice dragged me from my thoughts. "Let's go,

we can't sit here all day." We all got up together and walked out of the graveyard and through the village to our house.

The nights grew more and more difficult for me to cope with. Dreams of Peter were relentless and he was haunting me every night. In my dreams I would be playing with Peter and telling him stories, and that was wonderful, but my problem came at the end of the night when I would be forced to lie to Peter when he was pleading with me - "Don't put me back in the box, Daddy. Please don't put me back."

The concealed guilt and continual lying to my dead son were killing me emotionally and tearing at my conscience. I kept screaming out to God in my dreams "Why are You doing this to me? Why can't I have my son back? I'm sorry! Help me!" The echoes of my inner voice screamed out in the darkness, lost in the unfathomable echoes of my soul.

Sarah still refused to talk about Peter's death and I couldn't come to terms with having had to pay the terrible price for what I had done. Sarah's natural father, after whom Peter had been named, had walked out on her mother, Jane, when he discovered that Jane was having an affair with her now stepfather, Daniel. Jane and Daniel had travelled from Essex for the funeral and had stayed in their caravan in North Devon, which was in easy reach of our home. I had always disliked them as in-laws as their presence at the house always brought an unpleasant atmosphere; almost an odour that brought on a deeply sombre mood which was fuelled by their constant insensitive and hurtful remarks.

Jane tried to reason with me about Peter's death and the true meaning to life, not that I had invited her to do so. "It's the best thing really" she said. "If there was something wrong with the kid then it's best that he went when he was little. You don't get so attached to them then. It's true, you would have had all sorts of problems with him and anyway, you can always start again."

Sarah didn't attempt to correct her mother's hurtful remarks, but I couldn't let the moment pass. "You insensitive bitch! I can't just replace Peter with another child. We don't breed goats by the way, they are children! Peter is and always will be our baby!"

Jane pursed her lips in displeasure "There's no need to be nasty. I think we'd better go. Come on Daniel, let's get back to the caravan." Her gnarled face revealed her true nature. Twisted!

"I'm not asking you to leave. Just think about what you're saying." I was furious and really felt like throwing her and Daniel out. "You bitch. You really are an insensitive bitch. You've got absolutely no idea how we're feeling." Sarah decided to step in to defend her mother.

"They're my parents and you've said enough, Costa! Enough!"

I turned to face Sarah and said "I'm not a human sponge! I can't just say nothing. They've got no idea what we're going through." I knew that Sarah had no knowledge of my deeper feelings of guilt which I was now really struggling with and how I had allowed myself to betray her and the children in the way I did. No matter how I tried to justify my behaviour and the need to seek the comfort of another woman earlier in the year, I could not. I hated myself for the weakness of my own flesh, lack of self-will and control, and I was finding it more and more difficult to be in the house with her.

Sarah was now becoming visibly angry with me and snapped back. "Costa! Enough! Now back off and keep quiet!" Her mood was emphasised by her pursed thin lips and threatening eyes. Daniel had decided to keep very quiet. Sarah went on "Don't listen to him, Mum, he's upset. He's just a weak man, that's all. I don't want to hear another word."

Sarah was right about the 'weak man' but Jane wasn't going to let go. She still felt the need to justify her remark.

"Well it's true. He'd have to have had lots of operations, you know what I mean, operation after operation. You wouldn't want that would you? Anyway, as time goes on you'll eventually forget about him and you can always try again."

Jane was really pushing her luck. I snapped back "You don't stop do you? I'm never going to get 'over' Peter, you stupid woman! What planet do you live on?"

My words fell on deaf ears and they decided to leave. I resigned myself to ignoring her and Sarah and to flick off the already fading light of communication which was growing dimmer each day between us, before there was yet another argument.

The following evening I sat in silence in the lounge and Sarah popped her head around the door.

"I'm off. See you later." She was dressed in a short white sports skirt and a white T shirt.

"Where are you going?" I asked.

My question seemed to surprise her. "Badminton!"

Being somewhat surprised, I said "We've not long buried our baby and you're going to play badminton again?"

Sarah's attitude was brazen "Life goes on. I'm not going to just sit around the house like you, moping!"

Somewhat shocked by her demeanour, I said "I can hardly stand, and all you can think of doing is playing badminton."

Her response was instant. "Oh stop it, you pathetic man! You're using him as a crutch, for goodness sake. Get on with it!" She closed the door behind her and was gone. I wondered what it was that made her so strong. She seemed indestructible.

The feeling of guilt made me even more determined not to

lose another child. When I was at home in the evening I quietly walked in and out of the boys' bedrooms every fifteen minutes to see if they were still breathing. I had to hear and feel their breath before I was satisfied. I felt so guilty and empty. If only I had not gone out the night I fell from grace. If only I had turned left on the day he had died and not right. Each day that passed left me feeling more empty inside. I just wanted to die. "I could be with you then Peter. There's no one to look after you" I thought. When I was out I couldn't look at other people's babies because I kept seeing Peter in the pram. Dead!

I felt an inner panic when I saw a baby. I wanted to pull it out of its pram and shout "It's going to die!" They all looked dead to me. I felt sick in my stomach. I wanted to flee the scene rather than look.

The first day Michael went back to school was the first day I had gone back to work. My clients knew nothing of my loss, so I just carried on with my business calls as normal, hauling a numb, dead feeling around within me. When I arrived at Michael's nursery school just before the bell to collect him it immediately became apparent that the word had got out among the other parents, because they all fell silent as I walked through the playground. They didn't need to say anything. Their eyes spoke volumes as I trudged towards the door of Michael's classroom. It was so hard to lift my legs and walk in a straight line. Every step was a battle against the feeling of wanting to throw myself on the ground and wail in self-pity.

When I arrived at the house I found that Peter's room had been cleared and Luke's things had been moved back in to what had been his old room. Jane and Daniel were back. Luke was really upset and was crying inconsolably.

"I don't want to sleep by myself, Daddy. Can I stay with

Michael? I like being in Michael's room." He started weeping again.

I picked Luke up and gave him a cuddle "In a minute, Luke. I'll talk to you about it in a minute. Let me talk to Mummy first."

I turned to Sarah and said "So where are all Peter's things?" I was bewildered. I wondered why things had been changed without us having talked about it first.

Sarah looked at her mother for guidance and Jane answered my question. "It's best that all the kid's things are gone. It's a reminder and you don't want that, do you?"

I said "I didn't ask you, I was speaking to Sarah!"

Jane decided to carry on speaking. "You don't want to be constantly reminded of him, do you?"

"I'm sorry, but I do! I've told you this before, he's not a goat, so please stop calling him a kid. You've got no right to come in here and start making those sorts of decisions for me or for Sarah. Where've you taken Peter's things?"

Jane was still speaking for England. "We took some stuff back to the shops you bought them from" she said. "The rest we gave away. Believe me, it's the best way of dealing with this. You'll feel better once you've adjusted."

I responded instinctively "You evil bitch! You're behind all of this, aren't you!" I felt like hitting out at her.

Sarah could see that there was a problem with what they had done. Now she started to defend her mother. "Don't start on Mum, she's only doing what I wanted anyway. I'm the one who wanted to get rid of his things."

Still trying to control my feelings, I said "Well, you've made a big mistake, Sarah. It's heartless, that's what it is. Heartless! You waited for me to leave the house and without a word to me you got rid of all Peter's memories. Where are his photographs?" I looked them both in the eyes and waited for a response.

"What photographs?" Sarah replied and again she immediately turned to her mother for help.

"Don't you tell me you got rid of everything!" I snapped. I was gutted.

There was a silent moment and then Jane said "It's best. I know what I'm talking about."

I couldn't believe that anyone could do such a thing without even mentioning it or asking for my opinion beforehand. "No you don't, Jane! You don't know anything! What you have both done is wrong. It's evil! It's not normal behaviour and you should have known better. I can't believe you've done this! You must have planned it and you must have known what I would say because you didn't even have the guts to tell me to my face. You're a pair of evil bitches!"

After that Peter started appearing to me in my dreams every night. It was really wonderful to see him. As time passed on he was getting older, so he was the right age for that period of time. Every night it was the same dream and I was playing with him and telling him stories. The only problem was that right at the end of my dream, just before I woke, Peter would say "Daddy, don't let me go! Don't leave me!" I lied to him "I won't", but he kept on pleading. "Promise me, Daddy? Promise you won't put me back in the box?" and again I lied, "I promise, Peter."

The dreams and the lies were killing me slowly. As the nights went on I dreaded going to sleep. In the end I wouldn't even go to bed. My deep-rooted guilt was building up and up on my conscience.

"I promise you, Peter, I won't put you back in the box" I would say. How could I lie to him? I knew that he had to go back, and putting him there felt like a merciless thing to do. The guilt was harrowing. I kept breaking down emotionally during the day and was constantly in floods of tears. I didn't want to go to bed at night as the dreams were relentless. So Sarah and I threw ourselves into our work and I started to come home later and later until I was creeping in at 4 am. Sarah always woke up and said "Where've you been all night?"

The answer was always the same: "drinking". I had tried to be honest with her and now I was tired of her incessant whining. I knew that she would fail to understand why anyone in his right mind would feel the need to sit in a graveyard for most of the night, so I made the excuse that I had been drinking and I would take a swig out of a bottle of whisky just before I entered the house. In my mind I kept asking myself "Peter, how can I leave you alone in a place so dark and frightening?" Sarah could understand and accept my drinking, but grief, no. In Sarah's eyes Peter was just my crutch for my problems with alcohol.

I was now the brewery's top salesman and I wanted to know if I would be considered for promotion, but my manager, Alan Spooner, was unable to give me a satisfactory answer. So a meeting was arranged for me to meet the Area Director, Peter Hives, in the Bull Inn in Bridport. I arrived thirty minutes early and he turned up thirty minutes late.

Peter Hives had started his career as a vacuum salesman. He was about the same height as me, six feet four, and wore a cheap Prince of Wales check suit with a single vent in the jacket. He was about 55 years old with dirty-looking unkempt hair. He walked into the packed bar looking agitated and introduced himself to me. This was hardly an ideal place to hold a business meeting, but I assumed that the smell of stale beer, tired, nicotine-stained anaglypta wallpaper and dirty velvet curtains appealed to his sense of nostalgia.

"Hi, I'm Peter Hives and I'm your Area Director. Sorry I'm late, but the car park was full."

Well, I had been watching the cars coming in and out of the car park and there were plenty of spaces. Even so I decided to give him the benefit of the doubt. I looked him in the eyes and said "I'm Con, and I expect my manager has told you something about me?" I waited eagerly for a response.

Without hesitation he snapped back "I don't know anything about you. All I want to say is that I am looking to sack three people and at the moment you are likely to be one of them!" He raised his right hand and immediately started to click his fingers impatiently in front of me and continued "What do you want?"

My response was instinctive. "I asked to meet you so that I could discuss my future prospects with your company. I would imagine that you have at least booked a room where we can talk privately?"

He looked shocked at my response and carried on clicking his fingers. "I told you, I'm looking to sack three men and you could be one of them."

That was enough. I raised my voice loud enough to silence the busy bar and snapped "You arrive at our meeting thirty minutes late and start clicking your fingers at me and come up with a bullshit excuse about being late. Then you think I'm going to be prepared to talk to you about my future with your company in a grotty bar in Bridport! Let me tell you, you are very much mistaken!"

Mr Hives was quickly backtracking "Quieten down. There's no need to shout" he said.

I'd had enough. "Stop clicking your fingers at me! When you decide to give me the respect I deserve and arrange a proper venue for a meeting, just let me know!" I turned on my heels and walked out of the pub, got in my car and drove home. As I opened the door Sarah passed me the phone and said "It's your manager."

"Hello Mr Spooner."

I could hear the distress in his voice when he spoke. "What on earth's gone wrong? You can't talk to the Area Director like that. You'll have to apologise!"

I couldn't believe what I was hearing "Me! Apologise to HIM! He should apologise to me for threatening me and arranging to discuss my future career in a grotty bar in Bridport!"

Mr Spooner could hear by the tone of my voice that I wasn't going to budge. He said "Leave it with me and I will get back to you." He phoned me later that night. "I've made a proper appointment for you to see Mr Hives at head office at 2 pm tomorrow" he said. Although I was still annoyed, I was relieved to hear that I had been listened to.

When I arrived at the brewery the following day Mr Hives' secretary, Emilie, a smartly-dressed, attractive, middle-aged woman with clean, wavy, hazel, shoulder-length hair walked me to his office and opened the door. Mr Hives made good eye contact and I sat in the chair opposite him.

"What's all this about?" he asked.

"Well, Mr Hives, I'd like to know two things, firstly, when I joined your company two years ago my area was grossing £185,000 a year and I was able to administer this work from my kitchen table. As I have a small house and I don't have an office and my area is now turning over £2,300,000 a year, I am finding it impossible to carry on working off the kitchen table with a growing family. The depot in Taunton has three vacant offices and I would like to know if I could use one of the offices once a week to do my paperwork."

Mr Hives didn't even need to think about his answer. "No! If I give you an office I will have to give an office to everyone!"

"Well Mr Hives, what are the other areas producing in sales?" I asked.

"I don't bloody well know!" He now looked very uncomfortable.

"Sorry, I'm getting a bit confused here. I thought you were the Area Director, but you appear to be telling me you don't know what's happening in your distribution areas?"

"It's complicated. Only the Managing Director knows those figures" he said. I could see that Mr Hives had done 'uncomfortable' and was now getting thoroughly pissed off with my line of questioning.

"But I know them, Mr Hives."

"No you don't. Those figures are confidential!"

"Well, I can tell you what additional net profit was made on my area and it's £247,000."

"Rubbish! Where did you get that information from?"

"I receive four sets of computer sheets each month and they give me the production, distribution, sales, marketing and administrative costs. I also get a price list of all our products. I run my area like it's my own business and I have compiled a profit and loss account for it. As all the other areas are showing minuses of between 25-35% and my area is showing a 36% increase, I would have thought you might be asking me what it is that I'm doing that the rest ought to be doing."

"That's not true!"

"Well, ask me a question."

"What do you mean?"

"Ask me how I have made the extra profit."

Mr Hives was looking very uncomfortable. "It's just you."

"Wrong answer, Mr Hives. It's the way I'm working. Everyone could be working the same way and you would be showing massive profits instead of losses."

"You're still not getting the use of a desk at the depot!"

"Secondly, Mr Hives, I wanted to know whether I would ever be considered for promotion at some time in the future with this company. That's it."

He looked startled: "I don't know! How can I answer that question?"

I stood up and said "Quite clearly, Mr Hives, we are wasting each other's time and I have better things to do. I asked for an informed meeting with you today and you can't even give me a satisfactory answer to any of my questions. You clearly haven't got a clue what's happening in your business and I shall be looking for another job immediately. Goodbye."

I walked out of his office and drove home. When I opened the door Sarah passed me the telephone. "It's your manager. He doesn't sound very happy."

That was the end of my time with the brewery. When I left I was given my company car, references and nine months' salary as a settlement. I started my own business as an insurance broker. I also bought into a firm with clients in West Sussex, and this gave me the ideal opportunity to work away from home. I normally booked into a hotel for a month at a time at least three months of the year. I was earning large amounts of money, but my marriage to Sarah was failing quickly as my business continued to grow. I began to invest in property and I had soon built up a substantial portfolio in Devon.

Sarah thought the increased spending power was amazing. When I told her that I was going to leave her, she refused to let me go and continued to make the usual threats. "If you leave me I will make sure that you never see the boys again" she would say. Knowing Sarah as I did, I knew that she would be true to her word. This became her favourite weapon to keep me in check.

Finally, in February 1990, I felt I could take no more. One day I put two gallon cans of petrol, with the caps off, into the boot of my 7 series BMW and drove it into a railway bridge. I was so determined to kill myself that I held a match in one hand and a box of matches in the other at the point of impact.

Seeing that I had not succeeded in killing myself and smelling the petrol, which had fully discharged into the car, I struck a match and watched it ignite. Then I threw it over my shoulder on to the back seat and watched it burn on the rear seat - and go out by itself!

I was flabbergasted. The front nearside wing of the car was on fire and I was still sitting in the car waiting for it to go BANG when the fire brigade turned up. It had become evident that my destiny was not to die in a ball of flames in my car.

The fireman looked in through my driver's window and called out over the noise of the audible warning signal, which BMW install as an included extra in their package, indicating that I had indeed been involved in an accident.

"Are you all right?" he asked.

I opened my driver's door and stepped out of the car. I noticed that the roof had buckled under the impact, into a sort of concertina pattern. "Not really" I said. I stood back and watched the fire crew extinguish the flames. They pulled the shredded petrol cans out of the boot and came over to ask me "Why are you driving around with two gallons of petrol in the boot?"

I couldn't think of anything else to say except "They are for the lawn mower. I filled them up earlier today."

Two police officers arrived on scene and they requested a breathalyser, which was completely clear. Then they took me home.

When Sarah opened the door I could see by the look on her

face that she knew our marriage was finally over. I immediately started to pack my things into another car. Without a word, I left that night to return to West Sussex.

CHAPTER THREE

■ ■ ■ ■ ■ ■ ■ ■

MARION

JANUARY 1998

Events took a horrific turn during the eight years that followed; more of that in a moment.

In 1998, my life was about to be transformed. I was living in North Devon in a shared house with a group of total strangers. God only knows where the years had gone.

It was Friday January 23 1998 and I was off to start a new job. I caught the early afternoon bus from Bideford to Barnstaple, planning to get off at Yelland, which is about midway between the two. I was hoping to meet a woman who had given me a lead for my new job, and who lived in Yelland. All I knew about Marion was that she had four children, Terry, aged fourteen, Adrian, eleven, Samantha, nine and Jason, three.

When I first looked into Marion's eyes I saw the most beautiful woman in the world. Her blonde hair radiated the sun, with streaks of white light flashing through lighter shades of baby blonde which cascaded on to her shoulders like a crystal waterfall. Her fringe was brushed back like a gentle breeze, feathered into the natural fall of her hair. Her eyes, deep sky blue and clear, betrayed a deep sadness, briefly exposed through her unease and inner tenderness when she reflected on her inner pain.

I would describe Marion's figure as petite and her bone structure fine. She was five feet tall and showed absolutely no trace of having had four children. Marion had the sort of figure any man would die for. With me, standing at six foot four and weighing nineteen stone, with a bald head and an ugly rugby player's frame, I portrayed the complete contrast. I towered over her like a building.

Marion's soft nature and gentle way with the children made them respond immediately to her and they respected her every word. Such obedience in children I had not seen for a very long time. They reminded me of Michael and Luke, my own children, who now lived separate lives to me and were with their mother, Sarah. They had now grown into young men of seventeen and nineteen years of age.

As I prepared to board the bus, my attention was taken by a woman wearing a black T-shirt, striped tracksuit bottoms and trainers. She had a mouth full of black teeth and arms covered in tattoos, and she kept shoving her little son in the back to make him get on to the bus ahead of me. Her partner appeared to be in a state of panic, trying to fold the pushchair before the bus pulled away. He looked gaunt, with a skinhead hair cut, trainers and a shell suit. The little boy was about four years old and was wearing scruffy worn-out jogging bottoms, trainers and a grubby looking grey T-shirt. He was trying to ask his mother a question and his excited voice was desperate to be heard above the noise of the bus's diesel engine. The force of his mother's pushing kept breaking his flow of speech.

"Can I sit next to Daddy, Mummy?" His mother pushed the young lad violently forward again and his head flew back. She barked back "Just ignore your dad, he's an idiot! Now get on and be quiet!"

Her remark immediately triggered an old memory of me and my own children and my heart went out to this little boy and his dad. Sitting about halfway down the bus, I gazed out of the window on to the River Torridge and immediately caught the distinctive smell of mothballs wafting off a little old lady in a multi-coloured woollen coat and fawn bonnet who was sitting in front of me. The comment of the mother to her child, mixed with the odour of diesel fumes, sent my mind drifting back to Peter and that Thursday when I had lost him.

A sudden jab of the brakes and I snapped out of my daydream. We were coming into Instow, a lovely little village with small shops, a sailing club with rows of small yachts and dinghies with riggings and sails neatly secured. On we went past the wide lawns and terraces of the resplendent walls and columns of colonial grandeur which is the Commodore Hotel, set among palm trees and a stark reminder of our former empire days. The wind swept across the Torridge, tossing small boats clinging helplessly to moorings set deep into the slimy cold silt below. It was cloudy and cold, but thankfully a dry day.

As the bus started to come out of the village I abandoned my seat and swung from pole to pole towards the driver. The bus stopped, the door opened and I stepped out into the cool air of Yelland. I immediately felt the power of the cold wind, which was beating against my face so powerfully that I had to consciously steady myself. I turned to meet the wind head on and grimaced at the driver as I lifted my arm to thank him. Holding my clipboard tightly with the other hand I called out "Thank you driver." He nodded and called "You're welcome."

I crossed the empty road and began to knock on doors, dropping off leaflets in the hope of attracting interest in my new product range. My plan was to canvass up the left hand side of

Lagoon View and then back down the right. I was longing to meet Marion, who had brought her children to my barber's shop just before I sold it. I had no idea which house was hers and regretted not asking her for the house number, so I systematically knocked on every door as I made my way up the street of neatly-laid-out detached properties which lined both sides of the road. There were little side roads from left to right which revealed clusters of maybe five or six houses with small front gardens, leaded windows decorated with colourful curtains and blinds which lent a warm, intimate and neighbourly ambience to the estate.

When I knocked at one house the door was opened by a rather harassed, plump middle-aged woman in a tracksuit, with grey unkempt hair.

"Good afternoon madam…"

"No thanks!" She closed the door in my face, and I was left standing outside feeling quite foolish.

I eventually arrived at a neat three-bedroom detached house with oak framed leaded double-glazed windows. It had been a long haul up the hill and not everyone was being friendly towards me. Quite frankly they came across as hostile. I was going through a sharp learning curve with the double glazing industry and I really wasn't sure whether I was made for this type of work, but I needed to find another job quickly.

I pressed the doorbell of number 32 - and Marion opened the door. I stood there in my old green waxed Barbour jacket and cap, green cords and boots and stared into her beautiful blue eyes. Marion looked stunning in her neatly-fitted, dark blue pencil skirt, short lacy knitted fawn top and pretty patterned heeled sandals.

"Hello!" she smiled.

"Do you remember who I am?" I asked. I was fascinated by her charm and beauty. I wondered if she would remember me now that I was away from the shop.

"Yes, of course I do!"

'What a relief!' I thought. I remembered how I had felt when I had first met her. Marion's words were reassuring. I gave her a cheeky smile and said "Well, I did as you suggested. I have been banging on doors on your estate asking your neighbours about their faulty windows."

"Any luck?" Marion seemed very amused at my plight.

"Nope! They're a tough lot on here, I can tell you" and I nervously steadied my clipboard.

"Short of money probably."

"I've come to collect that cup of tea you promised me."

"Oh, right! You'd better come in then." As she closed the door behind us I could feel not only the warmth of the house enveloping me but Marion's magnetism and dexterity as a mother absorbed in the all-encompassing care of her four children.

"Look who's here, children!"

The smell of fresh bread was unmistakeable. Suddenly I was surrounded by four smiling faces who all spoke at the same time.

"Hello Constantine!"

"Hello again. It's been a long time since I last saw you all. October I think and it's January already."

"1997!" Samantha announced. "In the barber's. You cut my fringe and gave us all lollipops."

"Yes, I remember. It's been ages. I've got around to seeing you all again at last. What a lovely house you've got. We didn't have houses in the old days. We used to live in old cardboard boxes."

"No you didn't!" Samantha retorted. "You're pretending."

"Only having a bit of fun" I sniffed light-heartedly.

"Off you go and play then, I'm going to make Constantine a cup of tea" said Marion. The children seemed to melt away, leaving us alone in the kitchen, which was a large room also serving as a dining room. Jason, the quiet three-year-old, wandered up to me with a book hanging from his right hand and offered it to me, expectantly. As I lifted him on to my knee he showed no resistance. His mop of soft blond hair was light to the touch and I adjusted him on my knee to make sure that he was comfortable, straightening his corduroy dungarees.

"Shall I read you a story?" I asked. He raised his right hand to his face and put his index finger on his lower lip in a rather bashful way. "Is this your favourite book, Jason?" He nodded.

"OK, let's begin. Billy Goat Gruff, eh." My mind drifted back to my time with Luke when he was the same age. He had loved exactly the same storybook. "Do you promise not to get scared, Jason?" He smiled and I glanced over at Marion who just raised one eyebrow in surprise and Jason sat forward and listened attentively.

I watched as Marion went on working and helping the other children. I realised that they were a central charm, a glowing facet of her overall beauty. Finishing the story, I closed the book slowly and Jason opened it again for it to be reread, so I just kept on reading.

It was soon time for Jason to go to bed. When I closed the book he wrapped his little arms around my neck. Marion walked over to collect him. "Who's the lucky one!" she said. "Jason doesn't normally kiss anyone. Is that because you liked your story?" Jason nodded bashfully.

"Good night Jason." I lifted him off my knee and stood him on the carpet in front of me, giving him a big reassuring smile.

Marion continued to rush around non-stop until I had finished my tea. I was exhausted just watching her, a mother on her own trying to cope with four children through no fault of her own. I didn't want to leave, but at the same time I didn't want to outstay my welcome, so I said "I must be in your way, I ought to be going really."

Marion seemed disappointed, and I found that comforting. "I'll be done in a minute and the children will go up and then we can have a chat. You can tell me about some of your plans for the future."

I sat back in my chair and let out a sigh "OK" I said. I hesitated and then remembered that I had told her about my trip to Greece. "It won't be long before we're off to Greece to see what became of my mother."

"What's happened to your mother?" Marion enquired.

"It's a long story." I wasn't sure if Marion would really want to hear the full tale.

"Oh. Who are you going with?"

"My sister. We both want to know why they did what they did to our mum. It was all very gloomy and suspicious when she died out there."

Marion could see that I was hesitant to go into too much detail, so she changed tack.

"My mum's Greek" Marion gave me a beautiful, captivating smile.

"Yeah, I believe you!" I thought that she was joking and my face revealed my misgivings.

"Honestly! Look at all the ornaments in the lounge." Marion walked to the lounge door and pointed to her ornaments, neatly placed throughout the room. "Look! The Parthenon, the plates and vases. See?"

I stood up and joined her at the door and it was true, I could see them all.

"Really? You didn't just pop out and buy them did you?" I

laughed. Her aroma was soft, subtle, fresh and charming and I took that special moment deep inside me, wanting it to drift on forever. The moment was immediately secreted deep into the recesses of my heart.

"Yes, I'll call her if you like and Mum can talk to you in Greek. Maybe then you'll believe me!"

"I believe you." I was trying not to look too distracted as I made my way back to my seat by the dining room table. I was now in a bit of a tiz and quickly tried to regain control of myself. I wasn't sure if Marion had noticed, as she quickly changed the subject.

Marion was now standing in front of me and looking directly into my eyes. She asked "How's your back?"

I kept eye contact and gazed back into her eyes. "I've had thirteen weeks of physiotherapy and they've told me it's not responding to treatment. In other words, it's not going to improve. So they've advised me to find alternative work, you know, a different job. I told you all about that in the shop. Cutting hair all day was just too much for me and with the shop getting busier every day it was a good time to sell the business."

Marion made me another cup of tea and Samantha came through to say goodnight. Her nightdress was covered in little teddies and her hair was light and blonde and fell straight to the base of her spine. Her fringe was combed forward and rested just above her eyebrows. She gave me the sweetest smile.

"I'm off to bed now, Mummy. Goodnight Constantine." Her eyes wandering between us as she waited for Marion to reply.

"OK darling, I'll take you up in a minute."

I could see that Samantha was hoping I would include her in our conversation, so I said "What did you get for Christmas then, Samantha?" and she smiled sweetly again.

"Mummy got me a bicycle"

"What colour is it?" I asked.

"Pink."

"What, Barbie pink? Are you into Barbie?"

"I've got a Barbie!" she replied excitedly.

"It has been so good to see you again Samantha. Goodnight." Samantha hesitated, so I said "Are you too big for a hug?"

Samantha grinned and opened her little arms. Then she gave me a quick hug and scampered up the stairs excitedly, Marion following her up. A few moments passed and Marion floated back into the kitchen and gave out a large sigh.

"Are you OK?" I enquired.

"She misses her dad." She looked quite upset. I didn't want to make her cry.

"What happened to him?" I asked gently. "What could possibly make a man leave such a beautiful wife and four wonderful children?"

Marion's eyes were full to the brim with tears. "I don't know. Even the people he used to work with are amazed. They can't believe that he would just get up and leave."

"Why did he go?"

"I've no idea. Everything was going along quite nicely until he got ill, and then once his health improved he left us."

I could tell she still had deep feelings for him. He had clearly hurt her and the children profoundly. I tried to make sense of it, so I asked "Is there someone else?"

"I don't think so. He's been working away from home in Norfolk and he's been doing that for the last two years now."

While we were talking Adrian wandered in with his Liverpool football pyjamas on.

"I'm going up now, Mum. Goodnight." He gave Marion a hug and then walked back through the kitchen and as he passed me he nodded politely.

I couldn't resist making a comment. "I see, a Liverpool fan, eh?"

Adrian responded immediately "They're the best! Better than Man United, they're rubbish!" He beamed a great smile and I knew he meant it.

Suddenly Terry appeared at the door in his Manchester United pyjamas. His beaming face and expression hinted that he had the facts to disprove his brother's boast.

"Manchester United are the best and Liverpool are the ones who need all the luck" Terry declared with great pride.

Standing together, with their short-cropped blonde hair, I could see that this was clearly a subject for much light-hearted banter. So I asked "Which is the best team in the world then?" and they both responded immediately.

"Brazil!" Surprised at the immediate echo of their own voices, they fell about laughing.

"I'm going up as well, Mum" Terry announced.

"OK you two, I'll come up and say goodnight properly in a minute."

They both said "goodnight, Constantine" and wandered out of the door ribbing each other about various football players. As time was moving on I said "Well thank you, Marion, it's been really good to see you all again." and I got up to leave. I wondered how he could have left this beautiful woman. She really was a gem.

"It was lovely to see you again too, Constantine. Let me know how you get on in Greece."

"Yes I will."

"You can bring me back a good Greek boy!"

Marion saying that made me think really hard about what she had just said. Could I just pass this jewel on to someone else? It was a no brainer.

My reply was spontaneous. "I don't think so, Marion."

Marion looked astonished "Excuse me? I've just made you two cups of tea and you won't even recommend me to a good Greek boy?"

The room fell silent for a moment while I thought of what to say next. I knew that I was in trouble. "There aren't any good Greek boys. I'm the only one!" I said, and we both burst out laughing together.

"So you're a good boy then?" Marion gave me a probing gaze.

I thought carefully for a moment. I realised that if I wasn't careful about what I told her, I was quite likely to be thrown out of the house, and then I would never see her or the children again. It was a difficult one. I wanted to trust her, but it was just too much for her to take on board.

I could sense that Marion was watching me with fascination and intrigue. "What is it?" she asked.

"OK, I'll tell you something and then you can make up your own mind as to whether I am a good boy or not. I want you to think very carefully about what I am about to tell you and I'm going to ask that you keep it to yourself. If you want me to leave at any time, you only have to say the word and I will be gone. Agreed?"

Marion looked understandably concerned. "OK, but this sounds a bit scary."

"I'll tell you what happened to me from the start." I had to trust her. I don't know what made me even want to contemplate taking the risk, but I decided to open my heart to a woman I barely knew.

"OK. That sounds good."

"This is going to take a while. Do the children ever come down once they're put to bed?"

"No, they're really good. Let's go through to the lounge and make ourselves comfortable."

I walked through to the lounge and sat in the black leather armchair. Marion followed me and perched herself on the matching three-seater sofa. "OK, let's see. Where shall I start?" I hoped to God I was doing the right thing. Marion sensed my caution and prompted me to continue. "Go on, we have the whole evening, it's only seven o'clock."

And so I began to tell her my story.

CHAPTER FOUR

■ ■ ■ ■ ■ ■ ■ ■

FRAMED

Before I went into business I had been a police officer in London. I married Sarah and we worked together. She was on the Murder Squad and I was on the Crime Squad, and I also did some work alongside the Flying Squad. I saw them do some terrible things to people, you know, completely destroying people's lives. Unjustifiably.

One particular afternoon, there were about eight of us in the CID office when someone walked in with three carrier bags packed with booze. The stories began to flow and so did the drink as the sun fell across the windows that overlooked the main road. Panic ensued as they realised their dilemma. "We're dry! To the pub, guys!" Crashing the empty bottles together into the plastic bags, they called out "Come on, Con, you miserable bastard! If you won't drink in the office, have one with us across the road!"

I followed them as we left the office and walked across the fire escape and into the rear yard, dumping the bottles as they staggered past a huge bin with the lid open, through the rear gate. We walked up a side road and on to the High Street, crossed the road and entered a large pub. It was literally across the road from the police station. The need for overtime was of paramount importance and in their drunken stupor, DC Taffy Llewellyn,

AKA the Fridge, rolled his black beady eyes above his huge gut and let rip on his chair. Then he gave a sleazy grin and said in his Carmarthen accent "Get out and walk, you filthy bastard!" Then he slapped the backside of the young girl who was approaching the table to collect the dirty glasses. "Lovely arse, wench! You're wasted in here! *Dda iawn*! (Well done!) *Dalier ati* (Keep it up)!"

I wanted the floor to open and devour me. No sooner had the laughter died down than DS Brown, a tall, twitchy, narrow, pretty-faced Essex boy, who was referred to in his absence as 'the nerve in the suit' shouted: "Someone get me a telephone directory!" Miraculously one appeared. He called out "Con, choose a number. 440 or 449?"

I had no idea what was planned and chose 440. He turned to Steve, who was about thirty, stocky, oval faced with a home counties accent dressed in a leather bomber jacket, blue jeans, open neck lemon shirt and Puma trainers.

"Give me a name" he said. Steve was too pissed to even register what he was saying and carried on drinking out of his pint glass.

"Give me a bloody name, for Christ's sake!" shouted Taffy. Steve finally focused on the question: "I don't bloody know… Lion."

DS Brown was back in a flash: "You stupid sod, the pub's called the Red Lion! Use your imagination, come on!"

Steve thought harder: "What about Payne?" There was a raw of laughter and the Fridge said "You stupid bastard! He was looking out of the window when he thought of that one!" More laughter.

DS Brown opened the telephone directory at the name Payne and said "Initial? Someone give me an initial?" A voice from the group shouted "H! Hurry up and get on with it!" There was more laughter.

We have a winner, gentlemen!" said Brown. "We've got three under that name and we'll get three "Ws" for five o'clock tomorrow morning."

I caught hold of the Fridge and said "What was all that about?" He smiled wryly and said "Overtime, my boy, overtime."

Being the only sober one in the group, I asked "Why all the names and numbers?"

The Fridge's eyes opened wide: "Ah, I see. You've clearly not played the game before. We call it the Roulette Wheel of Life." He looked like a man who was proud of his labour. So I asked him "What have the numbers 440 and 449 got to do with the price of cheese?"

The Fridge laughed: "Don't you know anything? 440 is one side and 449 is the other side of the High Street. Simple really."

A smartly-dressed man in a suit approached the table. "I am the manager of the Red Lion" he said. "One of your group has assaulted one of my waitresses. I'm going to have to ask you to leave and not return. Your behaviour is unacceptable."

Listen, we're from across the road and we're having a bit of fun" said DS Brown. "So if you know what's good for you, piss off!"

The manager stood his ground: "You are all barred and if you don't leave immediately I will call the real police and have you all thrown out. Now please leave!"

This was the first and only time I have ever been barred from a pub. These men were crude, arrogant and a law unto themselves.

The next morning we all paraded at the police station to execute the warrants. Even though they were still drunk they were issued with firearms and raids were carried out on the unfortunate winners of their silly and cruel game called the Roulette Wheel of Life.

As we approached the first victim's house, The Fridge tapped so lightly on the door that I couldn't hear it and said in a whisper "Armed Police. Open the door or we will force entry." The Enforcer was used and sixteen kilograms of hardened steel created an impact of three and a half tons. The door went in and the team ran over it and poured into the house. A woman in her sixties ran out through the front door, screaming "My husband's just had a heart attack! They will kill him!"

I turned and threw up into the back of the hedge. I decided to resign with immediate effect. They all sauntered back out of the house and DS Carter said "That's a rap boys." He gave a card to the woman and said: "We were acting on information received. If you want your door fixed, you can call this number."

In my resignation letter I explained my reasons for resigning. I said I wasn't prepared to name names but I was ashamed to work with such a bunch of corrupt individuals and that it was up to their bosses to work out what was going on. It wasn't rocket science!

Sarah still kept up her friendship with one particular policeman she used to work with and I was a bit surprised that his wife never thought it a bit odd and warned her off. I had grown tired of the two women's conversation, which normally revolved around how much they hated sex and would prefer celibacy any day. I had cut off all links with old colleagues, though I always suspected that one day they might pay me a visit, because of what I had written in my resignation letter, but Sarah kept inviting this policeman friend to the house. Even though he and his family were visiting us, he still had himself signed on as being on duty and working in London. Quite frankly I found it annoying that this dishonesty was allowed to continue.

As soon as I left the police I started to work for a national brewery and then I eventually left to start up my own business. I trained as a broker and had quite a privileged life back then. I used to work away from home for about three months of the year and I acquired quite a lot of property; a farm, barns and an old rectory. This was about the time I left Sarah and started divorce proceedings. I had been trying to leave her for years, but she kept threatening me by saying that if I left her she would make sure I would never see the children again.

About this time I met a man in the hotel where I was staying called Brian, a six foot two ex-professional wrestler from south London who turned out to have some rather questionable friends. We didn't get on so well to begin with and after an argument in the bar, we resolved our differences over an arm-wrestling contest and then became properly acquainted. Brian asked me to go through his pension and life policies and in return I offered him some building work on my farm in Devon.

About two weeks later I had finished work early and I was relaxing in the restaurant of the Mayfair Hotel. I was reading the *Financial Times* and waiting to order my meal when I noticed Charles, the smartly-dressed waiter. "Good evening, Charles" I said. His freshly-pressed white shirt, black trousers and bow tie certainly made him look the part as he walked up to my table.

Charles smiled politely "Good evening, Sir. Can I take your order?" I had to smile because Charles and I had been drinking together the previous evening and I just thought he was having a bit of a laugh.

"Very professional, Charles, but you can cut out all the bullshit as Bernie's not here this evening and there's no one else around" I said. "I'll have the fresh salmon with a salad and a bottle of 1988 Chablis please. Oh yes, and one for yourself."

"Thanks Con!" Charles knew from previous experience that this meant he could have whatever he wanted and stick it on my bill without any questions being asked.

"My pleasure, Charles. By the way, you look like the bog's dollocks in that outfit. Well done!" He had even polished his shoes.

Charles gave me a cheesy smile as he left the table and headed in the general direction of the kitchen. I suddenly caught sight of Brian as he entered the dining room and I followed his progress to my table out of the corner of my eye. "Not again, I'm just about to eat, for God's sake! I really don't need this" I thought. I put my hands on the table in order to push myself up quickly in case Brian was here to cause trouble.

"Don't get up, Con! Please forgive me for interrupting your meal. I just wanted to apologise for my behaviour the other night" he said. He looked genuinely remorseful.

"It's me who should apologise, Brian. It all got very silly. Do you want me to give you your money back?" I reached for my wallet, which was still bulging with the money I had taken off him.

"Nah, I ain't bovvered about the money, Con. I'm really sorry and I shouldn't 'ave started on you."

"Or the other bloke you punched, Brian. Look, let's forget it. I just hope the other guy is all right." I could tell by his manner that he wanted to ask me something. He went on: "Bernie tells me you do investments as well. Is that right?" Bernie was the hotel owner and I had clearly told him too much while we drank large whiskies into the early hours.

I said "Yes I do, Brian, why?"

Brian now looked somewhat embarrassed: "Mine are all over the place and I want to sort them out, like. Can you help me, Con?" He paused for a moment and then went on "'Cos I don't read so well, see. I run a business and all that and I can 'ardly read. I feel really stupid. I can trust you, can't I?"

I considered the consequences of taking Brian on as a client.

"Oh." I was genuinely lost for words and I wondered if I really needed his business. But before I could reply Brian had interrupted my train of thought and said: "Have you got a card, Con? I'll get all my papers and policies together and I'll give you a ring. Is that OK mate?"

He looked quite humble as he spoke and I instinctively passed him one my business cards. I knew from experience that when a bully is reduced in size they usually want to be your best friend. I really don't want you as a friend, I thought, but I'll always take your money. So I remarked: "Yes of course, Brian."

Brian announced "Insurance broker, eh? Who'd believe it!" as he proudly studied my card "You're the boss then. Right?"

"For my sins, Brian. Anyway, I thought you couldn't read very well? Your reading sounds fine to me."

Brian pulled his shoulders back proudly and said: "Thank you, Con. Do you mind if I say something?" He was still looking uncomfortable as he stooped forward, lowering his mouth to my ear. At this point I wasn't sure whether he was going to try and kiss me or tell me something extremely profound. I found the whole situation fascinating.

"Of course, Brian. What is it?"

Brian lowered his voice to a whisper and went on. "I've never lost at arm wrestling before, mate. Can you believe it?"

I kept my eyes clearly focused on him. I waited for a moment and said: "Neither have I. What do you do, Brian?" He appeared to be extremely proud of himself at this point. "I've got a building firm in London and I've got loads of blokes working for me."

"You must be good at what you do then." Brian raised his right hand and opened it towards me and took hold of the lapel on my jacket and rubbed it in between his fingers, like a tailor feeling the quality of the cloth. "The best, Con. The bloody best! Nice suit by the way. I can tell, you know."

As if by magic, he produced one of his business cards and pressed it into my hand. He turned his head slowly to glance quickly around the empty restaurant. "It's quiet in here tonight, Con."

He was now starting to make me feel a little uneasy and I kept my focus on him. "It's early, Brian, that's all." He started to smile proudly and chipped in: "I'm so glad I saw you again, Con."

I spoke purposefully and reassuringly to him: "Me too, Brian. I think that inside you're a really nice bloke. You just get angry when you're pissed and you think someone's taking liberties."

Brian nodded slowly: "Yeah, Con, I don't like people taking liberties. That's me! Exactly!"

Brian suddenly remembered something and he shrugged his shoulders as he stretched to his full height. "Listen, I can't stop. Tracey is waiting for me in the bar. Thanks again mate."

Brian started to turn away: "Brian, listen, before you go. I've always believed that one favour deserves another." He moved forward and put both hands on the back of the chair opposite me and said: "This sounds interesting, Con."

I had now got his full attention.

"Well, I've just bought a farm in Devon and I'm developing it in stages. I want to re-roof some of the outbuildings. I'm looking for a fixed price, you know? I'm not made of money, so perhaps we could talk about the possibility of you doing some work for me in the West Country? Is that too far away for you?"

Brian's eyes opened wide and I thought "I bet he thinks I'm rolling in it".

He took a deep breath and spluttered "Yeah! Great! Blinder, mate! I mean, no, it's not too far." He then lifted his hand to his brow as he tried to think of what to say next. Any thought of Tracey had quickly vanished. "I'll give you a call and we can meet up, Con. Yeah?"

In a strange sort of way I was warming to this man. "Until then, Brian. Thanks for putting things straight. You know, apologising and all that. Don't forget Tracey!"

Brian raised his arm in acknowledgement as he turned and wandered out of the dining room, calling back: "Right! I'll be in touch".

Three months later, the phone rang in my office and I picked it up and said "Hello, Sally." She sounded a little confused.

"Hi Costa, I've got someone on the phone asking for you."

"Do you know his name?"

"He's called Brian and says he's a friend of yours?"

Sally knew from the name by which he referred to me that it wasn't a personal call and it had something to do with work.

"Do you want me to put him through?" I had to think for a moment and then realised: "Oh, Brian! Thanks Sally. You can put him through."

Brian's voice sounded anxious. "Hello, Con. Can you come up to my office in London so we can talk things through? I've got all my paperwork together and it's ready for you. We can shoot across to the farm afterwards and then I can sort out a quote for you."

I quickly glanced at my diary, thinking I could incorporate it with a weekend when I could see my boys: "Next Friday would be good."

I could tell that Brian wasn't happy. He snapped back "Nah. I want you to come over today, Con!"

Now this was very short notice. I made sure that my diary was always full for the following week by the Friday of the preceding week. So I said: "Brian, I've got appointments arranged. I can't just drop everything."

He sounded agitated by my response. "Come over tonight,

Con. It only takes forty-five minutes to get here and I'll tell my secretary, Billy, to hang on in case there's something else you need from him. We can go out for a beer and you can stay here in the flat if you want and we can set off early in the morning?"

I quickly checked my diary again: "OK Brian, I'll come over when I've finished my last appointment."

Brian appeared to calm down now and his attitude changed. "Pukka, mate. See you later."

I based my journey time on his estimate of time for the journey: "I'll see you around 6 pm then Brian." I walked through to see Sally: "Can you change my 7 pm and 9 pm appointments tonight and reschedule them for me please, Sally? I have to go to London tonight and I won't be back now until Monday."

Sally immediately reached for the diary. "OK. I'll rearrange the schedule for tomorrow as well."

I smiled sympathetically: "Thanks Sally. If there are any problems give me a call straight away. I know how much you have got on at the moment and I really appreciate all your efforts."

I finished work and then looked at the map and set off slightly ahead of time, following the A239 north towards London. I was grateful that the traffic was moving freely. Then I joined the A24 and turned right on to the A219 and into South Wimbledon, where I turned right on to the A238 and followed the road on to the A24 and then the B224. At Clapham Common I turn left on to Rookery Road and before I knew it I was parking the car behind some shops close to The Pavement. I looked at my watch and thought "Forty five minutes. No way! Someone has been telling me lies."

I left the car and walked up to his ground floor office, which had a clear, but not very clean, shop front window.

The place was a mess, with tools and equipment strewn across the floor. Brian was standing talking on his mobile against the far wall. A tired-looking guy with unkempt hair and unshaven face introduced himself to me in a soft voice.

"Are you Con?" I nodded.

"I'm Bill." He gave me one of those handshakes I often have nightmares about. His hand was as wet and slimy as a two-day old lettuce that has been left in the sun. It slipped and fell from my grip when I shook, it. 'Yuk!' I thought trying to maintain a 'pleased to meet you' grin. Lying through my teeth, I said "Nice to meet you Bill, Brian has told me all about you."

Bill offered me a seat and I glanced around his dishevelled office. The furthest wall from the front window was covered in photographs of men, mostly in dinner jackets, shaking hands and having fun at various social functions. There were photographs of boxing nights and wrestling events and also those which I recognised as Masonic Festive Boards. To the uninitiated, these are the formal dinners held after a Masonic meeting where there are speeches and toasts to various dignitaries. As I looked closer some of these faces were really familiar to me, but I couldn't immediately recall their names. As I continued to scan through the photographs I recognised one celebrity immediately; it was Big Daddy and he had his arm around Brian. They looked like they were buddies. As soon as Brian came off the telephone I said "You've met Big Daddy then?"

Brian laughed loudly at my remark and rocked back on his heels. "I used to wrestle with him! I was on the telly but you wouldn't recognise me because I fought with a mask on." He laughed some more.

I found this quite interesting because I used to watch the wrestling on the telly with my mum. My dad, being the Military Police boxing champion in his time, always said "Wrestlers are a load of pansies. It's all play acting! Like ballet. Boxing's a proper sport". But I thought bringing up my father's remarks at this point might be somewhat inappropriate, so I asked another question, pointing at one particular face in one of the photographs.

"I know some of their faces but I can't think of their names. Where do you know this guy from?"

"Christ, Con, you ask a lot of questions!" He put out his hand and gave me a strong handshake accompanied with another one of his broad cheesy grins and some advice. "Asking those sorts of questions can get you into a lot of trouble around here, Con."

"They just look familiar, Brian, I'm not prying or anything like that. I think I know some of them, that's all." I stood up and walked over to the 'wall of fame' and pointed to one face in particular "Who's he? What's his name?"

Brian laughed aloud "That's Charlie! Everyone knows Charlie. He's like a dad to me!"

"Charlie?"

"Yes, Charlie Kray!"

I moved on to some of the other familiar faces. As I pointed to each one Brian said "He's a copper and on the take. He's a copper and he's on the take. He's ex-SAS and owns a security firm and he's an arms dealer, if you know what I mean? He brings 'em in from Russia. He works for the government as well, out in Africa protecting the diamond mines. If you want anything in that department you only have to ask. Listen, Con, you used to be a copper, I'm going to the boxing on the weekend, do you want to meet some of my mates? We do loads of work for charity." The wall was smothered in black and white photographs and as I returned to my seat I had to think quickly.

"Thanks for the offer, Brian, but since I split up from the

missus I'm spending most of my time driving over to see my boys in the West Country. I've also got a girlfriend in Weymouth."

After I had taken a look through Brian's files and policies Bill left to go home and Brian and I sat talking together in the office. I outlined the work that I wanted done at the farm and showed him some photographs. I also gave Brian some telephone numbers of contacts that I had in Devon for sourcing materials, just in case he needed them. We carried on chatting about his work and I had a look through his accounts.

About an hour passed when a man who was about six foot one with short neat black hair, wearing an expensive looking suit, pushed his way in through the front door. In a strong South London accent he said "Everything all right, Brian?"

"No problems, Sid. He's a mate of mine. No problem at all." Brian motioned towards me and I looked inquisitively at Sid and then turned my gaze back to Brian.

"Give me a shout if you need me, OK?" Sid stared at me for a while and looked me up and down and asked: "Where are you from then?"

I answered him in a matter of fact way and said "Worthing."

Sid looked at Brian and smiled knowingly. "Not from around here then?"

"No, Worthing."

He flicked me a wink and then and as he was leaving he said: "I'll drop in a bit later to see if everything's OK, Brian?"

When Sid pulled the front door closed behind him, I said: "Who the hell was that, Brian?"

Brian looked a little bit nervous: "Oh, don't worry about him, he's the landlord. You know what they're like. He's just keeping an eye on things, that's all. He likes to collect the rent in person, if you know what I mean? Face to face, like. I've known him for years and he doesn't change. He's a lovely bloke when you get to know him. He doesn't know you though, so I suppose he's a bit suspicious, you know?"

I had met a lot of strange people in my time but Sid had really got me thinking. My mind was scanning over old memories of the 70s when I had worked on the Crime Squad in north London, and I thought of some of the characters I had met when I was stationed at Tilbury.

I thought for a moment. I had come across one of Charlie Kray's cronies before. He had been a minder in Grays and looked after a woman called Stella, who controlled most of the prostitutes in Tilbury and Grays for Charlie Kray when I pounded the beat down there. Mick had tried to drag me out of the window of my police car one sunny afternoon and, much to his surprise, I had beaten the crap out of him. He had only hit me once on the side of the head and that was it, goodnight Mick! I really wouldn't want to mix socially or make polite conversation with Charlie Kray, just in case he recognised my name.

Brian could see that something was playing on my mind. He said: "What's the matter, Con? You've gone a funny colour!" and he started laughing.

"The guy's a copper you idiot! He's on the payroll and he's sound! He's just keeping an eye on me, that's all. He's sound, I tell ya! Why don't you get your things in from the car and I'll give you the key to the flat? I'll leave the key to the office as well, just in case you want to go for a drink across the road."

I walked out of the shop, went to my black Golf GTI and took out my suitcase. Then I walked back into the shop. Brian was now on his mobile again and when he heard me enter the office he made some excuse and finished the call. "I'll leave you in the flat on your own tonight, Con, so if you want to bring a tart back you can. I'm staying with me girlfriend tonight. The missus shouldn't come around but if she does you'd best tell her I've popped out and give me a bell. I've told her I'm working late in here with you. Is that OK, Con?"

I dreaded the thought of meeting Brian's wife in such circumstances and being questioned about his whereabouts.

"No problem, Brian. So Tracy lives around here as well then?"

Brian found my comment most amusing. "No, it's another girlfriend, Con. That's one 'whack off' suitcase you've got there buddy! What the hell have you got in it?"

No one likes to admit they have problems at home and I was a bit embarrassed at having to explain my actions to anyone, so I just said: "I've been living out of a case since I left the wife. It's mostly clothes."

Brian looked genuinely concerned for me: "You poor sod. If I can help just let me know, eh?"

I nodded politely: "That's good of you, Brian. There's a few things I need to sell." As soon as I had said that I immediately regretted it.

Brian then walked over to take a closer look and said: "I know lots of people around here, Con, so if I can help you just let me know. What 'ave you got, mate?"

I was now grateful for his concern. I had noticed a familiar attaché case tucked just under his desk, so I had to ask him "Are you on the Square, Brian?"

Brian looked genuinely shocked "How did you know?"

Indicating the black case under his desk, I said "I've got one just like that."

Brian was now really excited. "I've only just joined and I'm taking my second degree in a couple of weeks. What about you?" He pulled out his case and opened it. "Look, here's me apron." He passed his regalia over to me.

I looked a bit serious, as one is supposed to do in such cases of carelessness, and said "I was always taught to be cautious, Brian" and we both smiled. Realising his error, he extended his hand towards mine.

"Do you have something for me?" Brian responded immediately. "Yes, I do." Still holding his hand I indicated the second degree and said "What is it?" Brian looked nervous and gave me a broad grin. "A word. What is that word? I will halve it with you."

Brian started to panic and snapped "Shit! I've forgotten it! Damn, damn, damn!"

"That isn't the word, Brian. You're going to have to polish up on your handshakes before your next meeting." We both laughed and Brian asked: "What rank are you, Con?"

The atmosphere was now quite congenial: "Well, I belong to two lodges, Brian. I helped to form one, which is mainly for farmers, and I'm due to go through the chair in the other in two years' time in the other, but with my problems at home, I can't see how I can do that now. I'm sure you understand."

Brian frowned: "Yeah, it's a bugger, Con." He appeared to be really eager to help me "Con, if there is a way I can help you, just say the word."

I lifted my case and walked it through to the flat, and Brian followed me into the lounge. "I need to give my boys a quick call to say goodnight and then we can have a chat. Is that OK with you?"

Brian nodded: "Yeah, no problem, Con. I'm just popping out for some fags."

Now that I was left on my own I tried to call Michael and Luke. Sarah answered the phone. She sounded rather excited to hear my voice. "Hi Sarah, can I have a word with the boys please?"

"The boys are already in bed and they're asleep, but I'm glad you rang." Nothing ever changes with you, bitch, I thought. I could hear Michael and Luke in the background. Obviously her immediate problem was more important than me talking to my sons. But again I wimped out, missing the opportunity to confront her on it.

I had had a strange feeling that the conversation would finally come around to money. I asked: "Why?"

Sarah's voice now sounded more serious. "I want you to send me £300."

By her tone I assumed that something had happened and said: "I've only just paid you your maintenance. What's gone wrong?"

Sarah was trying to dismiss my question: "Nothing. I just need £300."

"Why?"

Her voice went all dreamy. "I've been invited out for a meal and I've seen a really nice black dress that I simply must have!"

An image formed in my mind of the hours, which felt like days, waiting for her to put on her face. "That poor sod" I thought.

"£300 for a black dress! What's the special occasion?"

"I've got a new boyfriend and he's a policeman." Sarah said in a sly tone. Then she waited for my reaction. I found her remark rather predictable, as she liked to taunt me over my motives for leaving the Met. She knew that I despised their evil workings and conduct and the way they treated the unsuspecting public with contempt.

"I'm really pleased that you've found someone you like, Sarah." I considered what I had just said. Was I really pleased? Yes, I was.

"Yes I am" I said.

Sarah was straight back at me. "Yes I am what?"

"I'm pleased for you. Made up. Really!" Sarah sounded rather surprised at my reaction, considering how deeply I felt about the CID in London, but she was living in Devon, so there was no chance of her meeting someone from London.

"Are you angry?" she quipped.

"No, honestly Sarah, I'm really pleased for you."

"Don't you want to know where he's stationed?" It was that remark that struck me like a bolt of lightning. A twinge of concern flashed through my mind. Rationale quickly dismissed this reasoning from my mind.

Nah, I thought, I'm really not interested in your taunting and intellectual foreplay. I've really had enough of your silly head games.

"No, should I?"

"Well, I met him when I worked at Whetstone. He was a sergeant back then and we used to get on really well."

This was starting to make sense. Very interesting indeed. But now she was really starting to annoy me, and I wanted to say something nasty back. I managed to resist the temptation. "Sarah, if he makes you happy, I'm really pleased for you."

Sarah's voice sounded triumphant and I immediately felt the urge to strike her down with some sarcastic retort. I have to admit that she had scored a point and I was struggling to remove every inflection of her tone and the flashing images she had introduced into my mind. I focused on her objective of trying to annoy me and quickly dispelled her attack.

Sarah wasn't going to let me off her fishing line. She went on: "Well, can I have the £300?"

"Nice try, Sarah" I thought, trying to think of a way of dealing with her request. Why couldn't I just say NO to the bitch?

Somehow she always got her own way. All I wanted was to have a quick word with my sons. It was an honest, simple request. I really didn't need to have dialogue with her and at the same time pay for that concession. So I tried to deflect her request again.

"Can't you take it out of the maintenance money I've given you?" I said.

"No, I think YOU should have to pay. You left me, don't forget!"

Bitch, I thought, but instead of telling her that I said: "I'll send you a cheque."

"No! I need it now!" she snapped back. There was absolutely no compromise in her voice. "I want you to send it to me through the bank. I need it in my account today. Please? Please, please, please, bloody please?"

It was time to try to step up the reasoning, considering the hour, so I said: "I can't tonight. I'll send it through tomorrow."

Sarah's voice turned from venomous snake about to strike to the tone of an innocent child, all 'girly' "Promise?"

"Yes, yes, I promise. I'll send it across first thing tomorrow. I'm in London at the moment and I might drop in to see the boys over the weekend. Is that OK?"

I could feel the venomous snake starting to reappear. She barked: "Why? You can't just turn up without letting me know first. I need warning! It's just not fair."

"I'm giving you warning, Sarah. I'm telling you now. In advance!"

Sarah wasn't going to be happy until she knew my plan, so I said "I'm going to be down anyway, because I'm having some quotes done at the farm. So if you see people moving about as you drive past, don't worry, there's no need for concern, it will be me and the builder."

Sarah could smell the prospect of more money. She knew I was ready to start the building work, so she said "OK, I'll tell the boys you rang and you may see them at the weekend."

Trying to remain calm, I thought, there is a God. In a matter of fact way I said "Enjoy your meal."

Brian arrived back from the shop just as I hung up from Sarah. He nodded and gave me a strange look.

"Is everything all right?"

It was hard to disguise my frustration. "Have you ever rung home and wished you hadn't?"

Brian was most amused and let out a great roar of laughter. "Every time, mate!"

I really didn't want to mess around in the bank in the morning, so I said: "Listen Brian, I need to turn over a few quid and I was wondering if you knew anyone who might want a shotgun? I used to shoot clays at the back end of Tiverton, but when I left home I had to take my shotgun with me."

Brian looked surprised. "Have you got it with you?"

"Yes, Brian. I've explained my circumstances to Southampton Firearms Unit because my certificate was up for renewal. When I told them I had moved out of the Old Rectory they asked me where I was going to store my gun, so I told them it would be locked up in my empty farm house. They weren't happy, Brian. They told me that I had to keep it in my possession until I had actually moved into the property. How bloody stupid is that? I even told them I was living in a hotel in Worthing and this sergeant told me "It doesn't matter, you still have to keep it with you." So here I am walking around with a bloody shotgun in my suitcase. How stupid is that? I've left the ammunition at the farm, even though I'm not supposed to. He told me I had to pick it up as soon as possible, so going down to Devon this weekend fits in well for me."

Brian was very reassuring. "Listen, I've cancelled all my jobs, so I take it we're still on for going to Devon tomorrow?"

"Yes, Brian."

He pulled his mobile phone out of his pocket and was about to dial. "Listen, Con, don't worry about the shotgun, my mate Sid will take it off you. Do you want me to give him a ring and have a word?"

I said: "Are you sure? Do you think he'll want it?"

"What make is it?"

"It's a Purdey sidelock, a late model made with original chopper lump barrels. It's been sleeved to quite a high standard and it has a round bar action. I don't want to let it go really, but needs must."

"All that means nothing to me, Con. Is it a twelve bore?"

"Yes, Brian and a very unusual one. It's easily worth a couple of grand."

"Not around here, Con. How much do you want for it?"

"I'd take a grand for it, but it would have to be done legally, you know, whoever bought it would have to show me their shotgun certificate first."

"No problem, Con. Do you want me to call Sid now?"

"Yeah. If you can get hold of him."

Brian went downstairs as I unpacked the things I needed to stay over in the flat, and before I knew it he was back with his phone to his ear. "Sid said he'd buy it off you for four hundred quid. He's a copper, so you can have a butchers at his certificate as well. No problem."

"I can't let it go for four hundred, Brian, it's worth a lot more than that!"

Brian spun around on his heels while talking over the telephone and said "He wants a grand, Sid. It's a fucking Purdey, for Christ's sake!" He listened intently "Yeah. Yeah. That's your final offer?"

Brian turned back to me and said "He's sticking to his guns, Con. Get it? Guns? Seven hundred quid and that's tops." He chuckled away to himself as he waited for my response. "I should have been a fucking comedian, Sid."

"Yeah, OK seven hundred pounds, but it's got to be cash, Brian." I'd only just joined a clay pigeon club in Lancing a month earlier, so I was a bit pissed off with the deal really. But now that Brian knew I had a gun, it was best to get rid of it. It was now lying in three pieces among my clothes on the bed.

Brian went back on to his mobile. "Did you hear that, Sid? He'll take seven hundred quid but he wants cash. Yeah, OK, see you in a minute."

I assembled my shotgun, unfolded the case, slid the gun inside and took it downstairs. Within a few minutes Sid arrived and gave me seven hundred pounds in cash and showed me his shotgun certificate. He quickly signed a receipt, said "Nice doing business with ya" and left. Brian wasn't really paying attention to what I was saying as he now appeared to be in a hurry. "Thanks for helping me out there, Brian. I must admit that it's a stupid situation to get yourself into. It felt very uncomfortable walking around with a gun in my case. It's like something off the television."

"No problem. Listen I've got to dash, I will see you in the morning. Make yourself comfortable and help yourself to anything you find." Brian left, entrusting me with a key for the shop and the flat.

I must admit that after about an hour I felt a bit uncomfortable with what I had done and decided to go out and have a drink in the pub across the road. It was karaoke night in the main bar and it was packed and noisy, but the snug bar was virtually empty. I stood alone at the end of the small bar near the dartboard and looked around. The room smelt of old men, if you can imagine that, stale tobacco, pork scratchings and the afterburn of an old man's flatulence, like a sad, poorly-managed, bottom-end old people's home. The nuts on the bar were a kind thought at first glance and looked tempting, but I resisted the urge to eat them after seeing the old boy walk out of the toilet and dip his hand deep into the bowl. He must have the constitution of an elephant. The nicotine-stained walls and poorly-hung pictures of racehorses and greyhounds spoke of a misspent youth. The dartboard was well worn and the area around double top was positively bulbous.

The old man, who was about eighty-five years old, short, shrivelled with age and constantly bowed forward, was wearing a dirty, stained, pinstriped suit that has seen better days, a grey shirt and a Guinness tie. He sidled up to me chewing his cud and then raised his right index finger to my face: "Beware of strangers". Pointing his finger toward my face: "You're a fucking stranger!"

Having worked for the brewery for years, I knew all the ploys to solicit a free drink off a new face at the bar. At least, I thought I did. The only thing I could think of saying was: "Trust no one, Granddad."

"You ain't from round here, boy." His breath was stale but that was eased by the smell of peanuts, the residue of which was stuck all over the roof of his mouth, pushing his false teeth from his gums and making them clack around in his mouth. His voice sounded coarse and menacing and he kept licking his lips, a sure sign of a man's condition.

"I'm not from around here, I'm staying with my mate across the road. What part of Wales do you come from then?" I said in a light-hearted tone.

He looked shocked. "You cheeky bugger! I've lived around here all me fucking life! I've never been to Wales! I watched them build the 'ouses around 'ere. There was nuffink here then. Nuffink! The fucking Germans bombed the lot. Bastards! You're taking the piss, ain't ya? You think you're funny but you're a stupid bastard."

"Not as funny as you look in that suit, Granddad."

"I don't know if I want to drink with the likes of you!"

"That's good, piss off and annoy someone else."

"That's rude, you know. If I was younger I'd give you what for."

"I'm having a laugh, you daft bugger. You know? I was joking. Shut up moaning and have a drink." The old man smiled wryly.

"I knew you was, I don't mind a bit of friendly banter. I'll 'ave a pint of mild, but if a dickhead like you offers me a drink, I always insist on a large Bells to wash it down with. You ain't laughing now are you, you prick!"

"Well done Granddad, that's the nicest thing I've been called in a long time. I'll have the same." I reached out to shake his bony hand and he gripped mine like a set of mole grips.

"Me name's Jack, what's yours?"

"Con. Nice to meet you Jack. Drink up."

I lost count of the drinks I had with Jack and, give him his due, he stood his own rounds from there on.

As the night passed, young men kept walking up to Jack and asking after his wellbeing and wanting to buy him drinks. He thanked them and called out to the barman "Put that one behind the bar for me Allan!" and he made a note on a pad by the till.

There was a real sense of family in this place. Even though the punters in the other bar were singing their hearts out, they still dropped in on Jack to make sure he was being looked after.

They really cared about him, like he was family. Dad probably, maybe he was. I don't know.

I listened to Jack for most of the night reminiscing about his misspent youth. As I was about to leave his final visitor looked like a middle-aged thug with money, a hardnosed attitude, short cropped hair, nicely cut, single vent, dark brown woollen pin striped suit. He completely ignored me and spoke directly to Jack. Like a well trained dog, when he talked to Jack it was as if he was the only other man in the world. "Is he annoying you, Jack?"

Jack was in the middle of telling me about his boxing career and loving every minute of it. "Nah, he's OK, Frank. He's sound."

Still ignoring me, he went on "He looks like Old Bill to me and they ain't welcome in 'ere."

He turned and looked into my eyes for the first time and asked: "You're 'Old Bill, ain't ya?"

"No, I'm visiting a friend across the road."

Frank wasn't convinced. "Yeah, right" he said. Jack was quick to defend me saying: "He ain't Old Bill, Frank. He's a piss taker, but not a copper. He's sound, I'm tellin' ya!"

Frank left me listening to Jack. "I'd made a few quid selling stuff for the Government and after the war I offered to buy the bomb holes. Who'd want to buy a hole in the ground, Con? They thought I was mad but I ain't, see. I did a deal and it's done very well for me. Set me up, like. Frank's OK, he's just protective, you know, he don't like strangers either. We're like family around 'ere, Con. If we don't know ya, you ain't normally welcomed." He put his fingers on both hands together and emphasised "Family. We're all part of a family, Con."

We recharged our glasses and Jack said: "Come with me, Con. I'll show you somethin'." He led me through into the main karaoke bar and as soon as we walked in everyone cheered. I thought, My God, Jack's a celebrity. I felt proud to have been taken into his confidence and guilty for teasing him about his suit. The cheering continued and I watched as a microphone was passed through the crowd to him and he tried to pass it over to me.

"I don't sing, Jack. Sorry."

Suddenly the music started to play *My Way* and Jack was off. The crowd went wild as he minced towards the stage, and I slowly reversed out of the pub, crossed the road and returned to the flat. Jack sounded good from outside, but I was still feeling uncomfortable about the sale of my Purdey. I glanced through the photographs in the office on the way through to the flat and after what Brian had told me about some of the people he knew and what they did, I decided to telephone my brother John, a detective inspector in the Metropolitan Police, who at that time was attached to the Complaints Investigation Bureau (CIB 2).

John was surprised to hear my voice. "Is everything all right?"

"I'm in London at the moment and I am staying with Brian. He's the guy I introduced you to when we met up for our last reunion in the Mayfair Hotel. He was the one stood to your left with his girlfriend at the bar?"

"Are you in trouble?" He sounded really concerned.

"No. Brian seems fine, but I think that some of the people around him may be up to no good and there are lots of coppers involved. Bent coppers! I think they're on the make big time up here, John."

"How the hell have you got to meet up with them? Do they know who you are?"

"Yes, but they don't know I'm calling you. They all share the same interests in boxing, John. I recognised one of the guys in the photographs on Brian's wall and it's Charlie Kray. He's like a father to Brian, apparently."

"Costa, my advice to you is not to get involved! Keep well clear of that lot and anything illegal and if you think there are bent coppers involved give me a call in a couple of days and we can meet up. You can tell me all about it then."

"It's not just coppers, John, they're running a security protection firm and there are ex SAS personnel involved. They're bringing in guns from Russia and putting them on to the streets! Coppers and the military selling fucking guns to criminals! I've just sold my bloody Purdey to one of them!"

"Costa, don't get involved and if they are who I think they are you had better be careful. Keep in touch."

"I don't think Brian's involved, John. OK, I'll speak to you soon. They trust me, so don't worry. I had better go, they're coming back!"

"Have you got a phone number?"

I looked down at the dial on the telephone and the number section was blank. "I can't give you one, John. I've got to go, sorry."

I quietly put the phone down. I could hear Brian talking to Sid in the office below and he sounded really annoyed:

"Well, I don't give a shit! He's sound, I'm tellin ya! He's with me anyway, so trust me on this one!"

Sid was arguing back "It isn't worth the risk, Brian. We've checked him out and the lads on board aren't happy about him! He's not one of us! Do you understand? He wasn't in our unit!"

"I know him and I'd trust him with me life. He's on the Square with two lodges!"

I thought I should let them both know that I was around, so I made some movement in the flat which alerted them and I walked heavily to the door of the flat and went down to meet them both in the office. Brian and Sid looked very uncomfortable. "I've just popped in to collect a battery for me mobile, Con. Is everything OK?"

"Yeah, no problem. I thought I'd just touch base with you as I heard someone moving about downstairs."

"Blinder, mate. I thought you'd gone over the road for a drink. I'm meeting up with Tracy now, so I'll see you in the morning." They both left the office together talking quietly between themselves.

The following morning Brian arrived at the office at about 10.15 and we had a coffee together. I had already had the job on the farm priced up by another builder and had prepared a budget for the work.

"Listen Brian, Are you sure that you want to go all that way for such a small job?" I said. "I've only got a budget of about four grand to re roof the barns and I need the slates to match what I've already put up on the farmhouse."

Brian waved his hand in a matter-of-fact way. "I can get the slates cheaper from around here, Con. Trust me."

I wanted to be sure that we were talking about using the same quality reclaimed Welsh natural roofing slates, so I said: "If I pay for the slates and tell you the source, you can pick up what you need as and when you need them. They have to match the ones I have just put on the farmhouse, Brian. I don't want there to be any misunderstanding and it's always important to get the ground rules laid out correctly at the start."

"No problem, Con, we'll get the slates from wherever you want and you're paying for them anyway."

"The work is being done in stages, Brian. The architect has had a look over the place and he thinks it should be a grade I listed building but somehow it's been missed."

"Oh, I see."

"I've got planning to put in two new entrances to the farm because it's a busy road and I have full planning permission to convert the first barn. The idea is to reroof the first barn and then apply for a change of use and apply to convert the whole project into a business training centre, with an upmarket restaurant facility. So I will need a car park, diggers, lights and a proper working kitchen built out back with access to the farm house and then linking to the first barn."

"It's going to be a big development then, Con?"

"Oh yeah, not bad. There's about four acres in the top field and two in the lower field and I'm going to need to put in drains and tap into three wells in the grounds. I've already started to cut away a load of earth from behind the main house and we're pushing all the muck from there into the lower fields."

"All this sounds expensive, Con, if you don't mind me saying. You ain't going to do all that with four grand!" Brian was now looking extremely concerned.

I smiled. It was evident that I had to divulge more of my overall plan. "My accountant is going to partner me in the business and we've already set up a company to trade through. Peter, my bank manager, drives past my farm every day on his way to work and he keeps asking me how things are going because he knows my accountant as well. We've got a really good relationship and sometimes we meet up for lunch together."

"All mine does is write me shitty letters, Con." Brian started laughing aloud and the mood was quite relaxed.

"Brian, as soon as Peter sees the barns being reroofed, I'm going to tap him for some money. At the moment I don't owe anything on any of the land and I own the barns outright. He's offered to lend me some money but he will want some security from me. With a new roof on the barns it will mean that he will 'stump up' with what I need to convert the lot. See?"

"Got ya! You want it to look busy and he'll want to go along with it all. Right. You clever bastard, Con!"

"I want it done right, Brian, so I don't want a load of cowboys on the site."

"Say no more, Con. So there's going to be a few grand in it for me?"

"Of course, but to start with it's going to be four grand for two roofs. Agreed?"

"I've still got to see it though, Con. When do you want it all to start?"

"As soon as you can, Brian."

"We'll I'll come down next week with some of the lads and dump them down there. Have you got anywhere I can leave a motor for them to punt around in?"

"That's not a problem. The barns are big enough to stick a car in if you want to leave one down there."

"That'll save a lot of mucking around next week and we can all go down in one motor."

So I left my Golf at the back of the shops and, at Brian's request, drove around in his car to a friend's house where he picked up a blue Ford Fiesta and we followed each other down to the farm. Brian parked the Ford in one of the garages and I showed him around the farmhouse and explained the plans I had for development. Brian and I agreed a fixed price for the work and I gave him a key to the side door.

"You can start as soon as you like, Brian" I said. "I'll give you two grand up front and the rest when you've finished." We shook hands and I directed Brian to Exeter to show him where I had sourced the slates for the farmhouse roof. Later that afternoon Brian drove us back to London where I collected my car and returned to carry on with my work in Worthing. I went straight to the office in Tarring Road to check my diary. I arrived there at 9.30 pm and went upstairs to prepare myself for a meeting the following morning with the steering committee of BMI Ltd, my business management company.

When I got back to my car I found that the driver's door was unlocked and my coat was missing from the footwell on the front passenger side. I checked the boot, but nothing else appeared to be missing. I was just glad that I had sold my shotgun and I couldn't be bothered if my clothes had been stolen, so I didn't bother reporting the incident. I was too preoccupied trying to start the car and I had so many other things going on in my mind. I had remembered to telephone Sarah to apologise and explain that I didn't have time to drop in to see her and the boys, because Brian wanted to get back to London and I had an important meeting to prepare for the following day.

The next morning I parked in Harrow Road in Worthing as usual and got into the office at 8.30. I immediately noticed two uniformed policemen walking in and out of my office. Sally looked really anxious: "We were broken into last night." Both policemen followed me into the main office, which had windows across its complete width. It was the taller of the two who took charge.

"We're going to need a list of all that's been taken and we're going to need all your fingerprints for elimination purposes" he said. He kept ticking things off from what appeared to be a list in his notebook.

"I've got an important meeting in a few minutes and I really don't need all this right now" I told him. Fortunately I had prepared for my meeting at the hotel the previous evening and all the paperwork I needed was safely tucked away in my briefcase.

Then Sally's telephone rang and she lifted the handset to her ear and immediately put the call on hold. "They're here!" she called. She pressed the hold button again and said "Yes, Donna, show them up."

Sally said: "Your clients have arrived and they're on their way up." She managed to remain calm and professional. "Good morning gentlemen" she began. "You will have to bear with us as we've had a burglary and the police are taking details." Then she showed them through to my office.

"Hello George." I reached out and shook his hand warmly. George operated as a business strategist in numerous countries throughout Europe and he was keen to link into a business management company in the UK. He was a fit, good-looking Italian (aren't they all), clean shaven with a strong chin line, of medium height and with olive skin. He was a smart dresser with an eye for detail, and I could see that the canvassing, probably made of horsehair, had been finely cut to fit him perfectly, having been sewn delicately into the natural fabric of the cloth. The natural line of the sleeves fell perfectly to expose the contrast in colour with his crisp white handmade shirt. He gave me an enormous grin as his words dripped from his lips in a refined Italian accent, exactly as I had remembered him when we first met; precise, soft, and articulate. His diction was perfect; quite a draw, I would imagine, to the opposite sex.

"Hey, Costa! This is a first for me! I've never been fingerprinted before a meeting in my life!" George found my predicament most amusing, but for me it was embarrassing and very frustrating.

I reached out to shake another of my guests' hands. "Phillip! Good to see you again." Phillip Wilson was slightly shorter than me, around six foot two and definitely slimmer than me. He retained the older 'Southern Lowland' Washington accent which he revealed with the consistent r-dropping. Phillip was highly intelligent and extremely wealthy, but he paid little attention to his appearance or to how his clothes hung on him. He had told me that he was looking to invest in new projects and was keen to get involved in helping me fine tune the structure of my new business. Perhaps I could refer him to a good tailor in return for his support, I thought, returning his smile.

"Good to see you again, Costa. This is all very unfortunate for you, but, don't worry, we can still work through this distraction."

"That's good, Phillip. Take a seat."

My final guest was waiting patiently to shake my hand. "Hello Alan. Good to see you again." Alan had travelled from Warwick and looked like a typical 'bagman' with a rather bland and tired dark grey suit and loose chequered tie. He was carrying a deep, black, heavy document case, which he looked pleased to put down on the thick wine-coloured carpet beside his chair. Alan had a full head of shoulder-length hair, which glistened with the colours of gold as in the sun as he flopped back into his chair.

The same police officer returned and was now becoming very impatient. "Now that you're all here I need elimination fingerprints" he said. He turned to me and started rolling my fingers in ink, then proceeded to do the same to all those present. We took it in turns to try to wash the ink off our hands. He carried on doing this in my office in a matter-of-fact way. Before long he had fingerprinted all the members of the steering committee, Sally included.

I reached down to turn on my computer hard drive - and realised that it was missing. The screen was there and all the other equipment. It was just the hard drive that had been taken, which with hindsight appeared to be a bit odd.

"Excuse me officer!" I shouted. "They've taken my hard drive." At this point Sally came into the office. "Sally, can you telephone Preview Data Systems in Rickmansworth and tell them what's happened and ask them if they will drop off a new hard drive urgently?" Fortunately I was subscribed to a system which was backed up daily to an external storage system. Not being someone who believes in coincidence, I was starting to become a little suspicious about what was happening around me.

The meeting lasted for about two hours and we set a date for the next meeting; the three men left.

On the morning on Tuesday 16th April 1991 I was going through my post when I received a telephone call from Brian. "I want you to meet me at the farm today, Con. I'm bringing someone across who I would like you to meet." He sounded stressed and wouldn't take no for an answer.

"Brian, I'm in Worthing and I've got a full week's work lined up. The appointments have already been booked and I can't just drop everything and go over to the farm" I replied.

"You have to! I've got someone I want you to meet. You're going to have to reschedule! This is really important, Con. We're leaving now and we'll meet you there."

"Brian, I don't care. If you want me to meet the Pope, I'd still have commitments here!"

"Con, this is really important. We'll see you down there. Don't let me down on this one!"

I left my office to break the news to Sally but she was one step ahead of me and said: "Don't worry, Costa, I'm already rescheduling. I overheard your conversation." Brian had already started to bring chaos into my life and this wasn't a good sign.

When I arrived at the farm at 3.30 pm, Brian had already started to 'prep' the job with one of his workers. They were both dressed in jeans and casual shirts and wore short jackets, Brian in denim and his friend in brown cords. They both had smiles that could illuminate Blackpool on a cold winter's night.

Brian reached out and shook my hand. "Nice to see you again, you old bastard!"

Just a bit familiar, I thought and the look on my face must have shown how I felt about his little quip. I was thoroughly pissed off, as I was up to my eyes in work and didn't have time to mess around helping them orientate themselves with finding roofing materials. They both appeared to be like ducks out of water. Out of London and lost, I thought.

"Tim, this is Con, you know, the geezer I was telling you about."

I reached out to shake his friend's hand and he didn't want to let it go. I couldn't get it back! "You're real then, Colin?"

"I was real when I left Worthing this morning, so yes, I suppose I am, although I'm not sure what you mean?"

"Well, this prick reckoned that he had a mate who needed a job done. You know and he asked me to give him a hand, like. You know. Would I come down and give him a hand like." Tim was jabbering on about nothing. He was beaming and looked so pleased to see me.

"There's a lot of work to be done here, Tim, so yeah. If that's what you mean?"

"When he told me about you, you know, that he knew a 'toff' and all that. I didn't think he did, Colin, but you're real, like, ain't ya? You're bloody real!"

"I certainly am, Tim, but I'm not a toff, and it's Con." Tim was already starting to annoy me.

"Yeah I know. Well I'm a sparky, like, and I've got to do all the electrical stuff, you know, lights and power points etc."

"That's what sparkies do normally, Tim."

"Blinder! Yeah, you're right." He laughed nervously.

"Well, I'd better show you where to source the slates and I expect you want me to order them now? You need to follow me down the M5 as we don't have much time."

"Yeah, let's have a look around here first, Colin. It's lovely, ain't it?"

"I thought you'd already done that, and it's CON!"

"We ain't going to Exeter tonight! We want to book in somewhere and we can do that tomorrow." They clearly had some sort of a plan. "Where can we stay tonight, Colin?"

"I wasn't planning to stay tonight and Brian knows where everything is. I showed him the last time he was down."

Brian snapped back: "I'm from bloody London! It's all hills around here and I can't remember where nuffink is. Tell us where the nearest hotel is and we'll see you here tomorrow."

"The nearest and best pub around here is the Poacher's Pocket. It's a couple of miles back up the link road. Go straight over the roundabout and you'll find it on the right. It's a big white building. When you go in ask for John or Pat and they'll take good care of you. Just tell them that I sent you along."

"What about you Colin, ain't you coming along as well?" Tim looked really disappointed.

"No, I'm going to see an old girlfriend in Exeter, so I'll meet up with you both in the morning. Does ten o'clock sound OK?" I really didn't fancy a big drinking session with them and I found the thought of seeing Nancy in Exeter again more appealing. She had been an old friend for years and although we both fancied the pants off each other, we had kept our friendship intact by not getting involved in a sexual or romantic way, and strangely it worked. Nancy was an outstanding saleswoman and often worked away from home.

As chance would have it, she was out when I called at her house in Heavitree. It was getting too late to call on Sarah and the boys, so I returned to the farm and sat in the car for a while listening to it creak and groan as it cooled down. I loved thrashing the guts out of it on the back road up from Exeter to Tiverton and I felt a cold shiver go up my back as I passed over the bridge where I had wrecked my BMW.

Around midnight I left the car and went into the house. After rummaging through my case and making a makeshift bed I slept on and off on the floorboards in the bedroom next to the toilet. I kept hearing voices in the back garden, which was a bit odd because the property was completely isolated. I crept out of the house and walked around the farm in the dark to see who it was, but I couldn't find anyone prowling around. I sat in the car for a while and turned the engine on to warm myself up and then, after about an hour, I returned to the house to try to get back to sleep. I had absolutely no idea what was concealed in the woods at the back of my house and it was just as well that I hadn't walked up there to find out.

It was cold and windy the following morning and when Brian and Tim arrived we measured up the project. I threw some matching slates in a cardboard box and Tim put them in the back of his builder's van. This way I could be confident that they would match the farmhouse slates. Then, after having another look around the farm, Brian and his electrician friend Tim followed me in their van down the M5 toward Exeter.

Everything seemed to be going smoothly at this point and, once I had pointed out the various roofing merchants, we turned back and headed for the farm. About halfway through our journey Brian motioned for me to pull over and joined me in my car.

"What's up, Brian?" I asked. I was a bit surprised that the van pulled over as it did.

"I can't listen to that idiot prattle on! All he ever talks about are his ex-wives and how much money they are screwing out of him. He's doing my head in, Con!"

This sounded all too familiar to me. "Domestic strife with her indoors, eh?"

"You can say that again! So you're heading back to Worthing in a minute then?"

"Yeah, I'll just pick up some things from the house and go straight back."

"I'm going to leave Tim at the farm to manage things, you know? When my lads come over he'll make sure they do a good job stripping off the roof."

"No problem, Brian. I'll leave you to get on with it all. It's hardly rocket science."

"Skilled craftsmanship more like, you cheeky bugger! I'll keep you up to date over the 'blower'."

We continued to chat away about the building work as I drove up the M5 towards Tiverton and I was totally oblivious to everything going on around me. Every now and then I glanced back to see if Tim was keeping up with us in the van. The traffic was light and the sun was starting to break through an overcast sky and it looked like it was going to be a lovely day and I was looking forward to the drive across to Worthing.

It wasn't long before I started to approach the entrance to the farm, so I checked for oncoming traffic and looked into my rear view mirror, where I saw Tim in the van immediately behind me. As the road became clear I swung straight through the entrance and into the yard. Tim, on the other hand, had to pull up to allow for an oncoming vehicle to pass before he could cross over and follow me. It's not an easy road to cross and being concerned for the safety of Tim, I glanced in my rear view mirror. I could see his van stationary in the middle of the road just to the left of the heavy double white lines. He was signalling right to follow me into the yard.

As I turned around I looked through the front windscreen and I saw two men running towards me from behind the barn directly ahead of me. I immediately called out to Brian. "Are these your workmen?"

"No!" He snapped.

"Who the hell are they then?" I shouted. They looked tall and menacing, heavily built, scruffy and unshaven. I really believed we were being robbed. "What the hell's going on, Brian?" I shouted.

Then I heard the screech of tyres from the road and the roar of the van's engine as it sped away from the entrance. I thought about putting my foot to the floor to race past the men and down the new track that led to the lower field, but thought better of it when I noticed they were carrying pistols.

Brian leapt out of the car to confront the men, shouting: "Leave it to me, I'll sort the bastards out!"

There was no messing with this guy. I still wanted to get away, but I could clearly see that I'd be a dead man. Bastards! They had guns! Guns? Why guns, in Devon?

As Brian got clear of the car I could see four more armed men running at him from the left. They had been hiding in the other barn to my left. I saw another man carrying a heavy piece of wood and he whacked Brian across the back with it, sending him crashing into the gravel. Then four men piled in on top of him.

I looked again at the men who were standing in front of my car. The pistols they were carrying were pointing at my head and their hands were shaking violently. Suddenly my attention was drawn to my driver's window. I saw another two armed men, similarly dressed, pointing their hand guns at my head and their hands were shaking violently too.

I felt nothing now, no emotion whatsoever, only the feeling of weightlessness, a kind of floating feeling, while staring down the barrels of their guns. Instinctively I raised my hands above my head and pushed the palms against the windscreen. I didn't feel any fear, though I did realise the real danger in that one of these guns might go off by mistake. Look at their hands, I thought, they're bricking it. If I wasn't careful they would kill me in the car.

They were clearly pumped up with adrenalin and looked terrified. They held their weapons in their right hands and tried to use the other to steady their guns, but they were unable to stop their hands from trembling uncontrollably. Oh bloody hell! Just don't screw things up here, Costa or you're dead, I thought.

Even at this point I still believed that I was being robbed and that these guys were desperate. Why? I wondered. They must think I'm loaded.

I instinctively felt the need to try and reassure them, so I shouted out "You don't need to be afraid of me! You can have everything! It's OK! It's OK! My wallet's in my jacket! I mean it! Take it! You can have it all, I don't care!"

One of the men who were standing to my far right was still pointing his gun at my head and now he opened my driver's door with his left hand and reached over me and unclipped my seat belt. He shouted into my face "We're not robbing you, you prick! We're not robbing you!"

I was gobsmacked "What then? Who are you guys?" I kept my arms up in the air and my mind started racing wildly. "What do you want?"

As we were on an incline, the driver's door kept falling back on to me as I kept pushing it back with my right knee and the men in front of my car came to my driver's door to help, still pointing their guns at my head. At this point Brian was out of sight. Two of the men who were seeing to him suddenly jumped to their feet and returned to the firing position with their legs apart and pointed their weapons at me.

This was now getting rather silly. If all five guns went off at the same time we were all going to die here and no one would live to tell the tale.

The men who were standing to my right then started shouting orders at me.

"Keep your hands above your head!"

"Don't move or we'll open fire!"

"Don't get out of the car!"

"Look at me! Look at me!"

As we stared at each other I was unable to resist the temptation to look down the barrel of their guns as they were pointing at my head. "Look at ME! You bastard!"

I didn't know what I had done to piss him off so much. I was trying to reassure him, so I said "Calm down. Listen, everything's going to be OK. Right?"

He snapped back and leaned towards my face angrily, blowing frothy saliva all over me: "Shut the fuck up!"

The thing that concerned me most was that their hands were still trembling and shaking uncontrollably. I was at a loss as to how to calm them down. Suddenly everything seemed to calm down naturally and the floating feeling subsided. Up until this point it felt like everything had been happening in slow motion.

Against my better judgement, I said "If you're not robbing me, then who the hell are you?" My mind suddenly flashed back to my time working alongside the Flying Squad in London and then it clicked.

"You're the Met! What the hell is the Met doing all the way down in Devon?" I was totally confused and waited for a reply as my mind was turning somersaults. My comment was met with roars of laughter and the policeman on my far right leaned forward again and bellowed in my face:

"Shut the fuck up, you bastard! Why can't you shut up!" He walked towards me and leaned right into the car and I felt the cold steel of the barrel of his Smith and Wesson revolver. He pushed it into my face and snarled "Shut the fuck up! Shut it!" This guy was really pissed off with me now. I mean really, really pissed off and pushing the barrel in deeper he spat out: "Do you want to have a go? You do, don't you? Go on then! I'll blow your fucking brains out!"

A thought suddenly crossed my mind: "This guy's seen too many Clint Eastwood movies". But he had a real gun sticking into my face and this was no movie. Even so, I managed to mumble through the side of my mouth. "What's all this about then?"

He pushed the gun further into my face "You just don't stop, do you?" Seeing my lack of response to his demented outbursts of rage, he pulled his gun away and holstered it.

Two policemen then dragged me out of the car sideways. I could tell they were angry with me because they dropped me heavily on to the gravel and then the arresting officer pushed his size 10 boot into the nape of my neck, ramming my face into the gravel and barked:

"Not so clever now are you, you bastard?" I couldn't reply because my face was buried in the gravel. My hands were cuffed behind my back with plastic ties, the type they use for securing trees and posts, and all I could hear was the sound of their voices celebrating and congratulating each other. The whole situation was bizarre and as I listened I wondered why they were celebrating. They started to search the outbuildings and I heard my car boot pop open.

As soon as DS Bains took his boot off my head, I turned sideways: "So I'm right then, you are the Met. What's brought the Met all the way down here?" DS Bains was now trying to learn how to surf on my back and he snapped back in a rather agitated tone. "You start talking to us, son, and we'll start talking to you!"

"What's this all about? Why am I being arrested?

"I'm arresting you for conspiracy to rob" he said, and he gave me the usual caution.

"Rob who, for God's sake?" My question was met with more laughter. After being left face down for about half an hour I complained "You're killing my back. Can I at least sit up?"

I was then lifted up on to my knees and made to kneel on the gravel in the same position for about forty minutes. During this time the arresting officer tried to make conversation with me. "Is this all yours then?"

I wanted to say "piss off" but couldn't really see any reason not to reply. So I said "Yes, me and the bank."

His inquisitive mind prompted another question "Which bank's that then?"

"Nat West."

"How much do you owe them?"

"That's between me and my bank manager." I could see where his line of questioning was going and I was only too aware how things could be twisted to their advantage.

"You've done very well for yourself since you left, haven't you?"

"So you know who I am then?"

"Of course we do!"

"It's been a lot of hard work but it's been worth it."

After what seemed like an eternity a police traffic car suddenly swung into the yard and the wheels crunched into the freshly laid gravel and I heard someone shout: "Throw the bastard in the back!"

The arresting officer pulled me off my knees and walked me to the back of the police car. I had trouble walking because I had lost the feeling in my legs. "Get in!" With my hands cuffed behind me, he pushed my head down into the car and I managed to shuffle myself into the back seat. We then drove at speed to Heavitree Police Station in Exeter with the blue light flashing and the siren blaring.

I was led into the station, where the duty sergeant said "Strip and put this on." He gave me a white paper suit. As I took each piece of clothing off he searched it and bagged it. Then without further ado he motioned to the Custody Officer: "OK. Lock him away."

I was led to a large open grey door and he guided me into the cell with his arm around my back. Then the door crashed shut and locked behind me. I stood in the middle of the cold, empty cell for about ten minutes and then sat on the solid wood bed that was fixed against the wall.

About an hour later the hatch opened suddenly and a voice said: "You've got visitors". Two men, one in scruff order and the other in a suit, strolled into my cell.

I said "What's this then, a welcoming party?" and stared hard into their faces. I immediately recognised my arresting officer, but the other guy was a mystery. He had a full head of short-cropped brown hair and was about thirty five years old, shorter than my arresting officer. He wore a cheap dark blue suit and Paisley silk tie.

DS Bains was the first to speak. "Listen carefully to what the governor's got to say, if you know what's good for you."

"I'm Detective Inspector Stuart Badcock" said the other man. "I'm in charge of this case and you already know my colleague."

"So what's the bullshit charge then?"

DS Bains appeared to be very impatient, "Shut it you arsehole and listen to what we've got to say, if you know what's good for you." What was this, good cop bad cop? Badcock was clearly trying to convince me that he was the good cop. Unsuccessfully.

"We've spent a fortune on this job and we've come a long way and we have to get a result. Do you understand what I'm saying?"

"Yeah, I think so. I'm getting the picture." Now I was wondering 'Have you got a grudge against me personally or are you just trying to justify your overtime?'

Inspector Badcock went on "If you don't tell me what I want to hear you'll go away with the other two. Do I make myself clear?" The good cop shouldn't really be threatening me, I thought.

"If you really know who I am, which I know you do, you'll also know my brother." I motioned to my arresting officer. "DS Bains certainly knows him."

Inspector Badcock said: "Who's your brother?"

"Give me a break. He's a DI in London and he's worked with you lot! He's now on CIB2."

DS Bains added "Yeah, I know his brother, guv."

It seemed simple enough to me, so I said "Talk to him and he'll tell you everything I know."

"OK, I'll talk to him" said Badcock.

DS Bains looked serious for a moment and then said "Are you saying you're a 'snout' for your brother?"

"I don't know who you guys are and I don't trust you. So speak to my brother and he'll explain everything to you. That's all I've got to say."

DI Badcock said: "OK, we'll talk to him." The muscles on his face relaxed a little now. He nodded in agreement and they both left my cell and I returned to my solitude. About an hour later they both returned. DI Badcock said: "We've spoken to your brother and he's explained, but we can't do anything."

"Why?"

The inspector looked tetchy. "Because it's procedure."

"Procedure? What bloody procedure. Did you speak to him?"

"Yes, but our hands are tied. We can't do anything." The Inspector was being most unhelpful.

"That's bullshit!" I snapped.

DI Badcock said "We want you to help us put the other two away. If you do we'll let you walk."

"I don't know them. So what are you asking me to do?"

DI Badcock said: "Help us."

"Help you stitch them up, you mean?"

"We have to get a result! Do you understand?" My mind started racing. I had seen this before and I knew what a bunch of arseholes this lot were. I wasn't getting involved in their grubby little overtime racket.

"I know you lot only too well" I said.

"Well then?"

So I sealed my fate. "If that's what you've got to do to justify your overtime, that's what you'll have to do because I'm not helping you stitch them up. I don't know them."

DI Badcock said: "Here's my card. You can call me anytime. I mean at any time day or night, and I'll come all the way down here to speak to you personally. Do you understand? Just ask for Stuart."

"Yes, but you'll have a long wait. Now stick your card up your arse and piss off!"' I grunted.

"We'll see. You'll call me once you've had a few days in this place. You'll call me."

As they left I thought, I'd rather do time than kiss your arse, you bastard.

I was further interviewed, and confirmed in a brief statement why I had been at the farm. I answered some of their ridiculous questions. I was advised by my solicitor to answer "No comment" to most of their questions.

They charged me with conspiracy to kidnap, conspiracy to blackmail, going armed with a Section One firearm with intent to commit an indictable (serious) offence and no firearm certificate. I was remanded in custody to Exeter Prison.

CHAPTER FIVE

■ ■ ■ ■ ■ ■ ■ ■

REMANDED TO EXETER

I had often driven past the prison in Exeter, but I had never considered that one day I might actually be a guest of Her Majesty. As an ex-policeman I was warned by one of the escorting officers as we walked to the van to go to the prison. "Ask for the 43s when you get in there. You're going to need to, you've got no option, believe me."

I really hadn't understood what that meant, so I turned to Brian and Tim: "What's that all about?"

Tim looked concerned "I've no idea, Colin."

"Me neither." said Brian and he went on "No one's going to step out in front of you on the landing, you ugly bastard!" and we all laughed together.

"Hang on, did you just call me ugly? If you're not careful you'll get yourself into trouble" I said. There was more laughter.

Brian said "What, more than this? I don't think so, Con!"

"They've made a mistake, Brian and it's only a matter of time before they let us go."

The escorting office remarked "I hope you're right, mate, but it looks like serious shit to me. They came down with so many guns we couldn't get them all in our armoury. We had to find another storeroom. They didn't like us taking their guns off them either, but they're on our patch now and not in the Met. It was like taking a lollipop off a kid." He sniggered.

"They can't make these ridiculous charges stick, surely? Anyway, I'll be fine on the wing." I reassured myself.

"Rather you than me, mate. I personally think you must be mad to even contemplate going on to the main wing. You won't last a day in that place, I certainly wouldn't!"

I thought for a moment and tried to assess the risk "No, I'll be fine."

The escorting officer replied: "So you don't want to go on Rule 43 then?"

"I'm not a child molester or a grass, so I don't see a problem."

"So I won't mention the 43s when I take you in there then. Who did you guys piss off in London? We've never seen so many armed units in one place. Are you the Mafia?"

"No, we're not the Mafia! I'll be fine on the wing and I have no idea who we pissed off. I think it's just about overtime. You know the Met."

The escorting officer said: "I hope you're right."

When we arrived at the prison, the huge heavy wooden gates swung open and the van disappeared inside. We were driven through another large gate, slightly smaller than the first, and around to the side door. We were filed through one at a time into the reception area in silence. In total there were about eight new recruits and one by one we were called forward to be booked in and processed. The smell of disinfectant was overpowering and the atmosphere sombre.

Mr Evans, the duty prison officer, said "Right, Linehan. Strip!"

"What in front of everyone?" Tim was not impressed. "I ain't strippin' in front of this lot!"

The custody officer, a grey-haired, overweight, scruffy-looking screw with dirty shoes and a gut so large it was trying to push its way out of his shirt, sighed and said: "You can do this the easy way or the hard way. If I were you, I'd do it the easy way. Mr Evans won't take any shit from you lot and neither will I."

"I'm an old man, for Christ's sake! I've had a bleedin' heart attack and you can't treat me like this!" Tim pleaded.

Mr Evans tightened his lips and his cheeks went red: "Oh yes we can! You can't come into the prison unless you strip and get disinfected. For all we know you could be full of lice."

"Bloody lice! Who the hell do you think we are, tramps or something?"

Brian was trying to calm Tim down. "Just strip, Tim, you old bastard! We've seen it all before."

Brian started to take his jacket off. "Look, I'll start."

Mr Evans quickly let Brian know who was in charge. "We haven't called you yet, boy. Sit down!"

Tim could see that he was on to a loser. He started tugging at his clothing. "OK, I'll take me shirt off and here's me trousers" he said.

Evans shouted "Everything!" He glared at Brian and barked: "Fuck off until you're called!"

Tim started to do as he was told. The Custody Officer was now getting very impatient with him. "Bollocks! OK I'll take me kit off."

The Custody Officer snapped: "Come on! Hurry up." Brian returned to his seat in silence. It wasn't long before Tim was standing in front of everyone completely naked.

I'd seen the ilk of Mr Evans on the parade ground. If I gave him the 'rod of power', he'd scare the crap out of everyone by swinging his pace stick around and jamming it under his arm. He looked the archetypal drill pig, chin in, shoulders back and strutting his stuff. "Right, now get yourself disinfected through there, boy!" and he pointed to the de-lousing unit.

Brian chirped up "Go on you old bastard! It's as easy as falling off a bleedin' log." Brian followed next and then it was me. I prayed that he wouldn't call me 'boy'. I hate being referred to in that way, it brings out my nasty side.

Within a few minutes we were all standing in the shower area together, the mood hanging on us like a dark cloud. We were soon putting on our prison clothing. Once we were dressed, Evans said "Wait in there!" He pointed to a waiting area and we sat down on a wooden bench. Here I was spoken to by an inmate in prison blues who said "I'm the reception orderly, we've been waiting for you lot to arrive. You're the copper then?" He smiled deviously.

"I was a copper years ago, but I left."

Rubbing his hands together, he said: "News of your arrival has travelled. There's loads of guys who want to meet you, mate. Hundreds!" He started laughing. "As far as we're concerned you're still a copper. Once a copper, always a copper."

"They'll be all right once they've met me and I've settled in."

The reception orderly smiled broadly and said: "In our eyes you're the enemy. End of conversation."

"Like I said, it was a long time ago" I snuffed in reply.

Mr Evans screamed out: "When I was in the Welsh Guards I ate blokes like you for breakfast! Do you hear me?" The room fell silent. "Do you bloody well hear me?! If you do, say "Yes Mr Evans!" We were stunned and remained speechless. So he screamed out again: "Say Yes Mr Evans!"

We all responded immediately: "Yes, Mr Evans."

"Let's get this clear." He pulled his shoulders back, gave us a drill sergeant's glare and began his well-rehearsed speech. There was still some talking among the ranks.

"Shut it you arseholes and listen! You're the lowest form of life in here and we are your gods. So do everything we say and things will go well for you. You left your identities and personalities outside the prison gates and you'll get them back when you leave. From now on you mean nothing and you're worth nothing to us. You're just a number, nothing more than that. Do you understand? Nothing! You will continue to be treated as a number until you leave. Now keep your mouths shut and follow me!"

We collected our bedrolls and followed Evans to 'B' wing, the oldest wing in the prison. The facilities reflected it - there weren't any. Once on the wing, Mr Evans stopped off at various cells and locked away new prisoners. As he did this he checked them off on his list as he marched along the narrow passageways on the landings. We then climbed staircase after staircase to the top level, the 4s, and walked along a narrow gangway in the direction of the centre to the third cell from the end on the left. He unlocked the door and motioned for us to go in.

Tim said "All three of us. In here?" Mr Evans nodded and the three of us bowed under the door frame and filed into the cell one by one. It was dark and cold and about the size of a small bus shelter. It was filthy and the stench of stale urine was overwhelming.

I turned to ask a question - "What, all of us in here!" but it was too late. Evans slammed the heavy door closed behind us and I heard him grunt "Three more pieces of shit off the street."

I had done some bad things in my time, but I never thought I deserved to be treated or spoken to like this.

Tim snapped back indignantly: "How very rude, Colin. Did you get that man's number? I'm going to report him to the Governor! I can't believe that!"

Brian turned on Tim angrily "Don't be bloody stupid, you muppet! Stop acting like a bloody schoolgirl! This isn't a fucking hotel!"

"He's rightly upset, Brian, don't be hard on him." After having lived my life in relative luxury up until this moment in time it came as quite a shock to have to share a cell with what were effectively two total strangers.

"It's filthy!" I said. "Where's the toilet?"

"Don't know, Colin" said Tim. "There ain't no toilet in here. Hang on a minute - yes there is, it's this bucket. No sink in here either, Colin!" Tim was trying hard to think of ways to cheer me up by looking on the positive side of everything and it was getting to be a bit too much to listen to. "We'll have it all shipshape in a jiffy, Colin. Stop worrying, mate."

Brian was fumbling around to see where he was going to sleep. "I can't see bugger all in here and it stinks of shit! I can't stay in here! I just can't do it!"

"Yeah, it's overpowering, Brian. Perhaps they've got a better room. You know, one with a sea view. Should I ask at reception?" All three of us laughed.

Tim frowned and examined the wall above the single bed. "What's all these bleedin' drawings on the walls?" he asked. There was a pause while we all had a look. Brian said: "Dunno mate, No idea." I said: That's a clown, and that's a juggler." Tim was straight in with the answer and said: "It's a fucking circus, ain't it? It's definitely a clown by the door, ain't it? Pull that sheet off the light, cos we can't see nuffink with that covering it"

I reached up and pulled the red sheet down to reveal a small diffused strip light in the arched brick ceiling. Now we could see that someone had gone to town with crayons, as all four walls were covered in childlike drawings of animals and clowns. Even with the sheet taken down from the light, we found it hard to see clearly.

I turned to Tim: "Did you forget to wipe your arse this morning or did you piss someone off for us to be given a room like this?"

"Beats me, Colin. I'm 'avin' the top bunk anyway!" Tim threw his pack up in the air and on to the bed and started climbing all over it to make his bed.

"What time's breakfast, Colin?"

I snapped back "You're having a laugh! Food's the last thing on my mind."

"Well we've got to eat Colin, the big lummox is hungry." and he looked over to Brian, who was making up the single bed, against the wall opposite.

Brian swung round and dragged Tim off the top bunk and Tim started squealing for help. "Don't you call me names! I ain't no lummox!"

"Colin! Get him off! Get him off! I've not long had a bleeding heart attack! I don't want to die in prison."

Brian was clearly upset "You called me a lummox and you're out of order!"

"I called you a swanker earlier on and you said nothing then! What's wrong with a lummox? Go on Brian, what's your problem? Put me down for God's sake!"

"Yeah, put him down Brian. You can't kill him in here, if you do you'll get into trouble." I was trying to lighten the mood.

Brian hung on to Tim and asked: "So what's a lummox, anyway?" and he waited for an explanation.

"Well, it's someone who's strong and physical, like. Yeah, physical. Like you. See you lummox? See? Now put me down or I'll swing for ya!"

Brian lowered Tim on to the floor: "Oh. Well that's OK then. I thought it was something bad."

Tim immediately jumped back on to his bunk and carried on tugging at the green knitted blanket. He threw on the canvas cover. "I ain't got a pillow! I can't sleep without a bloody pillow!"

I sat on the edge of the lower bunk, which was to be my bed, and watched them both arrange their covers. I couldn't stay in there. I just couldn't do it.

Brian had finished making his bed and then sat on it with a proud grin on his face and said: "What about yours, Con, do you want a hand?"

"Come on Colin, shake a leg. I'll give you a hand and we'll soon have this place looking like home."

"Home! You've got to be sick in the head to think this is home, Tim. You can't possibly think you're going to ever make this place Home!"

"You know what I mean, Colin."

"Con! My name is Con! No I don't know what you mean, Tim. All of this just doesn't make sense. We need to work out what's happened instead of prattling on and trying to make beds in this dump!"

"You'll settle in before long, Colin. Try and look on the bright side."

"I'm not COLIN! It's CON! My name is CON! What bright side is that then? I'm not staying in here with you two. I don't even know who you are, for God's sake! For all I know you could be criminals."

"Colin, this place is full of criminals, you daft sod."

"Stop calling me Colin! My name's CON and you're starting to tick me off by calling me Colin all the time!"

"Sorry… Con. Yeah, you're right. Listen, I forgot, OK? I'm

an old man and all that and I'm sixty next year and I know nuffink. I'm stupid. Know what I mean? Are we OK, Con? I'm really sorry."

"Yeah, yeah, you're right Tim. I'm the one who should be sorry."

"That's OK, Colin, don't let it get you down, mate. Like I said, look on the bright side." Tim quipped.

"You're having a laugh, Tim. What bloody bright side? What bright side can you see that I can't?"

Brian was now lying on his bed looking at the ceiling through his heavy prescribed gold-rimmed tinted glasses. "Knock it on the head you two, I'm knackered and I want some kip."

"OK. As it's the last one left and if it's all right with everyone else, I'll take the bottom bunk then" I said in a sarcastic tone. I opened my bedroll on to the lower bunk bed and Tim helped me make my bed.

Once I'd finished making my bed I said "You never know, Tim, they might have room service." Tim gave me a wry smile but Brian lay silently on his bed facing the wall.

"He's asleep, Colin."

I got the strangest feeling that Tim had experienced prison routine before, because he took to it like a duck to water. "Have you been in one of these hotels before, Tim?"

His response was instant. "Nah! Not me mate. Not me. Never been in one before in all me life. The army, yeah, but not prison. Not in all me whole bleedin' life." From what I had seen thus far I wasn't totally convinced.

We seemed to sleep for hours on end, watching the light fall and rise again through the only window, a small vent at the top of the outer wall. All we could hear was the noise of people moving around outside, men shouting, doors being unlocked and banged shut and people moving around outside our cell door at certain times of the day. Lots of keys jangled and we were at a loss to understand why our door remained locked for so long. The bucket we used as a toilet was filling up quickly and there was no alternative for disposing of our urinal waste. We sensed that time was running out before it would overflow into the cell.

We tried to see if we could open the window further to see out but it was jammed shut and there were slatted steel bars blocking it. Brian stood on the back of the only chair to check the view and to get a bearing on where we were housed in the prison. The smell of three men without deodorant and urine was too much to bear and getting rid of the odour was proving to be a big issue for us all.

As I lay in my bunk I began to wish I was dead. At least I'd be with Peter. My mind started to churn over and over again the sequence of events that had led to us being arrested and the cheek of Badcock and Bains when they came into my cell in the police station. Bastards!

The following morning Brian made an announcement "No one is going to have a dump in here until that door opens. Agreed?" We all nodded in agreement.

"We're like bleedin' sausage machines. If you don't put any meat in nothing's going to come out the other end. Right?"

"Thanks for that analogy, Tim."

"As none of us have been to prison before, we have to assume that this door does open, eventually" I said.

Tim declared "I'm getting thirsty and you're getting hungry, ain't you Brian?"

"Yeah, I could eat a scabby horse."

"So let's form a plan. When we hear the sound of people moving about on the landing we'll kick the hell out of the door. Right?"

"Right. Good idea, Con. Have you got that you old bastard?"

Tim looked up in the air wryly and said: "Yes mate, no problem."

We had missed the first opportunity to join what sounded like the early morning rush hour, so when we heard the bashing of doors around midday, we did as we agreed and kicked the hell out of the door.

A prison officer opened the hatch. "What are you lads doing in here?" He put his key in the door and unlocked it.

Brian sounded very crabby. "Having a bleeding picnic! What does it look like! You've left us locked up in here for nearly two fucking days!"

The prison officer barked back in a grumpy Devonshire accent: "Hurry up, you haven't got long!"

As we stepped out of the cell there was a loud cheer and all the inmates started laughing at us. So I walked very carefully with the bucket, which was near to overflowing, to get it emptied and Brian managed to get a water jug from one of the cleaners and we all joined the queue for the bucket sluice and the water tap, which was set in a recess. The queue of inmates stretched all along the landing and we had to wait our turn to use the small urinal which was set to the right of two Thomas Crapper toilets partly concealed between two cubicles with half doors.

It was uncomfortable and humiliating trying to concentrate on moving your bowels with dozens of men, heads bowed, walking past you emptying buckets of urine and human excrement. The stench was unbearable. There were those who, even with having to use a plastic bucket, would prefer to defecate in the cell after sending their cellmates out on to the landing during 'Slop Out'. Allowing one's cellmate to do this did leave the cell humming with a ghastly odour. It normally followed that food would then be collected from the servery and taken back to the cell, so any idea of doing this was strictly taboo.

There were at least thirty to forty men carrying buckets, heads bowed, all doing the same thing. This scene was carved into my mind. Although I had seen it in films, nothing can prepare you for the shock and shame of living out this experience. The high arched ceiling and bars and the smell of stale urine were putrid and overpowering. The experience will remain with me for the rest of my life. It is impossible to adequately describe in words this powerful mix of human degradation, nor can one imagine the dishonour and humiliation one feels when, due to your confinement, you are expected to squat and defecate in a plastic bucket while your cellmates are sitting in full view of you trying to make general chit chat, attempting to pass off the experience as if you were invisible. The only other option open to us was to defecate in full view of everyone on the landing as the staff and inmates moved around during 'slop out'. This regime was both cruel and degrading.

Evans gave us one razor each, tissues and some soap. I asked "Why did you leave us in our cells for so long, Mr Evans? We were left in there for nearly two days!"

He laughed. "Some clever sod thought it would be funny to take your cards from outside your cell after we had done the count. We didn't know you were in there! You should have pressed the button."

I said: "I didn't see a button, Mr Evans!"

"Yes, there's a button. Cleaners I expect. You need to get along with them or you'll end up with all sorts of problems in here."

The queue for the recess was nearly at an end when suddenly there was a loud slosh of water and the sound of bells ringing and a loud bang as a door crashed shut at the other end of the landing.

Mr Evans shouted "All away! All away! Back behind your doors!" One of the inmates had decided that he had taken enough punishment. Rather than empty his bucket in the sluice he had chosen to throw it over one of the screws who was standing on the other side of the large arched gate that separated the wings from the Centre. Panic now ensued among all the staff and inmates

Bang – bang – bang… the noise was deafening as each door was slammed shut along the landing. It was a chilling and stark reminder of where we were.

I shot back into my cell and said to Tim "Mr Evans reckons we've got a button in the cell, I've not seen one, have you?"

Mr Evans turned up at our door to lock us in. "We've got a dirty protest!" he said.

"No Colin, I can't see one anywhere, no bleedin' button in here!" We started to search the wall near the door and we just couldn't see a button. Then Tim shouted out "It's the clown's nose, they've made the button the clown's nose! The clever bastards! Would you believe it, Colin?"

Tim pressed it. Two minutes later Evans turned up and opened the flap and said "What the hell do you three want, we're trying to clean up out here?"

I said "We've found that button, Mr Evans! We've found the button!"

He snapped back "You lot have got to get it together. You've lost the plot! Bloody idiots." He slammed the flap closed again and we heard him walk off.

In the late afternoon the door opened again and we climbed out of the cell to stretch our legs and join the queue for the recess. As we filed down the landing I noticed a lot of blood on the floor. The trail led away towards the end wall where there was a large window overlooking the hospital.

Tim said: "Hey Brian, look at all this blood! What's happened?"

The inmate in front of us turned his head: "Smiffy got PP9'd just before the bell. He's in the hospital now. Poor sod."

Tim wanted to know more "What's PP9'd then, mate?"

"It's a PP9 battery in a sock. You get whacked over the head with it if you piss someone off or get into debt. Smiffy was in debt, so he got it during slop out. He's a scumbag idiot anyway."

It was hard to ignore the constant threat of violence. One of the inmates had taken to kicking our cell door five or six times a day on a regular basis, shouting "Pig, pig, pig!" After some days I said to Brian, "I think it's a cleaner called Benny."

"It's hardly rocket science, Con. All the other prisoners are locked away when he does it, so it's got to be a cleaner."

"Yeah I know, but I'm going to catch hold of him, Brian."

"Why? What's the point?"

"The point is I want him to stop doing it. I'll give him a flying lesson, Brian!"

"A flying lesson? What are you on about?"

"Yeah Colin, where the hell is he going to fly to? Through the bloody roof? You've lost it you 'ave." My comment had clearly gone over their heads and they both found it very amusing.

"Not the roof! Over the railings, you pair of idiots! I want to see if he will go all the way down, you know, through the chicken wire at the bottom and land on the snooker table."

"From up here, Colin? You'll kill him! Ignore it, it ain't worth it mate. Honest. You'll end up doing a stretch for life."

"It won't kill him, he'll land on the net at the bottom. He's taking the piss and he's really doing my head in. I can't let him get away with it any more, Brian. I've had enough. It's definitely Benny."

The door kicking went on for weeks and I rarely left the cell. Tim and Brian went on their own to collect their meals and I stayed behind. I couldn't stand the smell, let alone eat the food. The thought of it turned my stomach. Cabbage boiled to nothing and the look and smell of diced swede, yuk! it makes me gag just thinking about it.

After a few days of watching Brian eat his diced swede, I said "Why can't they mash it with a bit of butter? That'd be lovely! Everything's overcooked!" So I kept waiting in the cell on my own until they returned to sit on the edge of their beds and scoff their food down like pigs eat swill, cunningly disguised as prison food. Yes, it was free and yes, I knew it was only a matter of time before I would have to cave in and eat it but not just yet!

CHAPTER SIX

■ ■ ■ ■ ■ ■ ■ ■

THE BLACK DRESS

I needed to see Michael and Luke, or at least talk to them. So I put in an application to see my Probation Officer and waited for him to call. About 11.30 am the same day I heard a tap at the door and the hatch opened and someone peered through. Then the door was unlocked and swung open.

"Probation?" He nodded and said "I'm Mr Patricks, follow me." So I tagged along behind Mr Patricks and he led me all the way down the various landings to the ground floor office he shared with his opposite number, Mrs Buxton. The walls were painted a cold lime green and I sat in a very uncomfortable upright chair opposite him.

"How can I help?" He had my file in front of him. He didn't bother to look up for eye contact.

"Well, I'd like to speak to my sons. I'm writing to them every day, but I don't get any feedback, so something must be wrong. I'm very worried and I need to know that they are OK." I was trying to hold back the tears of despair that were welling up in my eyes and crush the inner feelings of self pity.

Mr Patricks finally made eye contact with me and said: "Have you got a number that I can call?"

"Yes, but I've been told that my calls won't be welcomed."

Just as I said this a tear dropped from my eye on to my right cheek.

"Why ever not? That can't be right, surely? You really need to keep in touch with your children, don't you?"

"Yes I do and no, it's not right! I keep asking myself "Are they getting my letters?" I don't know! "Are they OK?" I don't know! I don't know! I don't know anything any more!"

He reached out in anticipation: "Let me call the number. Have you got it to hand?"

"Yes, it's a St Albans number." I passed him a piece of paper with Sarah's phone number on it and he began to dial. Suddenly I felt the urge to warn him. "I should let you know that my ex wife is living with a detective sergeant from Whetstone."

Mr Patricks looked puzzled "And?"

"Well, he's told her, apparently, that any calls from me are unwelcome. I even offered to call a phone box up the road, you know, at a set time and my sons could wait there for my call, but no she's not having any of that either." (This was before payphones were installed into prisons, which made contacting families so much easier.)

Mr Patricks dialled the number: "Oh, I see. Well I'll try it anyway and I will have a word with her."

"Ah, hello, my name is Gordon Patricks and I'm speaking from Exeter Prison. I'm Constantine's probation officer." He listened briefly: "He's with me at the moment and he has asked me to call you because he is concerned about the children. I can put him on briefly if you are prepared to talk to him?" Mr Patricks fell silent as Sarah spoke on the other end. After a few moments he said: "That's fine, I can relay a message to him if you prefer. Yes. I'm sure he realises that. Yes. Yes. Well, he informs me that he has been writing to the children and wondered why he wasn't getting any feedback from them." He listened intently to her talking: "I see. Yes. Yes. Yes. Fine. I'll pass that message on to him. Goodbye."

He put the telephone down and looked a little uncomfortable. "Well, your ex-wife doesn't really want to discuss the situation with you. She hasn't given your letters to the children because she feels that they will only upset them."

"And? What else did she say?"

Mr Patricks was wavering and didn't really want to say too much more. "I think it was probably a bad time to call her."

"Why, what else did she say? It's OK, I know what she's like. I would like to know what's really going on."

Mr Patricks locked his fingers together in front of him and rested his hands on the desk.

"Well, she told me that the children are now settled into their new school and they've got a new dad now. She also said that she will try and get them to sit down and write to you. She was quite specific in that she doesn't want you to write to them in London. If you want to write to the children you are going to have to send all your letters directly to her father and you've got his address. He will censor your letters. If he feels that they are suitable to pass on to the children he will forward them on. She's not prepared to do anything more at this stage I'm afraid."

I could see that he was in a very difficult situation: "It's very kind of you to try on my behalf and I appreciate your efforts Mr Patricks." As I got up to leave his office he moved forward and unlocked the door.

As he was turning the key he said "How long has she been seeing this policeman?" He pulled the door open and held it open for me to walk through.

"Six or seven months before I was arrested. I knew that

because Michael had said "Mummy's got a new friend and I can play games on his computer" and that was just before Christmas."

"It's a shame that she's taking that line. It must be very difficult for them as well. Let me know if there's anything else I can do to help."

"Great. Thank you Mr Patricks." He walked me back to my cell and locked me away again.

The door banging and name calling continued relentlessly and eventually I was convinced that I had narrowed it down to one man, Benny. I had finally reached the end of my tether.

The door banging that day was relentless and I was getting very short tempered. Brian said: "Calm down, Con, ignore the idiot. There's no way he's going to follow through with his threats. It will eventually calm down."

"I just can't see that happening, Brian. I'm not convinced they will eventually just accept me. I can't see that happening!"

Saturday was no different to any other morning and our door had already been kicked violently three times by Benny. I could hear his breath the other side of the door and he screamed through the gap in the door: "Pig, pig, pig. You're dead meat! Kill the pig!" He followed this up with the usual pig squealing noises.

As our door clunked open I quickly stepped out on to the landing and watched Mr Evans moving away from me along the landing. As luck would have it, Benny was standing right beside me, looking rather surprised. I grabbed him and turned him around and put my arm around his neck, shutting off his wind pipe and stopping him from screaming. I locked it on tight enough to restrict the blood flow to his head. He struggled for breath and tried to free himself. I grimaced as I growled in his ear: "You're mine, Benny boy! All mine! I'm going to teach you how to fly!" I twisted his head around so that he could see all the way down to the ground floor: "Will the wire catch you, Benny? Personally I don't give a shit whether it does or not! Do you understand? I don't give a damn!"

Benny's lanky six-foot-seven frame grew limp and I loosened my strangle hold to make sure I didn't knock him out. He drew his first breath after his near death experience. "Well?" I watched the colour return to his face as he gagged for breath. "Are you going to stop?" He nodded in panic and stared down on to the flimsy wire stretched over the 'ones'. He said nothing, but I could sense his fear and smell his bad breath and stale tobacco.

"Are we clear about where we stand, Benny?" I went on. He nodded and I let him go. He spent a few moments choking and considering his dilemma. I left him and wandered over to the recess and as I turned back I watched him skulk back to his cell. He didn't call a screw, which was good, and he never banged our door again.

Doug, the inmate who worked with Benny, appeared to be amused by what he had just seen, but in prison there are never any witnesses to rely on. This didn't stop the other inmates from making my life hell and making threats to kill me.

We remained in these filthy conditions for up to 23 hours a day. Trying to cope with the monotony and violence of prison life was horrendous. At first 'bang up' seemed like a lifeline to me as it was difficult to kill a man while he was locked away in a cell, but you can only stay in a cell for so long before the walls start to close in on you.

One Sunday we had all agreed to go to the chapel to see what it was like. Evans unlocked our door and we all followed each other along the landing in silence towards the chapel.

Mr Evans unlocked the large iron gate to the chapel and started to count us in. As he ticked us off his list he said: "I bet you three buggers have got some praying to do". His laugh reminded me of my father, as did some of his mannerisms.

Brian asked "What do we call you, Mr Evans?" Mr Evans snapped back: "You'll call me "Boss, Sir or Mr Evans. It really doesn't matter which one to me. Now fuck off and pray, you ugly bastard!" I thought: 'There's no way I'm calling you boss' and we walked into the chapel.

As we moved through the gate another inmate snarled at me. "What's up pig? It's bad enough doing bird in here without a pig watching us pray!"

I ignored his comment and carried on walking, but Mr Evans decided that he was going to speak up on our behalf. "Don't you idiots listen to the news? Don't go comparing yourself to these three men. They're professional criminals! They're the real thing! You, you're just a plastic gangster! So fuck off if you know what's good for you, and leave them alone or I'll have you down the block, Reynolds." Reynolds head sunk forward like a scolded dog as he scuttled off to his seat.

The Church of England service followed exactly the pattern I remembered, the only difference being the sermon and the hymns. The priest announced "As we are not allowed alcohol there will be no communion. If you want to come up to receive the body of Christ, which is represented here as a wafer, you can. If you want a blessing, please mention this when you come forward." When we were told to bow our heads for prayer, I watched the drug dealers suddenly spring into life. They started passing their 'wraps' around the congregation in exchange for whatever contraband they accepted as payment. Tobacco, watches, rings, chains and cash were the norm, things they had smuggled in from prison visits or deals done with those on remand. So after the usual singing of hymns, the sermon, bowing and handshaking on the way out, nothing much had changed in the services as I had remembered them. Then it was back to the cell and bang up.

"Waste of time, Colin. I don't believe in all that nonsense meself. I ain't going again. Can't see the point. What's God going to do for me? What do you say, Brian?" Tim looked over to Brian for some prophetic response.

"It's shit! I don't want to look stupid singing a load of stupid songs about nuffink. It's bleedin bollocks! Kids' stuff!" Brian gave a snort of indignation.

"Well it beats sitting in the cell on a Sunday morning with you two ugly bastards, so I'll see how I feel next week and I'll decide then" I retorted.

Although I had a strong physical presence, I knew that there was no way I could defend myself against 600 men and I was gripped with inner terror. I ate very little for the first three weeks and my weight dropped by nearly four stone. The food repulsed me and I couldn't bring myself to eat it. Tim kept on and on reassuring me "If you don't eat, Colin, you'll die in here, mate." He was right of course. I had already considered that as one of my options for early release.

The focus initially was on trying to understand how the prison system worked - how you can receive and send money and find work in the prison in order to get a wage. Jobs were in very short supply and if you couldn't find a position quickly the only option was to go into the workshop to sew mailbags for the post office for £1.90 per week or go on education. I thought initially that I wasn't going to be in prison for very long because I failed to see what evidence there could possibly be against the three of us, so I asked "What did you tell them, Tim?"

Tim appeared to be like me, genuinely at a loss as to why he was here:

"I told 'em everything, Colin. You know, how I met Brian and all that."

"Tell me exactly what you said in your statement, Tim?"

Jumping on to his bunk, he lay on his back with his feet up against the outside wall and continued. "They wanted to know if I knew you and I said nah, 'cos I didn't. Well I do now, Colin, but not then. Know what I mean?"

Brian was now becoming agitated. "Tell him what you said in your fucking statement you wanker!"

"OK, OK. I told 'em I had come to Devon to do a job for you, Colin, like." Tim was now waving the palms of his hands in the air above his head like an air traffic controller. He looked relaxed and untroubled by my questioning.

I said: "Job! What job, Tim?"

He was now doing circular movements with his hands and said: "Your job, Colin!"

"Con! My name's Con, not Colin! Enlighten me, Tim. Spit it out! Explain it to me so that I can understand."

Tim was now getting bored by me asking the same old questions. He was staring up at the ceiling.

"I've already told ya, Colin." He thought a moment and continued: "Well, Brian told me that he wanted me to run a job for 'im in Devon for you, like."

I was becoming more and more concerned as our conversation progressed, so I said "I need you to tell me what you think this job was. Can you remember what you said at the police station?" He twisted around and swung his legs over the edge of the bed, like a small child being questioned.

"Don't get angry with me, Colin. I didn't know what the job was when I spoke with Brian. It could have been electrical, 'cos that's what I do, you know, I'm a sparky, Colin. I told you that on the farm."

"I know you did, Tim. Go on."

"Well, they was trying to put words in me mouth, you know. Was it this or was it that and so on. I told them that you wanted your roof fixed and all that bollocks and Brian was going to leave me down there and stuff. You know, to supervise it. It wasn't until I got down to Devon that I believed he'd got a proper job for me. I didn't know he 'ad a mate who was a toff and all that. I thought initially, like, it was all bullshit, Colin. But it was true! All of what Brian said was true!"

"What else did you say, Tim? Was there any reason for them to lock us up like they have?"

"No Colin. Nothing! I didn't know, nuffink, I only just met you that day, didn't I?"

"Yeah, I know. Sorry Tim, I'm trying to work out what's happened. There must be something." I turned to face Brian "What about you?"

Brian thought for a moment and said "Nothing". I asked again "What do you mean, nothing?"

"I said nothing. I went "no comment", "no comment", "no comment", all the way through. I said fuck all about anything! What else was there to say?"

I perched on the edge of my bunk and racked my brains. "This is crazy. How the hell can they stick us in here?"

Brian grunted back "No idea, Con". He was reading his copy of the Sun. "Look at the tits on that!" he called out.

"Beats me, Colin. It really does. He's a fucking idiot, all he can think about is women. You won't get any sense out of him until his hands are covered in black ink."

I couldn't believe these two were being so matter of fact about the situation. So I said "We'd best wait for the depositions to arrive to see exactly what it is they're saying and we can go through it all properly then. I really can't see how they can keep us in here on what's been said so far. It baffles me!"

But the days dragged on into weeks and the weeks into months. It was so boring doing absolutely nothing all day and being left to lie in our cell for such long periods of time only made things worse. I kept going over the events that had led up to our arrest, over and over and over again. I remembered the conversation I had had with Sarah shortly before my arrest. "I've got a new boyfriend and he's a policeman." This made me wonder even more about why I was in prison. "Are you angry then?" She had asked. 'Why had she asked me that? "Don't you want to know where he's stationed?"

Well, I'd stopped believing in coincidences a long time ago and my suspicions grew more each day. Was Sarah behind all of this mess somewhere in the background?

Her words kept haunting me. "I met him when I worked at Whetstone, and he was a sergeant back then. We used to get on really well." Sarah's words kept lingering in the back of my mind. I was pleased for her, but she was enjoying winding me up. She was goading me and I knew it. She just couldn't resist rubbing salt into the wound by saying "I know how much you hate the police" and that just wasn't true. I didn't have a problem with the police. I didn't hate all policemen. Did I?

It was the way she laughed that bothered me. I had an inkling that she would be drawn back to someone wearing uniform. In all honesty, when she told me her new boyfriend was in the Met there was an initial feeling of anger, but not with her. I was angry with myself for waiting fifteen years to end my miserable marriage. She was pushing me for a reaction, and she was so good at doing that. She could administer her emotional surgery with the skill of a surgeon. Even over the telephone. Even though she kept pushing me for a response, I made sure that my voice remained detached and mindful not to speak in a way that might make her think there was some hope of a reconciliation between us. Sarah seemed determined to test me with her questioning.

"Well, he's a detective sergeant from London." Another spear aimed at my heart! I hated the way the Met treated members of the public and their atrocious behaviour was a contributing factor in me leaving the police. I had been a good, honest copper. I winced silently at the other end of the phone as she said "Don't do anything silly. Do you know what I mean?"

What had she meant by that statement? "Are you threatening me?" I asked.

"No no no! Just be careful, that's all." I had heard her laughing quietly on the phone.

"What are you talking about, Sarah?" She was laughing even louder now. So I asked her "I'm not stupid, what do you mean? You tell me that you're going out with a policeman and then you say "Don't do anything stupid!" I don't find that very funny." I paused and the silence at the other end of the phone began to really irritate me. "Like what?" Sarah began to laugh some more and her tone made me wonder what she was up to.

"Oh yes! Just before I go. Can I have the £300?" I had been surprised by her request and thought, the cheeky bitch! My mind flashed back to how she used to be and I was now struggling to control my temper.

When Brian and Tim fell asleep my attention turned to analysing my broken life. I wondered what my children thought about all of this. How on earth were they going to cope at school? How would they cope with the bullies? What about their friends? It was going to be all over the TV and the papers. Did they still love me?

As a result of all this mental activity I slept very little. "My life's a complete mess!" I thought. I kept beating myself up with mental anguish.

The cell walls were starting to close in on me and at about 2 am I climbed out of my bunk. I was standing on the back of the chair gasping for air at the window, having a panic attack. Tim jumped out of bed like a bullet from a gun and started grabbing my legs, trying to lift me up. The chair started banging against the wall erratically.

"Colin! You daft sod! Why didn't you wake me up?" he screamed.

I was still having trouble breathing and was barely able to talk. The room was really dark and I managed to get out a few words: "I can't - breathe - catch my…" I was really struggling to talk.

"Catch what, Colin? What the fuck are you doing up there?"

"Brreeath…." I wheezed.

"Thank God for that! You stupid bastard! I thought you were trying to top yourself! I thought you was hanging yourself, for God's sake!"

I still couldn't speak. I was fully occupied trying to suck air into my lungs. Tim was back at my ankles. "Here, Colin! Take this."

I reached out behind me "Whaaa… is it?"

"It's a brown paper bag, Colin, someone from the kitchen give it me yesterday." He forced it into my hand.

"What" I struggled for breath again "am I supposed to do with a brown paper bag?"

"Breathe into it, Colin. Seal it around your mouth and breathe in and out. You know, the same air, like."

'Lights out' was at 9 pm, and that was it for light until the morning. The security lights outside threw a faint amber glow through the top of the small window but this still left vast areas of total darkness within the cell. The cell stank of a mix of stale body odour, sweaty feet and rotting socks, with the ever-present and unmistakable stench of stale urine.

"Put the bag over your face, Colin and breath! Don't let any air out, just breath in the bleedin' bag or you're going to croak it in 'ere."

I muttered: "What bloody good is a paper bag going to be?"

"Trust me, Colin. You're going to be OK."

"It's such a mess, Tim." I tried a few more times to blow into his bag. "It's such a mess and I'm not good in confined spaces, Tim." I kept the bag over my face and kept blowing and sucking as the bag quickly filled and then crashed shut against my face.

"Colin?"

"What?"

"Stop talking, you daft sod. Blow in and out of the bag and don't take it off your ugly mush!"

The rustling noise of the paper bag inflating and deflating woke Brian, and he wasn't best pleased.

"What the bloody hell are you two doing at this time of night?"

"Colin's dying!"

"Tell him to do it quietly." I could hear Brian turn and he pulled on his blanket until it covered his head.

"How can I tell 'im that, you daft twat! He can't breathe, for God's sake! It's serious."

He snapped in a rather agitated tone: "Well let me know how he got on in the morning! Just keep it down!"

Tim leapt to his feet in anger and barked back. "Go to sleep you selfish bastard!"

"It's working, Tim, I can feel the walls returning to where they're supposed to be. They're not lying on my chest any more, thank God. How did you know about that, Tim?"

"Lovely, lovely mate. Everyone with half a brain knows that, Colin. Now get down and go back to bed. If it happens again, use the bag, OK?"

"Thanks, Tim."

CHAPTER SEVEN

∎∎∎∎∎∎∎∎

"SLUTS!"

Thanks to my problems with claustrophobia and panic attacks we had managed to convince Mr Evans that he needed us as cleaners for the wing, so we now got promoted and moved into a double cell at the end of 'B' wing. This was a great improvement and a very prestigious job to have, because our door never shut all day until final 'Bang Up' at night.

The following day Tim swanked into the cell and dropped a small, narrow, heavy wooden box on to our little table with a bang. He gave us all a rather cheesy grin which made his half moon reading glasses rise up on his nose.

"There you go. Entertainment! It's better than a TV."

"What is it? Can I eat 'em?" Brian asked and Tim shook his head. "Are they fags then?"

"Dominoes, you wanker!" Tim sat down on the only chair available in the cell by the small table and slid the lid back. He very noisily poured out the dominoes to form a pile in the centre of the table. "You'll never be bored again, my son!"

Brian retorted: "I'd 'ave preferred a TV."

"There's no fucking plug to plug a TV into you stupid bastard!" Brian went back to reading his copy of the Sun.

"Who gave you those, Tim?" I enquired.

"Well, I went down the bath house and this geezer wanted a haircut. I've not cut hair before but I gave it a go and it looked great when I'd finished. He was so pleased he asked me what I wanted in return. So I said dominoes."

"Bloody dominoes! Why didn't you ask him for some fags, you daft bastard?"

"I don't smoke, Brian, that's why, but I'm bloody good at dominoes. Dominoes is far better than fags. We can all get the benefit from them, can't we Colin?"

"CON, Tim! Anyway, well done! All we need now is backgammon and we've got ourselves some serious entertainment. Brian, we're never going to get bored again!" I roared and I laughed so loud my sides hurt and Tim giggled along with me.

"You know what, Colin, you ought to get into that game. I mean it! You can make a shedload in here."

"Yeah, right. Dominoes doesn't pay very well, Tim."

"No! I mean it, Colin! The current barber is shit and the blokes want to look pukka for their visits, they'll sort you out with all sorts of stuff. Especially the lads from the kitchens. Think about it."

"Yeah, I'll think about it, Tim."

Brian barked out an order from behind his Sun: "Get me a fucking cup of tea, bitch!"

Tim bowed politely and said: "Of course Brian, three sugars?"

Brian's voice sounded hoarse, which emphasised his east London accent. "Don't fuck around! Get me a mug of tea, now!"

Tim shot out of the cell and brought Brian a large mug of steaming tea and said: "Here you are, mate. I didn't think you wanted one, Colin?"

"Not at the moment, Tim. Thanks for the thought though."

"Come with me Colin and I'll introduce you to the barber in the bath house."

We both left the cell and waited by the gate for a screw to open up for us. I said to Tim: "What is it with you two? Why do you let him talk to you like that?"

Tim smiled and winked at me "Don't worry, Colin, he's not as clever as he thinks."

"Why?"

A screw arrived and let us through the first gate and then the second on to 'C' wing. We walked down the stairs to the bath house.

"Well, I hate him, Colin. He's an ignorant bastard."

"Yeah, so why do you act like you're his bitch?"

We reached the gate and the screw on duty let us straight through.

"Come over here, Colin and I'll show you why. Keep schtumm though."

Tim lifted a dirty old sock out of a cleaner's bucket that was tucked away in a corner. "That's why, Colin!" Tim looked at me in glee.

"It's a stinky, grubby looking sock!"

"It ain't no ordinary sock, Colin. It's me gingivitis Brian tea making sock!"

"What's in it, Tim?"

"One of my special treats, Colin. I crapped in it a week ago! When I've made him his tea he has this dunked in it before he gets it delivered to 'im and he loves it! He keeps asking for more! Ha ha ha!"

"You've gone nuts in this place, Tim! No wonder his breath stinks like pooh. You can't do that to him, Tim, he'll get ill."

When we got back to the cell Brian was curled up on his bed

in the foetal position facing the wall and Tim pulled me to one side.

"This don't look good, mate, he's seriously depressed. Look at him."

"Tim, you're a card. How do you do it?"

"What, Colin?" He looked genuinely confused.

"CON! My name is Con! Tell me about your family. Have you got one?" He took a deep breath and lifted both shoulders and opened his eyes wide and then raised the palms of his hands up in the air.

"Don't talk to me about family, Colin. I've got a daughter and she's a dirty, filthy, lazy, cow! I don't know how any bloke could put up with that!"

"What?" This wasn't the way a father should be talking about his daughter! I was intrigued.

"Well, she's not clean, you know. Dirty!" He waved his hands down towards his crutch. "She leaves her grubby knickers lying all over the place. She doesn't wash neither. She wears stupid clothes and she's a fucking mess, Colin!"

"Sounds like my sort o' girl!" Brian grunted.

"Shut it, arsehole! She's still my daughter."

"She's young, Tim, that's all." I could see he was genuinely getting upset.

"No Colin! Dirty, filthy, lazy! I don't know how anyone could even think about kissing her, let alone shagging her!" His attention drifted off.

"Don't be hard on the girl. I bet she can't wait for you to get home."

"I left, Colin. Her mother's the same. The pair of them. Dirty filthy cows!"

"So you left because of all the dirty knickers lying around,

Tim? That's one for the book."

I could hear Brian laughing from his stomach. "I like sluts."

"Shut it, you stupid bastard! I'm talkin' to Colin not you!"

"Yeah, let the man speak, Brian."

"Nah! It wasn't just the dirty knickers, Colin. I worked long and hard for 'em all. I worked for the Electricity Board, like I told ya, Colin, didn't I? I was a supervisor! A fucking supervisor!"

"Yeah, you told me, Tim."

"Well, I came home early one day and she was at it with one of the blokes I worked with, Colin. Bang at it in my own bloody bed!"

I could hear Brian laughing again but this time he said nothing.

"You've got time to meet someone else, Tim." I could see that he was really upset and I wanted to give him a hug but thought better of it. Not that he gave any indication that he was the sort of guy who would throw the soap deliberately on to the floor in the showers.

"Well, that's the funny thing, Colin. I did! I met five bloody wives and they all did the same bleedin thing to me!"

He looked genuinely pissed off now and I wasn't sure what to say. So I waited for a moment and then said "Oh, right. You poor sod. Cows!"

I could see that Tim was warming to me and he was clearly wanting to get something off his chest. "Dirty little cows they are, Colin. Dirty, filthy, little sluts. Brian's right I suppose."

Brian started laughing again "Sluuuuts. I like sluts. The really dirty ones are the best!"

Tim jumped up and screamed at Brian "Shut the fuck up! It's blokes like you who fucked my life up!

I stood up and put my arm around Tim as he was really angry

now. "Come on Tim, they can't have been that bad." I could see the top of his head now and his grey receding hair was held back in place with prison butter. It didn't matter, he needed a hug.

As I released Tim he rambled on. "You don't know 'em, Colin. I'm tellin' ya, they're lazy and good for nuffink, except sleeping and shagging their boyfriends. That's all they do! I couldn't stand it any more Colin, so I left."

Brian chirped up again. "I really like sluts. I mean I really, really like them. I've met loads. How many birds have you shagged, Tim?"

"I told you, you stupid bastard, I've had five wives. That's all! Five fucking wives!"

Brian looked really shocked. "Five?"

"Yeah, five. How many women have you had then, dickhead?"

Brian went quiet for a while and then started counting out aloud and he went up and up and I thought, "This must be getting too difficult for him".

"Nah, I can't count them all. I'm going to have to estimate a final figure, Tim. Anyway, it's at least a thousand."

I was flabbergasted. "Brian, are you saying that you've had sex with over a thousand women?"

"Yeah? What's the big deal? They're all sluts!"

"But you're married! How did you cope with Christmas and birthdays?" A logical question, I thought.

"That's easy. I had four Christmas dinners last year."

Tim was visibly shocked. "Four! What? All in one day? You greedy bastard!"

"Nah, I didn't eat all four. I'd be sick!"

Tim looked really confused and I could see that his mind was in a whirl. "How can you say you ate four Christmas dinners then, you daft twat?"

"Well, I went to see my wife and the kids for the first one and I gave them their toys and all that bollocks. I'd already told my secretary to call me at 1.15 pm."

Tim blasted: "Your fucking secretary is in on it! I suppose she was number one on your sleazy list of late night shags? You slag!"

"No, my secretary's a bloke!"

Tim quietened down to listen to Brian's reasoning and said: "Oh."

"Well, when I knew that we would all be sat down for dinner, you know, I told 'im to ring me and give me some old bollocks story about there being a crisis somewhere and that I needed to go right away. So I said my goodbyes and left. Then I went to the next house and apologised for being late as there had been a problem with one of me jobs. So it worked both ways. Do you get my drift?"

"Yeah, yeah, yeah. Go on, Brian" I replied, hoping that he would end this tale of deceit and debauchery.

"So as everyone was sat around the table and I had some more dinner, like. I'd already told me secretary to call me again at 2 pm. He had to think up another load of bollocks about another job and then I was off again! I'd done right with the missus and the kids first of course. Me girlfriends are only sluts, so they didn't matter. It went on all afternoon until I'd done all four of em."

Tim was flabbergasted and said: "Unbelievable!" and Brian looked at me with an immense sense of pride.

"Good eh, Con?"

"I don't think so, Brian. How could you? How can you live like that? It's insane!"

"Well I was knackered at the end, but I couldn't let 'em down, could I? That would be cruel."

Our enlightening conversation was interrupted by the door opening and a screw calling out "Legal Visit!" He looked directly at me. I got up and followed him down the side of the wing, down two staircases to the side door and out of the main building, past the hospital and into the legal visits room. He only spoke once during our journey, when he said: "It's your brief from London."

CHAPTER EIGHT

■ ■ ■ ■ ■ ■ ■ ■

LEGAL VISIT

Ian Perry was my third solicitor, and I had hoped that he would be a bit more clued up than the other two. They were both puppets for the local Crown Court Judge, who happened to have a close friend who was also 'On The Square' with the head of one of the lodges I belonged to and they both met regularly at Grand Lodge in London. The previous solicitors had kept saying "You're going to get eighteen years!" So they both had to go. I hoped Mr Perry was going to be different.

After a brief introduction, I could see that something was bothering him. "Hi Con, sorry I'm late but the train was delayed." Ian's approach was comforting. He was a slim man of five foot ten with short, dark brown unkempt hair and he was wearing a twelve o'clock shadow. His teeth were tobacco stained and he reeked of pipe tobacco. He was holding a black pilot's case which bumped off his thigh as he walked into the interview room. His dark blue pin-striped suit looked tired, but his attention to detail was electric.

I smiled and said: "No problem, Ian, I've got all the time in the world."

He moved his pipe into his left hand and we shook hands.

"They've found a map in your things and it's going to cause us a big problem" he said.

I was fascinated "Map? What map? What's on it?"

"I haven't got a copy of it yet but I can remember the layout. I'll draw it for you."

"Go on then."

He started by drawing two straight lines and above them he drew a double waving line. Then he marked the 'map' with four X marks. I immediately recognised what he was drawing and started to laugh.

"Ian, that's my farm! You've just drawn my farm and those are wells. That's the river and these straight lines are the road!" I could see that Ian was embarrassed.

"Well, the police think it's a map to a bank manager's house."

"Idiots! No bank manager lives around my farm!"

Ian opened his briefcase and pulled out a rather large bundle of papers. "I've now got the depositions through and I would like you to have a look through them and highlight any areas of concern, then we can talk again. You'll see what I mean when you read them. I've asked for the forensic reports and I have had some through. The rest should come over in the next few days. Nothing much there really. Your prints are on your car and in your house."

"Sounds very ominous."

"You need to find out more from the other two. You'll see what I mean when you read through the statements."

We then had a general conversation and Ian left to return to London.

The screw walked me back to the wing and locked me back into the cell and Brian and Tim leapt to their feet. Tim asked: "Well, Colin. What's it look like?"

Brian was slightly less enthusiastic and asked: "Have you had a chance to go through it with him? What did he reckon, Con?"

"He wants me to read through the statements because there

is something damning in them. I don't know what it is, so you are going to have to let me go through them all properly."

They both replied at the same time. "Yeah, no problem."

I wasted no time and went straight to the statements. I went through mine, which was as I had explained to them both previously. There was nothing incriminating in it.

"Mine's OK. Now let me have a look at yours, Tim." I started to flick through the papers one after the other. "Jesus Christ! You made a sixty eight page statement, Tim!"

"I didn't say nuffink, Colin! Nuffink!"

"You did, you stupid sod. You said sixty eight pages of something!"

I went straight into Tim's statement and read it slowly. "So you drove away from the farm when they tried to arrest you."

"That's right, Colin. I told you that!"

"You had a suspected heart attack and they took you to hospital in an ambulance?"

"That's right. I told you I had a bleedin' heart attack. They broke my teeth, Colin. They threw me in the back of a police car and asked me loads of questions."

"Like what? That's not in here!"

"They did! They told me everything, Colin. They knew about the job! They said they knew about the job!"

"What bloody job, Tim?"

"Your job, Colin!"

"What job? I'm sorry, I don't follow."

"They told me there was a job and that I was being brought into it. Well I was, wasn't I?"

I was struggling to find the right words to express my surprise. "A job on the bloody farm!"

"Yeah, but they said "Before you came down did you know

what the job was going to be?" and I said no, 'cos I didn't, did I, Colin?"

"Yeah, right. Stop calling me Colin, for Christ's sake! I keep telling you my name is CON! "

"I told you, Colin, sorry, Con, I didn't know you existed before I met you and they said "If you were going to go all the way to Devon to do a job, wouldn't you ask what it was?" So I said "Yeah" but Brian just said a job and that he knew a 'toff' with a load of money and there was some work. Well there was, wasn't there?"

"What else did he say?"

"He said "Didn't you think it was a bit suspicious going all the way to Devon, not knowing what sort of job it was?" and I said "No, not at all." So he said "Don't try and change the subject! Answer my question! Do you think that it might have been dodgy?" I said no, Colin, 'cos I'd met you by then, like I told you! I didn't know you existed then, did I?"

"So what happened then?"

"He got angry, Colin, and he gave me a slap in the car."

"In the car!"

"Yeah, Colin. He was over the top of the front seats, like, and he started slapping me about and they'd already broken me teeth on the road. He kept saying "Could it have been dodgy? Think about it and if you come up with the wrong answer you'll get another slap!" I was frightened, Colin, sorry, Con and he said that every time I said the wrong thing he would give me another slap. So I said "Before I met you, you know, on the way down, it might 'ave seemed a bit dodgy and all that. Lookin' back now, like."

"But none of what you have just said is in the statements, Tim?"

"I had a bleeding heart attack, Colin!"

"What do you mean?"

"I had a heart attack in the back of the police car!"

"That's not mentioned in the interview in your statement."

"No, 'cos they carried me from the police car on the main road into your yard and put me in the back of your car just before the ambulance arrived. You know, so that it looked like it had happened in your car."

"That's incredible! So they primed you first?"

"Yeah, I know that now. In my interview he went over it all again and it was the same bloke. So when he asked the same question I could hardly give him the wrong answer, could I?"

"So you told him what he told you to say about it "possibly being dodgy" on the way down?"

"Yes, Colin. Well it was sort of true, because I didn't know whether he really knew anyone like you at that time, did I?"

"This is unbelievable!" I sat back to carry on reading in disbelief.

I continued to read through 68 pages of total and absolute drivel that revealed absolutely nothing. It was no more damning than a confused electrician going about his normal trade and then, after being slapped and subjected to fear and intimidation, being coerced into making an already primed statement under duress.

"Tim, that's OK, I can understand what happened to you and the way they treated you is appalling. We can deal with all of these points in court. They've interviewed you contrary to PACE. All I need to do is somehow prove this in court. That's obviously what the solicitor was going on about."

I then started to look for Brian's statement. I went through the bundle and through it again and again. "Where's your statement, Brian?"

"I told you, Con, I didn't make one. I just said "No Comment" all the way through."

"Well, that's easy, they can't hold us in here with this crap! They're going to have to let us out!"

I then started on the police statements. The bundle was three inches deep. "How many bloody policemen were there at the farm?" I said. I started to quietly count the different statements and some minutes later I sat up with my eyes bulging in their sockets. "OK, how many policemen do you think there were when we were arrested, Brian?"

Brian thought for a moment and said: "Twenty?"

I looked at Tim and said: "Tim?"

"There were lots, Colin, 'cos I saw a load on the road outside and there was cars everywhere! I mean everywhere, Colin! It was like a car park out there!"

"Guess how many, Tim?"

"Forty?"

"Well, according to this there were over a hundred and twenty five! One hundred and twenty five! I cannot imagine who or what could have got that many policemen to travel all the way from London to Devon. It's ridiculous! I really don't believe this. I'm going to have to work my way through all of this bullshit in order to work out what they've done to us."

Brian appeared to be desperate to get back to his copy of the Sun and said "Yeah, go for it, Con." His head dropped back to marvel at the photograph on page three. "Look at the tits on that!" he moaned.

As I worked my way through the arresting officers' statements, I came across the one that related to Brian. "Hang on a minute! What were you going to do on my farm, Brian?"

"Your roof!"

"Come on, spit it out! What was it that you were planning to do on my farm that was illegal?"

"Piss off, Con, NOTHING!"

"Well explain to me why you have signed a policeman's statement saying "I've been such a fool, I was going to do it." and when you were asked "What were you going to do with the money?" you said "Pay off my overdraft with the National Westminster Bank" and then he asked you "How much is your overdraft?" and you told him "Ninety seven thousand pounds." Is that right?"

Brian jumped off his bed, pointed angrily at me and shouted "That's bollocks! I never said that!"

"Well, you signed a policeman's statement agreeing that you did, you arsehole!"

"Nah, that's bollocks. I never said that. I didn't, Con, honest!"

"Well they reckon you did."

"No, the only thing I signed for was for my property. They woke me up and said "Here you are mate, sign for this, it's for your property" and I didn't even have me glasses on."

"Why not?"

"Because I was asleep, that's why! They woke me up and me glasses were on the floor next to me bed!"

I was fuming. "Why didn't you put them on and read what you were signing, you prick?"

"It was only for me property, so I signed it and went back to sleep."

"You stupid bastard! If I get eighteen years because you just couldn't be arsed to put your bloody glasses on I'll kill you!"

The only avenue for us now was to try to dissect their evidence in order to disprove their allegations. I needed to get access to a computer, so I decided to go on to Education in order to see if the tutor would give me access to one. The classes were full so I volunteered to help out with keyboard skills for the other inmates.

Emily, the tutor, was brilliant. A tall, heavily-built woman of about 45 years with shoulder-length brown hair, she reminded me of my eldest sister and was very understanding. She turned a blind eye to what I was doing, saying "Just look busy and make sure you don't leave anything on the system when you log off. If you get caught, I know nothing."

I immediately went about trying to prove our case.

CHAPTER NINE

■ ■ ■ ■ ■ ■ ■ ■

SPECIAL DELIVERY

As remand prisoners we were supposed to be housed separately from the convicted prisoners, but the reality was that they lived on the lower floors and wore denim 'blues' while we were housed on the top landing and wore denim 'browns', or our own clothing if we chose to do so. Both convicted and unconvicted prisoners were entitled to a one-hour exercise period and we eventually took advantage of this together. It involved walking around the edge of a circle in one direction for an hour a day. If you were in a hurry you could take the inner circle, which would get you nowhere a lot quicker. So after six months we finally agreed that we would take our entitlement and walk around the larger circular area, because we had time on our hands.

I think it was Oscar Wilde who said sarcasm was the lowest form of wit but the highest form of intelligence. My mind wandered back to that fateful day when we were arrested and the sound of shuffling feet and whispered voices echoed off the huge outer prison walls that towered beside us. We were confined, like small children, to the naughty corner, but in my mind's eye I could leap mountains, which rendered these walls useless in holding back the power of my dreams and thoughts. In the flicker of an eye I could be anywhere of my choosing.

My silence was interrupted by Tim as he pushed in to walk alongside me.

"Hello, Colin!"

"Hello, Tim."

"You're deep in thought."

"There's nothing else to do but think, Tim. That's all I do all day and when the lights go out that's all I do all night. I keep going over everything. Everything!"

"Horrible place this, ain't it, Colin? I hate it too."

Brian shuffled in alongside Tim, looking dour.

"Have you worked it all out yet, Con?"

"I'm breaking all the logs down by times and I'm starting to see what they've done, but it's taking ages to go through them all. If one of the screws sees what I'm doing all hell will break out."

"I didn't know what I was signing, Con!"

"It's too late now, Brian. Don't beat yourself up over it. It's done!"

"I can't help thinking about me missus. She's going to come up with the kids to visit me next week. I was wondering."

I couldn't resist the quip. "Don't let your mind wander, Brian, it's too small to be let out on its own."

Tim and Brian laughed loudly. "That's a blinder, Colin. You're a card. It don't bother me that everyone hates you, I think you're a proper geezer. Know what I mean? I'd trust you, that's what I'm trying to say, Colin, but not this muppet, he's a fucking idiot!"

Brian snapped back "Shut it or I'll swing for you! All I hear all the time is your bloody voice and it's really starting to piss me off. Anyway, Con, I was wondering if you would cut me hair for me, you know, tidy it up a bit for my visit?"

"Me? I've never cut hair in my life. I'm bound to screw it up for you."

"Tim reckons you'll be good at it because you're particular, you know, attention to detail and all that. Will you give it a go? Cos I've seen the barber and Tim's right, he's shit at cutting hair. All he does is shave your head with the clippers and my missus will go crazy. It'll scare the crap out of her because I've got big ears underneath this lot." Brian lifted his hair to confirm what he was saying.

Tim looked shocked. "And who the fuck am I - Noddy? What's wrong with me then, you arsehole? If you'd asked me I'd 'ave cut it for you. I ain't going to cut it for you now, though! You can fuck off, Big Ears! You had your chance and you blew it!"

"If you can get me the scissors I'll give it a go for you, Brian."

"'Ere, Colin, I'll let you experiment on mine first and then you can do Brian's."

"Yeah, that sounds like a good idea, Tim. Are you all right with that, Brian?"

"Yeah." Brian turned to Tim and said "Shut it about the ears, if you know what's good for you, arsehole!"

Tim shrugged his shoulders and said "I don't give a shit."

Brian's head fell forward and he kept walking and snapped back: "Shut it, bitch!"

I spent the first fourteen months on remand walking in my own strength, unable to see my children and being systematically stripped of all my worldly possessions. You can't keep up your mortgage payments when you are in prison. Daily I sifted through my food, searching for pieces of broken glass and slivers of razor blades and smelling it for traces of chemicals. There are more ways of getting to someone that you hate in prison than you can imagine! I grew more angry by the day at the injustice done to me and wanted revenge against those who had stitched me up. I scoured my life searching for answers. Every day I mourned for my son Peter and for the welfare of my sons, Michael and Luke. I kept raking through the ashes of my broken marriage, trying to make sense of my life and in my mind retelling all the stories I had once told them. I clung to those images and memories and ached for a reunion with them.

At a meeting with my new probation officer she was sufficiently concerned by the rage boiling away inside me to suspect that I might be a risk, so my category status was increased to 'serious threat of escape' and 'high risk of being likely to seek revenge'. As I hadn't made any previous attempts to escape, I wasn't put in stripes (yellow strip down the side of your prison uniform) but I was put in an 'E Man' cell where I was carefully monitored while going to and from the court. The police took it upon themselves to escort us there and back in person.

My solicitor and barrister had advised me to go for an 'old-style committal', and this was arranged to be heard in Exmouth Magistrates' Court. On the first day of the three-day hearing we were taken to reception in order to change for court. When we were ready the grumpy, pot-bellied, ruddy-faced custody officer announced, with a silly grin on his face: "Can you three lads wait in the booth over there? You're marked down for a special collection and delivery service."

He found his remark very humorous. We were locked into a white booth and we waited patiently for our escort.

Shortly before 9.50 am the door opened. Four police officers were standing waiting for us with big smiles on their faces. Tim was really agitated by their presence and snapped: "What the bleeding 'ell's going on? What are you bastards up to?"

There was one policeman allocated to each of us. The beefy, head-shaven 'cuff man' made sure that the handcuffs were clicked on nice and tight. "Oh, you'll find out in a minute" he said.

"We're taking you three to court today. Have you got everything?" We all nodded. "Come on then." We filed out of reception along a narrow corridor and Brian moaned "Leave it out, the cuffs are cutting into me wrist. Loosen 'em off a bit!"

The 'cuff man' said "Can't do that I'm afraid. Follow us!" and we were walked to the side door and out into the yard, where there was a van waiting.

"What's that noise? Can you hear it, Colin?" The three of us raised our hands to shield our eyes from the sun to have a proper look. "It's a bleedin' helicopter, Colin! You don't need one of them, you stupid bastards! What's the matter with you?"

"Leave it, Tim, just go with it for now. It looks like they're after some fun. It must be playtime."

"It's not on, Colin."

"CON! I've lost count of the number of times I've told you, Tim!"

The helicopter was now hovering overhead and all the inmates were at their windows trying to see what was going on. As we were loaded into the van I heard one of the prisoners shout out "Your mates have come for you, pig!"

We were locked into separate cubicles and my knees touched the steel wall in front of me. I could feel my hip bones against the other wall. There was no cushion to sit on and I was jammed in tight as I heard him lock my door.

I heard the driver speak in an excited voice: "Radio through and tell them we're ready." The radio operator said "Hello India 99, all clear to move to the gate, over?" There was a crackle of the radio and then: Roger that, all vehicles are now in place, over."

As the police van pulled out of the last gate and on to the ramp down to the road I looked out of my smoked glass window to see a stream of cars and four motorcycle outriders.

"We're getting the works here today, boys" I said. "Let's make the best of it and try not to let them intimidate us. Brace yourselves!"

Tim screamed: "Bastards!"

The van accelerated away quickly and held first gear all the way down the slope. A screw opened the barrier with little time to spare. A traffic car took the lead and two motorcycle outriders overtook us, sirens blazing, and went up front to take the lead. To our rear was another traffic car and a second armed plain clothes unit. The other two outriders patrolled the rear, lights flashing and sirens blaring.

I could hear the three officers in the front whooping with excitement as we headed towards the High Street, all sirens blazing and lights flashing.

Brian screamed: "Who do they think we are, the bloody Mafia?"

"Hold tight lads, we're in for one hell of a ride to Exmouth."

"Thanks for that, Colin."

Our only contact with each other was by calling through the steel-plated walls of the van. I watched out of the window to see which route we took. We followed the B3183 into New Road, where the first two motorcycle outriders blocked the side road at Longbrook Street and the two outriders from the rear swept forward to block off the High Street as our van swept over the crossroads and into Paris Street. I was doing all right up to this point, even though I was bouncing up and down on the steel seat. I could see everyone in the High Street standing and watching us go by.

I heard Tim scream out "Slow down, you're going to kill us back here!"

It was now the turn of the other two outriders to buzz past us again with their lights and sirens blazing in order to get to the Western Way roundabout, where they completely blocked the traffic.

The policemen in the front of our van were screaming with laughter. They suddenly decided to go off road and mount the kerb, throwing us against the steel walls of our cubicles in the back. We banged up and down the kerbs and on to the pavement again. I was completely winded, and felt my back give way. I cried out in pain.

"You bastards have hurt Colin! Stop the van!" It was no use, they careered on regardless into Heavitree Road and we raced past the police station at considerable speed.

I could still see out of my window. As we moved down Heavitree Road the motorcycle outriders kept switching positions in order to keep the van moving. We then raced into Fore Street and on to East Wonford Hill, past Middlemoor Police Headquarters and on to the M5 roundabout, then into Sidmouth Road. As we hit the Clyst St Mary roundabout the van swung heavily to the right and we made our way along the Exmouth Road, blazing through Clyst St George and then through the small village of Ebford and into Exeter Road. By the time we finally arrived at Exmouth Magistrates' Court I was in agony. My head was buzzing and I was winded.

As we got out of the van we saw armed police everywhere. They were on roof tops and positioned in doorways, making themselves extremely visible. The court room had been closed for us and we were escorted through to the court cells.

When we were called into the court we were all handcuffed together, with me in the middle. Our barristers were sat at the front of the court and we were shuffled into the dock sideways. The only other people in the court were two armed policemen.

The magistrates entered the court and everyone stood up. The charges were read out and pleas were taken. A firm 'Not Guilty!' was the response from us all.

I signalled to my barrister, David Robinson, and he came over to talk to me. David, a rather dashing and well groomed forty-five year old David Niven lookalike, had impeccable manners. Beneath his wig he had a head full of honey blonde hair.

"Is everything all right, Con?"

I whispered in his ear "I was the only one who wanted this old-style committal and I've got a set of cuffs on each wrist. I want to make notes. Will they take my cuffs off?"

"I will ask the magistrates."

David returned to his place and said "Your worships?"

The rather grumpy looking stipendiary magistrate didn't look impressed. "Yes!"

"My client wishes to make notes. As the court is sealed and there are armed officers present, can we remove the handcuffs?"

The stipendiary magistrate announced: "The court will adjourn to meet with security to discuss this matter."

There was a sudden call: "All rise!" and we waited patiently for the magistrates to return. The court usher, not looking very impressed, called out: "All rise!"

The stipendiary magistrate said: "We have discussed the matter of removing the handcuffs with security and these men are too dangerous for us to allow the restraints to be removed. They will have to make do."

David looked at me and shrugged his shoulders and I called him over again.

He turned his ear to listen to what I was about to say and said: "Yes, Con?"

"I am listed as number three on the 'pecking order' and I am in position two. See if that will work?"

David smiled and returned to the front of the court.

"Your worships, it was by the request of my client that we should precede with an old-style committal. He finds it impossible to make notes. Your worships, where does my client appear in the pecking order?"

As I looked around the empty court room I had the feeling that our fate had already been decided. After much fumbling of papers the clerk of the court jumped up:

"He's number three, your worships."

David spoke again. "Can I ask why the jailer has put him in as number two?"

The magistrates were now getting more and more impatient.

"OK. Take them out and have them put in their proper places! Jailer!"

The three of us were then led out of the dock sideways and out of court and taken back to the cells.

I didn't consider it my responsibility to inform the jailer which was his left hand and which his right, so I remained silent. The jailer had now handcuffed me as number one, Tim as number two and Brian as number three. Then all three of us were brought back into court.

I signalled to David.

"Yes, Con?"

"They have put me as number one. I should be number three."

David raised his eyebrows and gave me a knowing look. "Your worships?"

I heard a rather agitated voice bark back "Yes! What is it now?"

"My client is right handed. It is his left hand that is now free. He should be in the dock in number three position and he has been placed in as number one."

"Get them out! Tell the jailer that if he doesn't know his left from his right hand I will come out and show him!"

All three of us moved out of the dock sideways yet again and were returned to the cells. The cuffs were now placed on us in the correct order and we were led back into court. The magistrate re-entered the courtroom and looked over to me.

"Are you happy now?" asked the stipendiary magistrate.

I smiled in acknowledgement and said politely "Yes, thank you. You are very kind."

The arresting officers were called individually. They all admitted that they had made their notes together at exactly the same time, but one said they had been done at Exeter Police Station and one said Tiverton, while the third said they had all made their original notes back in London. It wasn't just that. When we called their only independent witness, who happened to be off sick on the day in question, he confirmed that the detective sergeant who had said he had seen Tim in his white van stop outside the witness's house had been wrong. The witness said that the detective sergeant had not even been there. The only person in the car was a policewoman, who he had gone out to speak to. The DS just wasn't present, and the logs had placed him at that precise time in a completely different car which was over seven miles away.

The first day of the hearing was a disaster for the police, and it was due to run for three days. At the end of the first day the police evidence was already in chaos.

Tim smiled as we were led back to the cells and said "They're a bunch of muppets!" He was laughing to himself, and convinced that the case would indeed be thrown out. Most of the lies were proved to be what they were, lies.

The return journey to the prison was like the first, sirens

blazing and lights flashing as we three supposedly dangerous criminals were escorted back into the secure environment of Exeter Prison.

The custody officer looked genuinely pleased to see us. "Welcome back lads. Have a good day?"

"Not really" Brian replied. Then all three of us entered into deep conversation about the events of the day.

One of the local policemen said to the custody officer "It was so funny to watch. They made the Flying Squad look like the bunch of tossers they are. They'll walk, I reckon."

The custody officer removed our handcuffs and then turned to the policeman who had just finished speaking.

"Can I have their warrants, please?"

"Warrants?"

"Don't tell me you didn't get their warrants from the magistrates?"

"No. I didn't realise they needed them."

"I assure you that they do. We can't accept them without a warrant. You will have to take them back!"

This time the journey from the prison was a lot more sedate. The three of us were taken to Heavitree Police Station, where we were held until the next morning. There were no sirens, flashing lights, armed escort or helicopter, only a lot of red faces. We were let out of the back of the van in the dark and allowed to walk into the police station without handcuffs on, a great surprise to the three of us. We were then placed in separate cells for the night. In the morning we were not given the opportunity to wash, change or shave and we were taken back to Exmouth Magistrates Court, this time without the usual cavalcade.

David, my barrister, visited me in the cell. As soon as he saw me he said "You look a mess, Con."

"I feel like one. I've not had a wash or cleaned my teeth and they have damaged my back in the process."

"That's disgusting. How is it that you haven't had an opportunity to wash?"

"These plonkers forgot the warrants and the prison wouldn't let us in. Can you believe that?"

David said "That's down to the Clerk of the Court."

"Well, I'm not being funny, David, but I want to wash and have a shave and clean my teeth before I go into court."

David put his hand on my shoulder reassuringly "Leave it with me."

When we were called into the court I refused to go in. Tim and Brian, like a couple of sheep, went through by themselves. The magistrates entered the court and David jumped to his feet to explain.

"There was an administrative error last night and warrants were not issued for my client to re-enter the prison, so he has had to sleep in an uncomfortable police cell overnight. Consequently he has been unable to wash, shave and change his clothing. I therefore ask that he is allowed time to wash and shave and have a drink and that a clean shirt and underpants be brought to him so that he can put on fresh clothes. I also ask that the driver of the police vehicle that transported him to court be spoken to and advised to slow down and to remain on the road during transportation."

The senior magistrate went bright red. With a look of thunder he barked "See to this request immediately! Court is adjourned for thirty minutes!"

The clerk of the court shouted "All stand!" and Brian and Tim were dragged back through from the court room and were locked away in separate cells.

Tim called out "Good on you, Colin. You've really pissed

them off!" and Tim started laughing uncontrollably. "Did you see that judge's face? He was fumin'. Bloody fumin'!"

"He's a bloody magistrate not a judge, you moron!" Brian didn't seem quite as impressed as Tim.

I carried on shaving and put on my clean pants and a nice fresh shirt. When I was finished I said to the custody officer, "That's lovely. Thank you so much for that. Can you let the magistrates know that I am ready to see them now."

We were all cuffed together in the right order this time and filed back into court. David came over to see me: "Is everything OK now, Con?"

"Yes, thank you so much for organising this, David. I feel so much better now. All I need now is an apology from the bench and I'll be happy."

"Of course. Leave it to me."

Within a few minutes the magistrates returned to court and the clerk called out "All rise!" and everyone stood up.

The stipendiary magistrate was keen to proceed "Right! Can we continue now?"

David jumped to his feet "Yes your worship, the only thing left for my client now is an apology from the bench for their error in failing to issue the warrants and we can proceed."

"Yes, you are quite right, please accept our apologies for the dreadful way in which you have been treated."

I nodded: "Thank you your worship, I appreciate and accept your apology." I thought David wouldn't mind me responding directly and he turned and nodded politely.

We were still in the process of cross-examining police witnesses and it was becoming obvious to us that the case should be thrown out, but the magistrate butted in halfway through David's cross-examination of my arresting officer.

"I've heard enough! This case is going to Crown Court!" He banged his gavel and the magistrates stood up together and marched out of the court room and closed the door behind them.

David came back to me and said "They're an incestuous lot down here. Our suspicions were that it was going to go through in any event. I will speak to you in due course."

The officers in the case were now extremely annoyed as a result of what had happened and when we arrived at the prison they made sure they had the warrants with them this time. We came in through the gate with the full police convoy together with the helicopter as per our first day. The Governor was there when we passed through the first gate and he approached the van.

"I'm the Governor, what's all this noise about?"

The police driver wound his window down. "We've overheard these men plotting to escape from the court and I've been told to tell you that we want their category status raised to 'A' as they are extremely likely to escape."

The Governor didn't look convinced at all. "Don't be stupid! I'm the Governor and their categories are staying as they are. Now get them inside and stop pratting around out here! You're in my prison now, so don't tell me how to run things in here!"

When I left the van I was sent straight over to the prison hospital as I was virtually unable to walk due to my back having collapsed. The male doctor examined the base of my spine and in a matter of fact way said. "You've got piles that's all. I can lance it now if you like. It's very common at your age."

I couldn't believe what he had just said. "Well that's funny, I never had piles yesterday!"

"These things can happen, I promise you. There's nothing else wrong with you. You can go back on to the wing."

CHAPTER TEN

■■■■■■■■

PADDED CELL

After hurting my back in the police van during my 'old-style committal', my back collapsed again while I was in the gym playing volleyball. I was carried over to the wing on a stretcher and I managed, with great difficulty, to climb off it and on to the bottom bunk. I was unable to get up to the toilet on my own or get food or medication and Tim was my only lifeline. He fetched and carried for me as best he could, until it became a problem with the staff. They refused to let Tim collect my food or medication and this exposed his position badly to the staff and inmates for helping a 'pig'. I thought that it was best for me to go over to the hospital wing in the hope that I would at least get some help.

I was carried over to the hospital on a stretcher wearing a pair of prison shorts and a T-shirt. I was placed in the strip cell and the door was locked behind me. I now felt totally isolated, alone.

I raised my head and looked around the cell; it was unbelievably dirty. The walls were covered in food stains and human excrement and the floor was no better. It was covered in a thick layer of grime that no one had tried to clean for a very long time. The smell of urine was the first thing to hit my sense of smell, followed by disinfectant. My head flopped back on to the hard plastic-coated table I was lying on.

I thought: "Christ, what have I done? I couldn't survive on the wing. I was a sitting target for the thugs and there's no way I'm going to survive in here! Fortunately the window's open and I can breathe but it's freezing!"

On closer examination I could see that the window frame was in place but there was no glass, only bars. I scanned the room again, looking for something to cover me, but there was nothing. No pillow, no sheets, no blankets. My whole body started to go into shock and I began to shiver uncontrollably. There was a cardboard chair and table and a paper pot to urinate and defecate in but I just couldn't get up because of the pain in my back.

The food trolley arrived outside the door and the screw shouted: "Your meal's here. Get up and collect it!"

I turned my head to face him and said: "I can't move. I'm stuck." He waited with the block orderly for me to get up for about fifteen seconds and the screw sighed. "You don't want it? That's fine. See you in the morning." Then he slammed the door closed. I called out "I need a blanket! Please can I have a blanket?" The block orderly opened the hatch and said: "I'll ask one of the cons you stitched up when you was a copper to bring one over for you." He slammed the hatch shut and I lay helpless as he wandered off down the corridor laughing.

Some distance away I could hear other inmates screaming in agony and crying for help. It was very distressing to listen to. I heard a cell door open next to me and another inmate was brought in to one of the other padded cells. He was groaning in pain and pleading for help. "Please don't lock me in here! Please, I can't do it!"

I heard the cell door slam shut and the noise of the hatch opening and the screw said "Shut it, you piece of shit!"

It was a young lad's voice and he sounded like he was in pain. He started to cry. I lay helpless on my bed, still unable to move. I felt an urge to comfort him with words as he sobbed his little heart out. I felt like a piece of meat on a butcher's table. Helpless.

As the shift changed this young man's sobbing was clearly annoying the night shift, who appeared to be chatting in a rest room. One of them shouted out: "Shut the fuck up! Stop whingeing, you little bastard!"

I thought, My God, that's my dad's voice. It had exactly the same resonance and it brought back harrowing memories and images of him returning home from work drunk. I tried to call out to the lad: "Quiet! Please be quiet or he'll hurt you!" But he couldn't hear me above his own plight and crying.

The screw's voice grew louder: "Shut up you little bastard! Shut up! Shut the fuck up!" But the lad was too distressed to take in the seriousness of his situation. I heard a chair crash against a wall and the stamping of feet along the corridor. "I'm not listening to this little bastard whinge on all night!" His cell door opened violently and there were several impacts and groans, then silence. A heavy silence, full of fear, pain and anticipation.

I thought: 'Please be OK, my silent, wounded neighbour. Please be OK'.

The night passed slowly, and I was freezing. The wind blew in huge gusts of freezing air that fell on me like a blanket of ice that crushed the air out of my chest. I heard a young lad's voice cry out in his sleep "Mum, mum, mum! Where are you?" Then silence returned in the chill of the night. I thought of my own mother and wondered where she would be. Now I knew where the expression "killing time" had been born, in the belly of this place, hell on earth.

After what seemed like an eternity, first light appeared

through my window, extending my torment for another day. I had had one night in Hades and I had taken enough. The thought of living for an eternity in a place like this was too much to bear.

I could hear the noise of the breakfast trolley wheels as they squeaked along the corridor delivering meals. This time I was ready. I had managed to drag myself out of bed and was leaning against the door, sweat dripping from my forehead, when the hatch opened. The food was of no interest to me, but I was gagging for a drink. The orderly smiled nastily and said: "Feeling better this morning, pig?"

I remained silent and watched as he ladled out the food on to a blue plastic plate, lifted it up for me to see, growled in the back of his throat and then spat in it. He slapped another plate over the top and passed it through the vertical grill in the door. Most of the food fell through the side of the plate and on to the floor and I let the plate drop to the floor inside the cell. "Enjoy your meal, pig!" He then poured some tea into a polystyrene cup and said: "One lump or two?"

"Neither. Just as it comes, thank you."

There was no escape from this man. He snorted again and gave me one lump and I let that drop to the floor to join my food.

I never bothered to make the journey to the door again for food. I just said something witty like "Thank you so much, but I've already eaten." This response always seemed to hit the spot and annoy him enough to grunt a reply. "Fuck off pig!"

I had always found that by trying to love them back, even though they clearly wanted to do me harm, always seemed to do the trick. "I'd love to keep talking to you, but I must really get on now. Things to do, you know? Goodbye then."

The orderly was clearly getting agitated as his response was always the same. "You're a piece of shit, pig!"

Well, I knew the answer to that one "Thank you, that's the nicest thing that anyone has ever said to me. Goodbye then."

Each day the Senior Medical Officer, a woman of about 45, shoulder-length mousy coloured hair, with a knowing smile and wearing a brilliant white doctor's coat, would enter my cell to do her inspection. She immediately turned on her heels and remarked "Everything OK? That's fine" and left without giving me the opportunity to reply. I asked one of the screws for some paper and a pen and wrote a letter of complaint to her, while lying on my back. My complaint was about the condition of my cell and my treatment while being taken to court.

The following day she came to see me with two screws. "I understand you're not happy here. Is that right?" she said. I had finally managed to get her attention.

"This is supposed to be a hospital" I said. "It's a disgrace to humanity! I came in here with a back problem and now I don't just have a back problem, I've got depression as well."

The SMO turned her nose up in disgust. "Well, let me see, you could be here for a week, a month, maybe even years. It's up to you, really."

I don't take too well to being threatened and that's exactly what it felt like. So I said "I have hurt my back. It's freezing in here. Can I have a blanket, please?"

The SMO snapped back "There is absolutely nothing we can do for you I'm afraid. Goodbye." They marched out of the cell and closed the door behind them.

Much against my better judgement, I decided that this was not good enough. So I wrote another letter and the following day they returned with a slightly different attitude.

The SMO did all the talking. "So, it's the police who hurt your back and not the prison staff."

"Yes."

For some strange reason she now sounded a bit more interested. "You want to complain against the police?"

"Yes. I don't have a problem with the prison service. You are creating one by not responding to my needs."

"We have told the cleaner that you're not happy with his work and he's not very impressed with you either."

I said: "I don't care about the cleaner. I'm not looking for friends. I have a back problem! Please help me to get back on to my feet and then I will be out of here."

Later that afternoon I heard someone calling me through the hatch. "Costa! Costa!"

I couldn't believe what I was hearing. Only friends and family called me by that name. His voice was familiar. It was a man I had met when he had called at our home several years earlier selling life insurance. He had a pretty-boy face, blonde hair and a gentle manner with him and he stuck his face close to the hatch when he spoke.

"Chris?"

"Costa, I can't hang around here, it's too dangerous for me and you. I'm one of the orderlies in here and I've heard you have written to the Senior Medical Officer to complain. You really can't do that in here."

"Why, Chris?"

"Listen, you are in very real danger. I really want to talk more with you but I have to look after myself first. You're in big trouble. Please believe me!"

"OK, Chris, I believe what you're saying."

"You have to get out of here as quickly as you can. People die in this place. Do you understand what I'm saying?"

"They won't do that."

"Believe me, Costa, they do and you're in a lot of trouble. Big trouble, for complaining! Don't eat any of the food either."

"I'm not."

"Get out of here my friend. The other orderly is looking to sort you out. I must go now, we can't speak again. Good luck."

"Chris, can you get someone to bring me over a blanket? I'm freezing."

"I'll see what I can do."

An hour later I heard Tim's voice. He was talking to one of the screws and said: "I'm the barber. The Governor has said it's OK to cut the inmates' hair over here. Where do you want me to start, boss?"

As my cell was the second along the corridor I had to assume that the young lad had been discharged. The Screw opened my hatch and said "Do you want a haircut, Buller?"

My reply was instant: "Yes please, officer." The door was unlocked and Tim walked in carrying his barber's kit with a very serious look on his face.

The screw said "I'll leave the door open, if he's any problem just shout."

Tim turned on his heels and said "Thanks boss. He won't muck me around."

Tim pulled open his bag and pulled out a blanket and some clothes for me to wear, two apples, four Mars bars, an orange and a packet of ginger nut biscuits. He said: "Chris told me you was in bovver and you needed help. Throw all the rubbish out of the window, Colin."

I started to well up with tears and said: "You're like an angel, Tim. Thank you."

"Colin, listen to me. I'm putting all this stuff in a plastic bag and I'm going to hang it on this piece of string and hook it up on the window. The screws won't see it then. Right? All you 'ave to do is pull on the string and eat what you want and then hang it back out of the window again. See?"

"Thanks, Tim."

"Listen, I've got to give you a haircut." Tim pulled out his clippers and extension lead and went out into the hallway to find a power point. Fifteen minutes later I was shorn like a sheep and Tim packed his gear up and swept the floor. Before he left he said: "Colin, you've got to get out of this place. They're going to kill you in 'ere!"

A week later, there was a rattle of keys and a clunk and the officer in charge stood in the open door frame. He was a dead ringer for Christopher Lee and he didn't say a word. He just pointed with his finger toward the entrance to the main wing, so I climbed off the bed and staggered to the door and walked out of my cell and into the hallway. I stared down the corridor to the gate. I looked back and neither of us spoke. I started to hobble along in the direction he was pointing with his bony index finger. He nodded slowly, so I assumed I was doing the right thing. I kept walking in silence along the highly-polished red-tiled floor towards the locked gate at the end that led out to the main wings.

Once I reached that point I looked back. He now indicated for me to turn right. So I now moved out of sight and I saw a door ahead of me with 'Senior Medical Officer' on it. I knocked gently and waited.

I recognised the SMO's voice: "Come in!" I opened the door and staggered into the room. The SMO was sitting in her chair. She made no attempt to get up to welcome me but politely said: "Sit down."

I slowly lowered myself on to the upright pine chair, which was upholstered with a plush, deep, wine coloured material that seemed to grab hold of the material on my prison issue trousers.

I looked at the floor and commented: "carpet!" My remark was made quietly to myself. I had no thought or concern as to whether I would be heard or not. Natural surprise I suppose, and marvel at what I saw, overwhelmed by the comfort they worked in behind the cruel scenes and conditions I had witnessed. "Comfy chair."

"Yes, yes." She was now trying to be calm and reassuring. "I understand you are still not happy here?"

"I've really hurt my back. Can you help me please?"

"Oh, you've hurt your back have you?"

"Yes."

"Let me take some notes." She then proceeded to record my complaint regarding the police and my stay in the hospital. "Let me get this straight. Your complaint is solely about the police and this has nothing to do with the prison's treatment of you?"

"That's right." Thoughts of my friend's visit to my cell earlier made me err on the side of caution.

"So if I arranged for you to see a physiotherapist, would that help?"

"Oh, thank you."

"I can't promise when though, and you might have to pay. Can you afford to pay for a physiotherapist?"

"Yes, that's fine. If I need to I will find the money."

"We don't want you here any more. I want you to leave. Now!"

I had a very strong suspicion that this episode in my life in the prison would be given a red ink score. I walked back to the cell and the Christopher Lee lookalike approached me. I stopped and waited, as he clearly wanted to say something to me.

He said: "You know what?"

"What?"

"You've got some balls. I respect you for that. She doesn't like anyone standing up to her. Nothing frightens you, does it?"

"I wouldn't say that."

He reached out to shake my hand.

"Respect."

I took his soft warm hand and we looked coolly into each other's eyes.

All I could think of saying was: "Thank you."

He said: "I'll take you back to the wing. I think it's the best place for you. She's not very happy with you at the moment. Trust me, it's the best thing."

"Thank you."

I was then walked slowly back down the highly-polished corridor to the main wing, where I spent a month trying to walk again. When I eventually saw the physiotherapist, she examined me and said: "Oh dear, you have a twisted spine and your right hip is out of line. How on earth have you been able to walk about?"

"With great difficulty."

The sound of cell doors opening and closing, gates slamming and men trying to attract the attention of screws by shouting, banging and kicking doors felt never ending. It even carried on after the lights went out at nine. This enforced confinement drove the men to calling for drugs to be delivered in other ways, either by calling for a cleaner to pass things on from cell to cell or by dropping a line out of the window and swinging it in a pendulum motion until the person in the next cell caught hold of it. The only real period of silence was in the small hours of the morning and that too was dependent on whether someone, who was 'off his face' on drugs, had left his radio or rap music blaring throughout the night. If the screw on duty was able to rouse this reprobate from his stupor or the batteries ran dry, peace was again possible. The younger inmates could sometimes be heard crying and calling out "Mum!" in their sleep.

'Slop out' was like market day in Tangier. Every day was market day! They poured on to the landing like demented shoppers looking for deals, with credit scoring gauged on the promise of what might get through on the next visit. You could buy anything on the wing; prescription drugs, such as Temazepam, and non-prescription drugs such as black, squidgy black, blow, cannabis resin and marijuana, hooch and cocaine, crack cocaine, ecstasy, opium, heroin and meth. Then there was the tobacco, handmade cigarettes, matches, models made from matchsticks, knives, PP9 kits, coshes, radios, batteries, cigarette papers, gold and diamond rings, chains, pendants, watches and sexual favours.

The list seems endless. Where there is degenerative life, there walks a fallen man, like a blind fool, cascading oblivious towards his own misery and doom. I wondered what it was that compelled them to this fate, and resolved to discover the answer to this ancient mystery.

If you wanted anything, all you had to do was say what you wanted and it was brought in for you - at a price of course. The most common method of bringing drugs into the prison was to pass a condom containing the drugs from mouth to mouth by way of a kiss when greeting or leaving a visitor. This type of transfer was made more difficult if the visitor was male of course, and then it became a definite conversation killer, particularly if the goods were transferred at the beginning of the visit. When this happened it would normally bring on a theatrical display of emotion and the visit was terminated. So the preference was to wait until the end and then go for it. If the drugs had been swallowed that meant bringing them up again on the wing; and if that wasn't possible, they would have to wait for it to pass naturally through the body. This appeared to be the least favoured method of smuggling drugs into the prison because it was slow and messy and there was the risk of inadvertently flushing them away. For easy access, the more dedicated prisoner usually plugged the package up his anus or left it jammed between the cheeks of his arse until he returned to the wing and then his first job was to go back to his cell, cut up the drugs and sell as many 'deals' as he could on the wing for contraband or cash. This trade would then generate enough cash to pass out on visits for more drugs to be brought in and the cycle would continue endlessly, unless the chain was broken by someone being caught or they consumed all the drugs themselves.

Another favourite way was to fire the drugs over the wall with a catapult. The inmate would linger near the fence and try to catch them, or root around for them in the grass on the other side.

It wasn't just taking drugs that I found repulsive, but the extreme risks that were taken to bring them into the prison and the journey the drugs had to take before they finally reached the end user. It was easy enough to spot the drug dealers, as they walked with a particular swinging action, a cheek clinging roll, which most of the screws recognised. This swinging motion was more obvious immediately after their visit even though they had gone to enormous lengths to put on a brave face with a couple of ounces of 'squidgy black' jammed between the cheeks of their arse.

I would tell the men who offered me drugs: "Sorry, I prefer to do my bird neat. I want to remember what they did to me and I am not prepared to push it to the back of my mind by watering it down with some mind bending concoction which more than likely has been up two or three arseholes before it arrives at my cell door."

Those who took the drugs swore by the effects they derived from taking them, but personally I wasn't convinced. Once they had run dry they were left to face the trauma of prison life and reality without help.

Studying the mindset and the tactics they used to influence their wives, girlfriends, mates and associates, who had often only just been released themselves from prison, was fascinating for me, and so was reading all their depositions. I watched closely and wondered what it was these drugs did for them. Perhaps they substituted for some elevated state of consciousness. Up to this point I had never experienced this, nor had I even bothered to think about it. Where do you go when you're off your face? Why do it? You've only got to come back and face reality again. I was fascinated how effective emotional blackmail could be and that they were so desperate they were prepared to exert this form of emotional abuse on their loved ones, who appeared compelled to act immediately to their call and at the same time risk everything by exposing themselves and their children to trade with the drug dealers outside the prison, and after all that they still had to smuggle the drugs in. Such dedication!

Why? What was it that drove them to such lengths? The reality was that the screws preferred the drugs coming in. They chose to turn a blind eye. When drugs were available on the wing it made their job easier and the prison a lot calmer and safer. They could sit quietly discussing how many years they themselves had left to serve. You could see them sitting together trying to estimate their projected pension earnings. In so many ways they were killing time too. Many were ex-servicemen who wanted to bridge the gap in their lives up to their own retirement.

The only avenue for escape from the cell was to choose some form of prison entertainment, and there was so much to choose from!

Although Tim and Brian had resigned themselves to avoiding the prison Chaplain's services, I carried on attending them all. There was the 'Chaplain's hour' once a week in his office and the usual drug dealers' meetings in the chapel on a Sunday morning, which started with the Roman Catholic service, followed by the Church of England service. The entertainment in the Anglican service was increased by the second in command, a Pentecostal minister, who joined the service for some lively hand-waving and clapping sessions, which made it even easier to pass the drugs around and harder for the screws to see what was going on.

I believed I was a Christian, maybe not a good one, but I had beliefs. I kept my beliefs to myself of course, mainly because, if I was honest, I didn't know enough about my faith to be able to talk about it. I had helped out at Sunday School with my own children, but it hadn't made any real sense to me back then and it still didn't. It was just something I did on a Sunday and Brian was right, I suppose - it was stories for the children. I couldn't see how it would help me in the here and now. How could Jesus help with what was happening to me in prison every day? The hatred towards me was not only from the inmates but from the staff.

When I attended these meetings with the other prisoners I stared blankly at the minister as he spoke and I felt nothing, because I had heard the stories so many times before.

I thought "All these words! What do they mean to me?" I kept listening. These words of wisdom must be meant for the rest of the prisoners, not for me. I looked around and studied all their apathetic faces. I listened to this meaningless bilge week after week, until one particular Sunday I asked myself a question. "Perhaps this guy is talking to me?"

I thought about what that might mean. I still failed to understand why I had been incarcerated and I asked myself if there was a reason. I pondered that idea for a long time. If there was a reason, I needed to find out what it was. The quicker I found the answer, the quicker I would be released.

I didn't normally read a newspaper as I had enough reading matter with all the depositions that kept being dropped off to me by illiterate inmates searching for some hope of a reprieve. They wanted me to see if I could help them in some way, "being an ex copper and all that." One of my 'clients', Andrew, who happened to be well educated and was from a wealthy family, had been to court in the morning. I had suggested that he write a personal letter to the judge, as he was expecting a long sentence. He was on a drug dealing charge for being caught with a lot of cannabis resign (nine bars I believe, it matters not), so I made a point of referring to the drugs as marijuana in the letter. The judge had commented on Andrew's letter by saying "Quite clearly this man is not a dealer, because if he were a dealer he would not refer to cannabis resin as marijuana! He's clearly a user and not a dealer." Andrew was given a very light sentence and was expecting to be discharged by the end of the week. Again the news travelled quickly and my stack of depositions grew deeper. Some of the tales of woe were quite bizarre.

While reading through other inmates' court papers, I thought 'If only I could do this for my case. If only it were that simple!'

I was standing on the landing looking out over the wing during 'slop out' when I overheard three inmates making plans to attack Andrew in his cell. Their voices were lowered but I could clearly hear their reasoning and intention.

"He's got to be a grass, Clint. No one gets six months for dealin'!"

His cellmate responded "Listen, Derek, does he think we're stupid? He's a grass. He has to be! Nine bars he got caught with, scales and everything!"

I heard a deeper voice with a Welsh accent grunt "Let's PP9 the bastard. Let 'im 'ave it! What cell's he in?"

As soon as they stepped on to the landing I turned to face them, blocking their path. It was the Welshman who spoke first. "Get out of the fucking way, copper!"

I kept eye contact with them as they stood bunched together in front of me. "If you think I'm going to get out of your way so you can PP9 my friend, you're very much mistaken. If you want to do him, you will have to take me out first!"

It's normally the ringleader who does all the shouting and my main target appeared to be the man with the Welsh accent.

"What's it got to do with you, pig? He's got to be a grass to get six months for dealin'!"

"Not if he's got me helping him write letters to the judge he hasn't. I've seen his depositions and he's no grass, nor is he a nonce! Now pack it up and wish him well, can't you? He's got a result!"

Clint looked very agitated. "When you was a policeman did you ever arrest anyone?"

I could immediately see where this was going, so I said: "Thousands!"

Clint's jaw dropped at my response and he was now looking very uncomfortable. "Did you ever send anyone to prison when you was a pig?"

I snapped: "Of course I did, Clint!"

My Welsh bully wanted to know more. "How many?"

"Hundreds! But the judge sent them to prison, not me. I just took them to the judge."

Clint was back in a flash "How can you stand in here and say that! How can you?"

I leaned against the railing nonchalantly, "Listen, this is how

I've always seen things. It was only ever just a game of cops and robbers. If you decide, in your mind's eye, that you want to play the game and if you had half a brain you would have worked out the odds of winning and losing, you know, the odds of being caught or catching someone. So let's say you choose to be a robber and the odds of a robber being caught might be 10-1 and you decide to play? Is that reasonable so far?"

All three nodded and Clint said "I didn't want to be caught though."

My body language demonstrated to Clint that I understood how he felt and I raised my palms and nodded. "Nobody wants to be caught, Clint, but you must have known that there were odds of being caught. Agreed?"

"Well I didn't know what the odds were! I just did it."

"I see, Clint. That's fair enough, but you joined the game, didn't you, and the game has odds?"

Clint nodded "Yeah."

"So let's say they were 10-1 in your favour and you got caught. That means the game is over. So let's say it was me who nicked you; you would know that you have to go to the judge?"

"Yeah." Clint nodded

"Well, before we do, I'd sit down and tell you that you've lost the game, right? I'd then say to you "Listen, Clint. You have to go to the judge because you lost. So tell me what you want me to tell the judge, you know, put it in a statement and the judge will give you whatever the penalty is, not me, because I'm not the judge, right?"

Clint nodded and the other two were captivated "Yeah."

"Am I going too quick, Clint?"

"Nah."

So I went on "I loved playing the game. If you wanted to keep playing the game as well, I needed to have you back on the street as soon as possible, you know, so that we can carry on playing the game, right? I'm not taking any of what's happening personally, I just like playing the game, but if you get fed up with losing and you want to spend more time at home with the kids and the missus and maybe decide you want to get trained up to do a different job, then you have that option. It's not personal, it's just a game. Do you understand what I'm saying?"

My Welsh friend interrupted "You sound like you were a good copper, so why'd you leave?"

"Good question, my friend. I left because the cops started to cheat and the robbers got pissed off with them cheating. I could see that this could only end up in war and I didn't want a war, I just wanted to play the game, you know, cops and robbers. So if your odds were up, we sat down and talked it through before we started another game. You'd have to pay whatever penalty you were given by the judge of course before we could start again. It's only fair, eh? So now, because of all the cheating, the robbers feel cheated and are angry. Are you lot going to hate me because I was good at playing the game?"

Clint's mind glazed over and he said "I wished that it was you who nicked me. You sound OK."

"Are you going to leave my friend Andy alone? Maybe you can all just wish him well, because he got a result. Now if he wants to carry on selling drugs, I'd have loved to have seen his face again in the police station if I'd just nicked him again. We could then have had another one of my chats."

All three nodded and Clint said "You sound like you were a decent copper."

"Thanks Clint, that's the nicest thing anyone's ever said to me."

Andrew left Exeter Prison that Friday and he honoured his promise to look after me when he was 'on the out' even though I insisted that he didn't. I received a *Daily Telegraph* and *Sunday Telegraph* in my cell from that moment on.

One Sunday I was reading an article I found interesting. I read it several times and ordered a book from the library. When it arrived two weeks later I read it with great interest. For the first time it revealed to me the mystery of why Sarah had held so much power over me.

When my girlfriend Heather visited me in the prison the following week I was excited to see her and tell her my good news. As soon as I gave her a hug and a kiss I couldn't help but blurt it out.

"I've worked out how Sarah had so much control over me for so many years and why I put up with it" I said.

Heather was wearing black cords and an old sloppy jumper and her long blonde hair was held back with an elastic tube. She laughed and threw her head back in amusement. Before I could say another word she said: "It's taken you all this time to work that out? It's easy, you married your mother!" She gave me an incredulous look. "Come on, Costa, surely you didn't need to read a book to work that one out! I knew that the moment I met her."

"How did you know?"

"I bet the first thing she wanted to do when she met you was to meet your mum. Am I correct?"

"Yes! After the third date and that was it, she never wanted to see my mother again until Luke was a year old."

"You men are so easy!"

"Have you known all along?"

Heather puckered her face in a knowing way, which left me mystified. I thought to myself 'Well, Heather's never met my mother, so she can't have done the same thing'.

CHAPTER ELEVEN

■■■■■■■■

CROWN COURT

I met David in a small room deep in the bowels of Exeter Crown Court before my trial on May 18 1992. He was quiet and to the point, reassuring and compassionate.

"David, this is my final draft of my understanding of what happened" I told him. "I have managed to secretly type these notes in computer studies. Please try not to disclose this fact to the court as it will get me and the class tutor into trouble."

I produced the final breakdown of all my notes on the logs that would prove my innocence and said: "We must have the forensic results from the items found in the boot of the car. Where are they?"

"There are none, Con."

"David, there must be!"

"There aren't. I will check again with the prosecution. I have to go as we will be on in a minute."

Tim, Brian and I were brought up a narrow stairway from the cells into a crowded courtroom. I couldn't resist looking up into the gallery and smiled at the familiar faces I recognised. The jury of five men and seven women were sworn in and I listened to the prosecution's opening address.

"Your Honour, ladies and gentlemen of the Jury, the three

accused stand charged with the following offences: conspiracy to commit blackmail; conspiracy to kidnap; possessing a firearm with intent to commit an indictable offence; having a firearm with intent; possessing a firearm without a certificate.

"They have all pleaded not guilty. The prosecution will prove to the jury that, without any doubt, these men planned to carry out these offences on the day they were arrested, namely 17th April 1991."

The first day passed quickly. I had a meeting with David after the court had been adjourned. We met in the same small room below the courthouse.

"That's the first day over with. Is there anything that you feel is important to tell me at this time?"

"Yes David, I need to see the forensic reports. You promised me that you would get them for me."

"Yes, I did. Why are they so important?"

"I believe they will prove that I have nothing to do with these charges. When will I get to see these documents?"

"The prosecution will produce them tomorrow. Listen, there isn't much we can do today. I have to go as I am meeting your bank manager this afternoon. He's agreed to meet with me to discuss the case."

"That's good news! He will tell you that I have always conducted myself in a professional way in my business and personal dealings with the bank."

Our meeting concluded and I was able to see my girlfriend Heather for a few moments with my sister Coralia. Heather was emotionally distraught, as was Coralia.

"I saw the judge in the car park and had a word with him" said Coralia. "He was putting his black labrador into the back of his Volvo estate. I told him 'My brother's innocent!' and he said

"I can't talk to you about his case." Then he left."

Heather was dressed in a smart dark blue wool suit with her skirt just above the knee and a floral blouse and black court shoes. Her curly blonde hair was tied back in a pony tail and she appeared to be composed, but she was clearly concerned as she spoke "The court staff said that we can only see you for a few minutes."

I embraced them both and within a few minutes the screw told us to "Finish your visit!" We were led to the back door and handcuffed and then taken to the prison van. As we left the court the press were jumping up at the windows, trying to get a photograph of us.

During David's cross examination of Detective Sergeant Bains, he asked:

"Did you send the gun and masks found in the bag for forensic examination?"

"No, we didn't think it was necessary."

"You didn't think it was necessary!"

"No."

"Didn't you think there might be some evidence on these items which would assist you in this case?"

"No. The items were examined at the point of arrest and we didn't think that it was worth subjecting them to further examination."

"Was there any forensic evidence on these items which relate to my client?"

"No."

David turned to look at me, confused, and sent his clerk, Duncan, over to talk to me.

"They say they never examined the items and the prosecutor confirms this as well" he said.

"They're lying, Duncan. They are holding this evidence back from me. I want to see the continuity of this evidence! They went to the laboratory in Chepstow and I can't believe that they never examined them, it just doesn't make sense!"

"OK I will tell David for you."

The trial continued and officer after officer detailed how suspicious the movements were of the three of us. The detailed logs showed every movement, yet there was an innocent explanation for each one. All were perfectly normal activities that in no way constituted anything illegal. Buying milk, collecting papers from the shop, parking the car, carrying boxes, etc, etc, etc, but there was no bag.

The prosecution had only one independent witness, Philip. He had been seventeen years old and at home with the flu when the doorbell rang. Upon answering the door he was confronted by WDC Alison Lovell. She wanted to look out of the bedroom window in order to observe the white van parked across the road. Philip didn't believe that she was a police officer and asked her for her ID card.

"I've left it in my car" she said

"I want to see it before I let you in."

I thought 'Clever lad'.

So WDC Lovell went back to her car and retrieved her handbag and produced her warrant card. While she was walking to the car Philip looked over the fence and saw her silver Golf GTI parked at the side of his house. It was empty.

In court, Detective Sergeant Edward Pratt was cross examined by David.

"Detective Sergeant Pratt , you have said in your evidence to the court that you followed the three defendants to a house some three miles away from the witness's house where the witness and other officers have said the van was parked?"

"Yes, I dropped WDC Lovell off at the bottom of Satchel Drive. I was able to keep the defendant's vehicle in sight at all times. I followed it up the A380 to Exeter Race Course and then back down to Cherry Tree Cottage, the home of the intended victim."

"What vehicle were you driving?"

"A Golf GTI."

"What colour was it?"

"Silver."

"Who was driving that day?"

"I was and WDC Lovell was the passenger."

"Did you remain in that vehicle at all times?"

"Yes. WDC Lovell had gone to the witness's house in order to keep observation on the white van."

"What happened then?"

"I followed the defendants. There were road workers outside Cherry Tree Cottage and they drove past the cottage slowly, looking up the drive to the property. They then returned to the van, signalling to the driver to follow and then they returned to the farm."

"You weren't even in the Golf that day, were you Sergeant Pratt ?"

"I was!"

Your witness has already stated that the Volkswagen Golf you say you were driving, was in fact parked and empty outside the witnesses house the whole time."

"He must be mistaken."

"He's your witness. A witness for the prosecution. We also have Detective Sergeant Anderson and another officer, who were writing down your transmitted logs, who have said that the sighting that you have mentioned never actually happened!"

"I can't answer for them. All I can say is what I saw. I saw them at the intended victim's house."

"You are a liar."

"No, I saw them at the house!"

Detective Sergeant Pratt left the witness box and as he passed me the Court's secretary, who moved closer to me in order to wave, giving a silly girly smile to DS Pratt, said: "Bye darling, I'll see you later". Then he smiled and walked past me, giving me a devious look.

I immediately called Duncan over and in a whisper asked: "What the hell's going on with them two?"

"We saw them together in the pub last night and she was all over him like a rash, God knows what's going on there, he's got to be giving her one."

"That can't be right, surely? They're definitely taking the piss doing it right in front of me! Who does he think he is, James Bond?"

I called David over: "Why hasn't Badcock been called?"

"We don't need to talk to him. He had nothing to do with the arrests."

"I want him here. He's a liar and I want him cross examined, he came to see me in my cell and offered me a deal if I helped him stitch the other two up."

David left me and addressed the Judge: "Your Honour, we would like to question the officer in charge of the case."

"Why?" Judge Neville looked agitated.

"We believe he is required to attend and answer questions about this case that are important to my client."

"Very well, I order that he attend."

The following day Detective Inspector Badcock arrived in the witness box.

After being sworn in, David stood up to question him: "Are you the officer in charge of this case?"

"Yes."

"Did this operation have a code name?"

"Yes it was called Operation Dolby."

"Where did the information come from that instigated this investigation?"

"I'm not going to reveal our source, all I can say is that we were acting on information received."

"Who was the main target of this information?"

"Long. We were told that he had a gang."

"When you went into my client's cell, you offered him a deal if he helped you stitch up the other two men, is this right?"

"No, we don't do deals with criminals. I never went into his cell."

"My client insists that you did."

"It never happened."

"My client requested that you speak to his brother, did you talk to him?"

"No."

After hearing that the only civilian prosecution witness had now become a defence witness, plus the two officers who wrote the logs, the judge summed up the case tentatively and then dismissed the jury.

After seven hours of deliberation and reconvening for the occasional question from the jury, they had reached a decision.

"All stand!"

"Members of the jury, have you reached a decision?"

The chairman of the jury rose from his chair and the other members of the jury looked straight forward, several with their heads down. It wasn't a good sign of what was to come for us and we knew it.

"How do you find the first defendant, Long, on the charge of: Conspiracy to blackmail?"

"Guilty, Your Honour."

"Conspiracy to kidnap?"

"Guilty, Your Honour."

"The charges of possessing a firearm with intent to commit an Indictable offence and having a firearm with intent to commit an Indictable Offence have been recorded as not guilty under section 17 of the Criminal Justice System and will be included in sentencing these men with the other charges."

The chairman of the jury nodded, as if he had already been primed with this information.

"Yes, your honour."

"On the charge of possessing a firearm without a certificate, have you reached a verdict?"

"Yes, Your Honour, guilty."

Brian looked visibly shocked and swayed in the dock. He looked like he was about to collapse.

Judge Neville then looked at me and I remembered the last time I had seen him on an early morning shoot at Tiverton, lifting the boot of his Volvo estate and letting his black labrador jump out of the back. It was now his turn to lift his sights to me.

"How do you find the second defendant on the charge of conspiracy to blackmail?"

"Guilty, your honour."

"Conspiracy to kidnap?"

"Guilty, your honour."

"The charges of possessing a firearm with intent to commit an indictable offence and having a firearm with intent to commit an indictable offence have been recorded as not guilty under section 17 of the Criminal Justice System and will be included in sentencing these men with the other charges."

The chairman nodded, as if he had, yet again, already been primed with this information.

"Yes, your honour."

On the charge of possessing a firearm without a certificate, have you reached a verdict?'

"Yes, your honour. Guilty."

I stood silently with thoughts of the festive board: "Point, left right; Point, left right; Point left right, Bang! Bang! Bang! Bang! Bang! Bang! Bang! Bang! Bang!" So mote it be. I resigned myself to the fact that the officers of the Flying Squad had won this particular battle. I really hadn't stood a chance against so many and David knew it too. At least he'd been straight and honest with me.

The members of the press stared hard trying to record some sort of reaction from the three of us in the dock.

"How do you find the third defendant on the charge of conspiracy to blackmail?"

"Not guilty, your honour."

"Conspiracy to kidnap?"

"Not guilty, your honour."

"The charges of possessing a firearm with intent to commit an indictable offence and having a firearm with intent to commit an indictable offence have been recorded as not guilty under section 17 of the Criminal Justice System and will be included in sentencing these men with the other charges."

The chairman of the jury nodded again. "Yes, your honour."

"On the charge of possessing a firearm without a certificate, have you reached a verdict?"

"Yes, your honour, not guilty."

"You are free to leave the court."

Tim, visibly shocked staggered out of the back of the dock and was escorted below. David looked shocked, as did the judge.

As he left, Tim could be heard weeping. He stood still for a moment and faced me.

"Colin, they can't do this to you. You're innocent! You can't let me go and not Colin!"

At this point the prosecuting barrister leapt to his feet.

"Your honour, in mitigation!"

The Judge looked stunned. "Mitigation! Mitigation! Go on."

"I would like to point out that the kidnap could not have happened on the day in question."

The judge looked even more confused. "You said that it was. Are you now saying that it wasn't going to happen on that day?"

"Yes, your honour, the bank manager's wife wasn't at home. She was playing golf."

"Playing golf!" The look of amazement on his face said it all as he stared over his half moon glasses.

"Why did you say that it was definitely going to happen that day?"

He thought for a moment and said "Forget it."

After a short address, he turned to me and Brian.

"You have been found guilty on all the charges. I hereby sentence you for conspiracy to commit blackmail: twelve years.

"Conspiracy to kidnap: Twelve years.

"Possessing a firearm without certificate: Three years.

"Take them down!"

CHAPTER TWELVE

■ ■ ■ ■ ■ ■ ■ ■

"COPPER, COME OUT HERE AND DIE!"

The screw collected me from my cell and I met David in the dark passageway that led up to the dock. He reached out to shake my hand.

"Let's go in here and have a chat." We were shown to a door that led into the interview room.

"We must appeal! Leave it to me. I will start the process immediately."

"It's not worth it, David. There are just too many policemen. You were right. Thank you for all you did, you couldn't have done any more."

"I will try. Please trust me?"

"Conviction only. Not sentence!"

"Con, I don't have to stay in these sort of places and I can't imagine what you must be going through. You must be in a lot of danger. Take care of yourself in there!"

"Yes I will. Can I return to my cell now?"

"Yes, of course."

"I want some time for all of this to sink in, David. I need to consider my future."

"Of course, I will visit you in Exeter Prison next month."

We shook hands and he knocked on the door and I walked

back with the screw to my cell. It was a large cold room where I had spent the last three weeks eating nothing but fish and chips. The others thought I was quite mad, but I insisted upon it. I was like a pregnant woman with an inner craving for some hedonistic banquet. We were offered a choice of meals, but if they couldn't get me fish and chips I went without. The stainless steel walls were covered in graffiti and scribbled messages, 'Al, on tour June 1988 - 2 years. Bastards!' and 'Biff - On tour 1990 - "Not Guilty!" 5 years! Tossers!' This scrawl went on seemingly endlessly around the main holding cell.

My sister Coralia was the first private visitor; she just wept. Then Heather joined us in the visiting room for a few moments and we were walked to the van and the escorting screw, who I had seen being dragged into one of the cells on the main wing by an inmate. He appeared to be genuinely upset by our case. "I have been following your case, Buller. I saw what they did to you and you should have walked today!"

"Yeah, tell me about it."

"There were too many of them. It was just too much for you to take on by yourself, son. You put up one hell of a fight. Sorry."

"It's hardly your fault" I said.

The mood in the prison was sombre as Brian and I passed through reception. There was a lot of head shaking and many sharp intakes of breath, accompanied by profound glances of deep empathy and absolutely no squibs from staff or inmates. As we walked back from the reception area in our prison blues there was a silence, which I took to be some kind of mark of respect for taking on three out of the four London Flying Squads. The result had been inevitable. They knew that we had put up a fight and any man doing a 'twelve' was doing 'heavy bird'. This tariff commanded respect among the inmates. They also knew that as an ex-copper my life was about to take a nose dive into a completely new level of misery, one that I was unlikely to survive unscathed.

I would now have to wait for an allocation to a long-term dispersal prison. There were only a certain number of prisons which would accept a man doing a twelve-year sentence, and I dreaded it. I had it on good authority that there were two prisons, should they be allocated to me, from which, thanks to my police background, I might never walk away; Long Lartin and Wandsworth. The only prison where I 'might' survive would be HMP Maidstone. So I set Maidstone as my objective.

I now believed that it was a good time to prepare myself for death. I sent every personal item of emotional or sentimental value that I had out of the prison and my sister Coralia collected them from the property office. If I was going to go out in a body bag I wanted nothing with me from my old life. I kept the letters from my mother in a thick plastic bag with HMP inscribed on it. The only other thing was my crucifix, which I wore at all times. If anyone wanted to take that from me they would have to stand in my way on the wing or pull me into a recess and take it by force.

Early lessons learned inside prison were harsh. If someone wants to kill you they probably will, and there will be no witnesses. No one 'sees' anything in prison, but at the same time everything is seen. I had a long, lonely and dangerous walk ahead of me and I would be a fool to think otherwise.

Policemen are considered the lowest form of life, after the sex offender and child molester. What lay ahead was an impossible walk for someone with my background. A mini life sentence had been passed on me and the fellow inmates knew it. I would be held at Exeter for a few months and then I would enter the Dispersal System and get moved to a secure prison.

The men knew that even if I was guilty no physical crime had actually taken place. It was an allegation of a thought in process, in that we were 'thinking' about committing an offence. One of the defendants had been acquitted and the sentence was hard and cruel.

Now began the period when the staff look to 'red ink' the prisoners. If the staff can get any part of your report written in red ink, because you've been problematic, the next prison gives them the opportunity for 'payback'. It's the first thing they look for when you move to a new prison and I knew I had some 'red ink' on my file already. The Governor thought I was a cold and calculating person and had told me so on several occasions. To top it all off I had pissed off the Senior Medical Officer.

I quickly submitted an application to see the Locations Officer, Mr Hodgson, a tall, slim and rather well-spoken man with a rosy complexion and pleasant disposition. He had grey short fuzzy hair parted down one side and he always spoke slowly and calmly to everyone around him. He was not, however, to be underestimated in my opinion. Mr Hodgson wielded immense power in the 'futures' market' for me and my life depended on it. I just hoped that he would realise the same thing and be kindly toward my own disposition.

"You're going to Long Lartin, Con." Screws didn't mind calling me 'Con' because as far as they were concerned we were all 'Cons'. They found that opportunity quite amusing because they could call me to my face what they thought and called us all behind our backs and I didn't give a toss! It was, after all, my name.

"You don't have a choice I'm afraid, it's because of the length of your sentence."

"You know that with my background they'll kill me in Long Lartin!"

"I don't think so."

"I think so. I want to go somewhere else. I've got twelve years and you wouldn't want to turn it into a death sentence, would you?"

"Where though? No one will take you!"

"Please, there must be another option?"

"I'll ring Maidstone, but I don't think they will take you either."

He lifted the telephone and dialled through to speak with his counterpart in Maidstone Prison.

"Mr Hodgson, allocations officer here from Exeter. We've got a decent chap doing a twelve who won't be any bother. Do you want him?" He listened for a moment.

"You will! Are you sure?"

"Good. I'll send him over in due course. Can I have your fax number and I will send you the paperwork."

"Yep. I've got it. Thank you."

"They will take you." He looked pleasantly surprised. "Will you take Maidstone?"

"What are the facilities like?"

He looked at his prison handbook.

"They've got a swimming pool!"

"Sounds good to me!"

"Good. I'll send you over there then."

"Yes please. Thank you so much!"

I wanted to kiss him, but thought better of it. I was now naively looking forward to my move.

I had held various positions within the prison for work. I had been a wing cleaner, library orderly, computer orderly and part time prison barber. I took Tim's advice and started cutting hair, starting off by cutting his first and then Brian's and then I moved on to some of the shorter-sentenced prisoners, because of the risk of screwing one up. I then progressed to the more intricate cuts of the lifers. What I really liked about being the barber was that I was allowed to carry a very large pair of scissors in my pocket. I had two sets of scissors and so I adjusted one of the pairs so that they were stiff to open and used them for demonstration purposes only. I made sure I was near a dart board. The conversation normally came around to my background:

"You're a copper then?"

"Yes."

"Did you ever arrest anybody?"

"Yes. Hundreds."

"How could you do that? Did you put anyone in prison?"

"Loads."

"Bastard!"

"I met my father, and he was married to my mother when I was born. So there is no chance of that I'm afraid."

"Ain't you frightened walking about in this place?"

"No."

"Why?"

"Because I always carry these in my pocket."

I would then take out the scissors and throw them neatly into the centre of the dart board, then walk over and pull them back out again, wipe off the residue of plaster from the wall and put the scissors back in my pocket.

"You're fucking crazy!"

"Good at cutting hair though. What would you like to be today, sir, a solicitor? Bank manager? Doctor? Footballer? What's your fancy? I will transform you!"

The word soon got around. If I was going to become their victim they would have to choose the battlefield well.

Cutting hair brought with it certain privileges and spoils. There was always tobacco, jewellery from burglaries (committed prior to coming inside), watches, engagement rings, drugs and favours from the kitchen orderlies, offered as payment. I declined all those in favour of tea bags, or if it was an orderly, I would accept hot chocolate poured through my cell door via a folded piece of card. It trickled through the door and into my plastic mug on the other side nicely, just before bedtime. Should I be pushed, a piece of fresh cheese would be just dandy. It was the scissors I wanted to possess the most.

There was a rumour being spread by the Chaplains that a bishop was coming into the prison from Africa. I had given this visit some thought and made a mental note to attend should he arrive. I went to as many church services on a Sunday as I could and watched the drug dealers sing a few songs while swapping their deals in the sparse chapel. I listened to the priest go through the sermons he had prepared and memorised at theology college. All of it left me feeling empty. I understood what they were saying, but so what?

The following week I wrote to Sarah:

Dear Sarah,

I hope that you and the boys are well.

My time in here seems to be drifting on and on. I have been sentenced to twelve years and I have no idea when I might be released. Please tell the boys that I miss and love them very much and I enclose ten pounds pocket money for them. As I only get paid £1.60 per week it's hard to be able to save money any quicker.

I understand that you still want me to send all my letters to your parents' address as you are unwilling to release your address to me but I would like to make contact with them both.

I would be prepared to telephone a public phone box in order to talk to them, if you would prefer? You've already told me in a previous letter that you wouldn't want me phoning your house but all I want to do is talk to the children and hear their voices. Please don't cut them off from me.

If you want to sell some of the paintings to raise some money, please go ahead and do so. While I am in custody I will not be able to continue to pay you any maintenance.

If you have got any photographs of the children I would love to see them.

All the best and please send my deepest love to the boys.
Costa.

The following week I received the following letter from Sarah.

Con,

You never cease to amaze me with your stupidity and selfishness!

You left me and your children on our own and wonder why I am refusing you contact with them.

When you left me I sold everything! I mean everything! I now live in London and want a clean break away from you. I told you that if you left me you would never see the children again and you won't!

So you can sit in your cosy little cell and hide away from all your responsibilities. The children and I are settled into a new relationship with Gordon and he is very kind to us.

I am sure that you have a nice warm cell and that you have made lots of new friends that you can sit down and play silly games with.

Please find enclosed two letters from the boys, which they asked me to include in my letter.

I live in the real world and I have to get on with my life, so please leave us alone.

Sarah.

The frustration of my situation and her forbidding any contact with my children made me lose my temper. Sarah knew exactly which buttons to press to wind me up.

I ran at the bars in my cell window and took hold of them, lifting myself off the ground. Then I screamed out.

"If You are there, God, show me that you're real! SHOW ME!"

I immediately felt a voice come out from deep within my stomach that was not my own and it came out of my mouth with a disabling power that instantly calmed my anger.

"You started it!"

I was shocked, frightened, and at the same time I was at peace. In an instant! I sat on the edge of my bed. I remembered that I had indeed written a letter the previous week to Sarah and it was as a result of my letter that I had received hers.

I sat back in my chair to read the letter from my youngest son, Luke.

Dear Dad,

I hope that you are O.K. I miss you like crazy.

I am forgetting what you look like so if you have got anything that you can send to me that will remind me of you I would be really pleased.

Lots and lots of Love

Luke

I immediately started looking around my cell to see if I had anything I could send to Luke. I remembered that they liked to hear me play my harmonica, so I said goodbye to them both the next day in letters I posted to her father's address. My mouth organs were really all that I had and they gave me great pleasure, but I didn't hesitate to send them to my boys. I missed them and so did the men who heard me play (especially *Danny Boy*), but I missed my sons more and I desperately wanted them to remember me.

The following Wednesday I felt drawn to attend the Chaplain's discussion evenings on the education wing. So I pressed my bell and followed a strange calling from deep inside my unconscious mind.

This black bishop was visiting the prison from Africa and he had asked for the opportunity to speak to the men. The room was packed full of inmates who were mostly taking a break from 'Bang Up' and they all jeered as I walked in with comments like "Fuck off pig! You don't belong here. God ain't going to help you."

The Bishop was introduced by the Chaplain and he stood up to address us all.

"I am from Africa and I am personally responsible for two hundred and eighty churches. I have come here to give a message to just one man. This man will know who he is once I have spoken."

He then went on to describe me and my situation exactly.

I called out and I stood up: "That's me! It's me!" Everyone stared at me in silence.

When the Bishop had finished talking, he said.

"Will you come forward to me please? I have been asked to pray with you."

I made my way through the crowded room and approached the bishop. The men watched me curiously.

I said "Your message is for me. I'm definitely the one that you have come for!" I don't know why, but my whole body started shaking.

The bishop spoke in a whisper to some invisible person and said: "Do you reject the devil?" I must admit that I found this question a bit freaky, but all the same I answered: "Yes!" He mumbled some more and said "Say it!" The whole room went silent and I said "Say what?"

The Bishop looked concerned and said "Say 'I reject the devil!' and spit on the floor three times." I immediately spat on the floor three times and in a raised voice said: "I reject the devil!" He then placed the palms of his hands on my head and said: "Repeat this after me: 'Oh Father, Lord of Heaven and earth…'"

I held my eyes shut tight and said: "Oh Father, Lord of Heaven and earth"

The Bishop went on: "I confess to you all the hidden and open sins of my heart and my mind".

"I confess to you all the hidden and open sins of my heart and my mind."

"which I have committed unto this very day."

"which I have committed unto this very day."

"Wherefore I beg of You, the all righteous and compassionate Judge"

"Wherefore I beg of You, the all righteous and compassionate Judge"

"forgiveness of all my sins and grace to sin no more."

"forgiveness of all my sins and grace to sin no more."

The Bishop said a blessing and then said: "Open your eyes."

When I opened my eyes he appeared to be searching for something within me and held his stare for some time before he said: "Your life will never be the same again. Amazing things will happen to you."

That night I walked back to my cell in a daze.

I didn't feel any different. I didn't feel any better. I asked myself "Is this just another lie?" I felt nothing.

Simon, who had wandered out of the library, joined me and we walked to the gate on 'C' wing together and waited for a screw to let us through. He said: "What's the matter, Costa?"

"I don't feel any different. I should, but I don't!"

"Feel any different about what?" Simon was only about 23, and being on remand he wore his own clothes and liked to dress well. Today he had on some black loose-fitting silk trousers and a patterned long sleeve silk shirt.

"My promise."

Simon remarked: What are you on about, Costa? What's the matter? You look weird."

"A black bishop came into the prison tonight with a message for me and I've promised to serve God and to be a faithful witness, but nothing's happened yet!"

He patted me on the back: "Don't be so hard on yourself, give Him time."

I nodded my head: "Yeah, you're right, Simon. I will do just that; however long it takes! I made a promise."

The following day I was sitting on my bed listening to the incessant bang-bang-bang on the steel cell door next to me. It was a relief when the screws opened all the doors along the landing for 'slop out' because then the banging stopped. I overheard two men talking just outside my cell. One was a

Devonian and the other a deep, rasping Rastafarian.

"So, you're next to the pig then?"

"You serious, man?"

"Yeah, you've got a copper as a neighbour." He found this most amusing.

'Bastard!' I thought.

The mood changed instantly as my Rastafarian neighbour called out: "Come out here piggy, wiggy, piggy! Can you hear me, pig? I've got something I want to give you!" There were hoots of laughter. Then he grew impatient and the Rastafarian voice called to me again in a raging voice, "Copper! Come out here and die!"

He clearly wanted to kill me and he kept calling to me. So I rose from my bed, lowered myself through the short doorway and stood outside my cell. I looked him straight in the eyes and said: "Did you call me?"

He let out a long, deep laugh. "We don't want any coppers on our wing. Fuck off and go on the 43s, man!" The landing was full of inmates all looking on and laughing.

So I kept looking him in the eyes and calmly and politely said: "Well, if you want me to go on the 43s, you are going to have to put me over there. I'm not going to volunteer to go on my own."

This was an invitation that he found hard to resist. To 'put someone on the 43s' usually meant that you retired with that person into a recess and then beat the crap out of each other.

He walked towards me and as I spoke I turned to go in my cell with him and he shouted: "Don't go in your cell, I'm going to kill you!" I said: "Don't be stupid, you can't kill me out here, the screws will see you. Come into my cell and you can kill me in here without any witnesses. Come on, you'd best come inside!" He smiled broadly, knowing that his friends across the landing were watching, and walked into my cell. I could see that he was about the same height as me, broad and very black.

There was a chair on the other side of a small table pushed against the wall and I sat in it and I invited him to sit on the edge of my bed.

He shouted "I ain't sitting on your bed, man! I'm going to kill you!"

"In a minute, there's plenty of time. You can try to kill me when we've finished our game of backgammon." I smiled and continued speaking "Before I beat the crap out of you, I'd better at least know your name?"

"Ha, ha, ha. Good one. My name's Gary. You've got some arse man!"

I reached for a board game and said: "Nice to meet you, Gary. My name's Con, but my friends and family call me Costa. I'm talking strictly backgammon here, right? Do you fancy a game or not?"

"Yeah, man."

We both sat chatting and played backgammon and the prison staff, who were having difficulty controlling Gary, locked us in together. I said to Gary "I made a promise to God a couple of days ago to serve Him and that's what I'm going to do."

Gary was more interested in the cross hanging around my neck on a gold chain. "Where'd you get that cross from?"

I threw my dice and took my move: "I was baptised Constantine in the Greek Orthodox Church in Malta when I was five years old, Gary." I took hold of my cross and turned it over. I showed Gary my baby teeth marks on the back and said: "Can you see that?"

Gary leaned forward: "Yeah, man!"

"I did that when I was five. Going some, eh? This cross is solid gold."

I sat in my chair and Gary perched himself on the edge of my bed and we both sat happily playing backgammon.

"You're supposed to be on the other side, how come you've gone from cop to robber?"

"I pissed off the Flying Squad, Gary. They wanted me to stitch up the guys I came in with, so I told them to piss off. I wouldn't do that to anyone."

"You never stitched anyone up then?"

"As a policeman I liked to look at it all as a bit of a game, you know, as you described it a moment ago, cops and robbers."

"So you got fed up playing the cop then?"

"No, I really enjoyed playing the game, Gary. I didn't like it when the rules started to get changed though, you know, they started cheating. So I decided to get out. It was the only thing to do really."

"You enjoy locking people up then?"

The screw looked into the cell to check on us.

"Yeah! They lost the game, didn't they? Listen, Gary, if I decide that I want to play the game of cops and robbers, I have to decide on what side to be on, don't I?"

Gary nodded: "Right, but I do drugs. I don't rob banks. I couldn't do the bird for robbin' banks."

"That's exactly my point, Gary. You chose drugs. Let's say I choose 'cop' and you choose to be a drug dealer. Before you start the game, if you've got half a brain, you'll sit down and work out the odds of getting caught first. Right?" Gary nodded. "If you choose to take the odds and go out and become a drugs dealer, say, without fully considering the risk, whose fault is that?"

"Mine, Costa. It was all my fault. I just didn't want to get caught, that's all."

"Yeah. Like I said, if you've got half a brain you'd sit down and work out what the odds are of getting caught. So you then engage in the game knowing that you had say a 1 in 10 chance of getting caught. If it 'came on top' and I caught you, I'd say "OK Gary, the game's finished. I've won. Right?"

Gary nodded. I went on: "You'd probably say something like "Shit! I knew that taking short cuts didn't always pay off." So then you would know that you are going to have to go before a judge and maybe do some bird. Right?"

"Yeah, I'm following you."

"If you didn't think it all through, then you are an arsehole and you deserve to get caught anyway, because you never considered the risks involved and you always have to suffer the consequences. Right?"

Gary started to laugh aloud. "Yeah man, you're an arsehole, Costa. Ha, ha, ha!"

I had to see the funny side of his remark and laughed with him and the atmosphere in the cell warmed.

"So what was the problem, Costa?"

"There wasn't one really, I just said to the robber: "I like playing cops and robbers. I don't want you to take this personally. You have probably got a stack of shit propped up behind you and that's why you wanted to play the game in the first place. Right? So I'll tell you what I'm going to do. I'll let you tell me what you want the Judge to hear and I'll help you get the lightest sentence possible, because it's not personal. It can't be personal, Gary, can it? What do you think?"

"It shouldn't be personal, Costa. I agree with you, maaan."

"So I'd ask the guy "How do you feel about that?" and they would normally agree. So I'd sit down with the robber and paint a picture for the judge and try to get my robber back into the game as soon as I could, so we can get right on with the game again. Right? That's if he still wants to carry on with the game of course."

"Sounds fair."

"It's not personal, Gary. That's my point."

"So what went wrong?"

"The rules changed and the players began to cheat. The cops took it personally and doctored their evidence to gain convictions and planted evidence. The robbers got pissed off because they realised that if they got caught the key would be thrown away. What happened, Gary, was that in 1978 I could see war approaching. The guys I worked with in the Met were playing stupid games and cheating. One of their games for example was called the 'Roulette Wheel of Life'. Most of them were heavy drinkers and during bouts of drunkenness they'd do underhanded things to stitch people up. For example, they would then send someone to wake up a magistrate and get three warrants issued and at 5 am the following morning they'd kick the doors in! I didn't want to play that new game, Gary. They were changing the rules. Innocent people were getting hurt. I didn't like playing that game. The victims never asked to play that game either, did they?"

"Heavy shit, man."

"So thirteen years later they came back for me, Gary, and I have had everything taken away from me. My family, job, money and all my possessions."

"I've got nothing either, man."

"It's OK for them, Gary. They're the untouchables. They're allowed to carry on playing their silly corrupt games and everyone turns a blind eye on them."

"Yeah, I know."

"The public wonder why they don't see any real results. It's because they are being lied to, Gary. They think there are coppers on the street, but they're at home watching television or building houses or fitting windows on the side when they should be at work or they're out with their girlfriends pissing it up, making out that they are at work. Their bosses only need to do tests on the duty rosters and they'll have all the evidence they need. The trouble is that they are all at it on CID and their bosses are doing the same thing."

"What do you mean, man?"

"If you guys really knew the truth there would be chaos on the streets. Let's say that there were fifteen burglaries on a Friday night."

"Yeah?"

"There should be four or maybe five CID officers on duty and they would be expected to investigate them and make enquiries. The boys on CID don't agree with that! Oh no, Gary. I'm talking about London here mainly, right?"

"Yeah."

"They take it in turns to cover. One guy goes into the office and he goes to the duty roster in the CID office and forges the names of the rest of the shift, booking them all out on investigating the burglaries. You know, house to house enquiries and all that shit, but really they are all still in bed. So the public think the police have got it all under control, but in reality they've got jack shit for their money."

"Wow man, they should be out catching us guys! Ha ha ha ha ha! I like that, they're doing us a favour man."

"So this one copper races around all the burglaries, right, and then goes back to the office and keeps the duty roster up to date for the day."

"Sounds like a cushy job, man. Why didn't you like it?"

"Because it's wrong, Gary! Some of the guys were up to all sorts of things they shouldn't be but they protect and cover for each other. Some get caught, but that happens very rarely and the Commissioner just covers it up and pays off the person who's complaining. The police station is a bit like a hotel revolving door. The bad ones retire, but they like to live and work among the others in order to stay in favour and be on the pulse in case a problem rears its ugly head and then they can warn the others. So they get jobs in security and hang around playing cricket and golf, being another one in the 'Old Boy Network' linked up through the Masonic Lodge. That's why they are called the untouchables."

I held up the small cross that hung from my neck and said: "The only thing they won't take away from me is my faith, Gary. I made a promise to God and I will keep it."

"Blood clot! I'm not into all that god shit, man." He looked deep into my eyes: "You really believe this shit, don't you?"

This was to be the start of a short but lifelong friendship.

As the date for my move to Maidstone got closer, I became more and more apprehensive about moving. I was now well enough to go over to the gym again and started playing a little badminton and volleyball.

On Sunday afternoon I was collected from my cell with about thirty other prisoners and we were taken over to the gym for a game of volleyball.

In the changing rooms after the game, the supervising screw disappeared. This was a bad sign and I could sense it. I knew that when this happened, it would normally follow that there would be a beating and I felt sure that it was me who was going to be the victim.

The men were of mixed race. There was a group of about nine blacks. Their self elected leader, Sammy, shouted at me "What you looking at, pig?"

I ignored the remark as he was clearly trying to start a fight. I decided that if I was going to get a beating, I didn't want to wet myself, so I walked through the changing room and into the area where the urinals were. I could hear the men speaking.

"Listen, man, he's going to Maidstone. What will the brothers say if we have let a copper walk around unharmed in here?"

I could hear several blacks arguing among themselves, so I closed my eyes and looked to the heavens and said:

"I made a promise to you that, as your son, I would witness to you and I have been faithful to that promise. If you want me to have a kicking then I will receive it."

I walked back into the changing room area and all the men were waiting for me. I managed to remain calm in the confidence that these men were now dealing with a far greater power than me.

Then Sammy stepped forward. He was heavily built with long dreadlocks.

"Come on, let's give it to the pig!"

I remained calm and said nothing. Sammy moved closer. He had something 'palmed' in his hand, which appeared to be a prison-machined knife.

Suddenly I heard a voice I recognised. "You leave the man alone. He's a good man!"

Gary moved between me and the gang and Sammy and Gary began to argue wildly.

"Are you a brother, or what?"

"Yeah, I'm a brother but this ain't right. He's a good man. He loves God and he's OK."

"Fuck you, Gary. You won't have any respect from the boys in town if we don't do him!"

The men began to push each other around. Gary stood his

ground and the other men watched in amazement.

"Shit, Gary, you're not right in the head, man! This ain't you!"

Gary wouldn't budge. "If you're going to mess with him, you will have to do me first" he said.

"This ain't your fight, Gary!"

"It is now! Leave him alone!"

The screw returned and things quickly calmed down. When we all returned to the wing, I went to thank Gary for stepping in to help me and said:

"I appreciate you helping me, Gary. You did something really special today and I'm proud of you and grateful."

"Shit, that ain't nothing. He wanted to cut you to get your cross and chain, man. I wasn't going to let the man take the only thing you had left!"

"Thanks Gary."

Gary's look was of deep shame and he said: "He wanted to sell them for drugs! That ain't right!"

CHAPTER THIRTEEN

■ ■ ■ ■ ■ ■ ■ ■

WANDSWORTH

I left Exeter Prison in a private coach, ironically with little fuss, and we journeyed north up the M5, picking up more prisoners at Bristol and then moving on to Onleigh, where we stopped for refreshments prepared by young offenders. The food was slop, and everyone left it. I no longer believe in coincidences. I found it strange that on this coach all fifteen prisoners had had the same London barrister as me.

Tim had chosen a local barrister from Devon, who happened to belong to our presiding judge's chambers in Devon, and was acquitted. (My barrister had already warned me of the incestuous links within the judicial system in Devon and from what I could see he was right to be cautious.)

At Onleigh I was put in a secure van and taken to Wandsworth Prison in London. I arrived quite late with seven other inmates and we were marched in military style through a dark enclosed yard into the reception area. I was then marched in double time in front of a miserable screw who was about five foot ten, clean shaven and reeked of Brut aftershave. The slashed peak on his cap appeared to be nailed on to his forehead as he barked out his commands.

"Where's your property, boy?"

I was tired and eager to get on to the main wing.

"It's here." I lifted my plastic HMP bag.

"Sir! Say Sir to me! You piece of dogshit! You're in Wandsworth now, so don't fuck with Daddy!"

I stared into the screw's eyes, which clearly made him feel uncomfortable, searching for some hint of humanity. I focused on the back of his head. I could sense that this screw was now searching for a reason to 'nick' me, which would then expose me to their evil torturous regime, about which I had already been warned by my new friend Gary. If you get 'blocked' in Wandsworth you are thrown from the top of the stairs that lead down to the 'Block' and the screws are waiting at the bottom of the stairs to give you a good kicking. After 28 days, once the bruising has gone down, they ship you out to another prison. Gary had clearly experienced this misfortune. You poor sod, I thought. I later discovered that this was standard practice at Wandsworth and they took great pride in their torturous regime.

I was not going to allow them to abuse me in this way. Not if it was within my power to stop them. For the benefit of my own health, I said: "It's here, cur." I made sure that, in my mind's eye, I expressed the true meaning of the word. This screw was indeed a contemptible, ill natured, mixed-breed of dog.

He snapped again "Don't look at me when I am talking to you!"

It was a strange request and an odd feeling came over me being ordered to look in another direction when addressing this peculiar man, but, for the sake of my own health, I conceded.

"Where's all your property?"

I half raised my upturned palms to explain and said: "That's it. All of it."

"Sir! You address me sir! Do you want me to nick you?"

"No cur, that's it. All of it, cur."

"It's all prison gear! Where's your gear, you worthless piece of shit!"

"I don't have any, cur." It was true. I had sent everything bar my cross and chain out of the prison, because I really believed I was going to die in the prison system.

As there was nothing to enter into the property book, I was marched through on to E Wing, which is the Hospital Wing and the hardest to live on because it houses all the inmates with psychiatric problems. Everyone starts on E Wing as it's a 'grounding wing' for the new boys.

The same screw marched me and two other inmates on to the wing and placed us in different cells. When it was my turn, the screw opened a cell that already contained one inmate - his card was on the door.

It was fear that prompted me to speak, as I really wanted to be on my own. "I'm doing a twelve, cur. I'm entitled to a single cell. Can I have one, please?"

"You go where I say, you useless piece of shit! That's if you know what's good for you! This is your cell, so shut the fuck up and get in!"

The door was slammed closed behind me and I moved deeper into the urine stinking, damp, poorly lit cell. When my eyes adjusted to the light conditions, I could make out a bed with a body on it against the outer wall under the high window. Whoever my new cellmate was, he appeared to be asleep.

The other bed, I assumed, was mine and it was to my left. I felt the bare mattress and it was wet to the touch. Not damp but wet. It smelt like it had been urinated on. So I rolled out my bed pack without making the bed and lay on top of the hard sheets, blanket and green cover.

Until I knew the identity of the man I was in with, I wasn't going to even contemplate going to sleep. I sat up and waited for him to wake up, drifting in and out of consciousness. I waited until morning and finally at first light 'Sleeping Beauty' woke up. His first words were: "What's the time, mate?"

I wanted to be helpful and tell him the time, but I said "I don't know, I haven't got a watch."

He started shivering, which distorted his Geordie accent as he spoke:

"What's your name?"

"Con."

"Mine's Harry. Have they told you what I'm in for, Con?"

"Not directly. I did overhear someone say shoplifting, Harry, but that doesn't bother me."

He appeared agitated by my remark. "I'm not a fucking shoplifter! I killed three diggers who owed me money."

"What's a digger Harry? Sorry for my ignorance."

Harry smiled nervously and his shivering increased until he was shaking uncontrollably. "You don't know what a digger is?"

"No."

"A heroin addict, man! We stick needles in our arms and dig around for veins, so we're called diggers, you fucking idiot!"

"Oh. Now I understand."

"Have you got any gear, Con?"

"Just prison stuff. I don't have anything of my own." I knew that he didn't mean personal possessions; I was just having a bit of light-hearted banter with him while I let him assess whether I was a threat to him or whether he could use me in some way to feed his grubby little habit.

"No, have you got any drugs or fags, mun? I've got a visit and I need to think straight."

"Oh, no, I don't do drugs! I like to take my bird neat. Who's coming in to see you then, the missus?"

Harry laughed and his whole body shuddered uncontrollably.

"No! It's a legal visit and my barrister's coming in to see me. I'd like to do my bird neat but I can't, Con. I'm a junkie. Look at me!" He lifted the sleeves on his shirt to show me all his needle marks, but I couldn't see them in the poor light.

"You could if you wanted to, Harry."

His whole body was now shaking more violently and he started clucking like a chicken. He stood up and staggered up and down in the cell.

"Are you cold? You can have one of my blankets if you are, Harry."

"No, mun, I'm starting to go into cold turkey. I need some drugs and quick! I've got to score a deal. Have you got any money or telephone cards?"

"Just prison clothing, Harry. Sorry, I'm all out."

"Haven't you even got a 'blim'? You know, enough for a joint? Anything!"

"I can't help you, Harry. Sorry."

"I'm a triple fucking killer, mun! I'm a fucking psycho when I go cold turkey, so you'd better find me some drugs, Con or you're dead!"

I kept a deadpan expression, and said:

"Damn!"

"What's the matter?" Harry enquired in a concerned voice.

I put my hand around to the crack in my arse and felt between my cheeks and said: "I think I've just shit myself."

"Don't fuck around with me you bastard! I'm dangerous!"

"Harry, you are scaring the shit out of me. I won't be able to sleep tonight if you carry on threatening me like this!"

Harry quickly realised that his attempt at trying to frighten me was futile and he kept pacing up and down the cell, shaking more and more as the time passed.

A screw shouted "slop out!" and the door opened long enough for us both to use the toilet and empty the bucket. Our cell was really close to the Centre and as I looked down I could see a large star delineated on the floor. The Centre in Wandsworth is quite different from Exeter. It was like a large roundabout, with a huge brass star inset into the middle of the floor. Gary had told me the same story that Harry was now elaborating on. "You are only allowed to walk around one way and you can't overtake. Don't even try it mun. The bastards 'll 'ave ya. All the wings meet in the middle, which make it a huge star. Massive!"

Harry shook more violently and went on: "There's over sixteen hundred cons in 'ere and the screws are evil bastards, Con! They're cruel, Con, really cruel, mun, I'm telling you this to warn you. Don't cross the screws in Wandsworth, it would be a big mistake!"

"Did they hurt you, Harry?"

"Big time, Con. Two screws stand back to back, protecting the Star which the Queen has walked on! So if anyone tries to walk around it the wrong way or cut across the centre, you get rugby tackled to the ground and thrown down the block. Walking on the Star the wrong way is heavy shit, mun."

Harry was helpful in explaining this rule to me in such detail, so I was prepared for what was to come. The food was brought on to the wing on a trolley and the cells were opened, a few at a time, for us to collect our trays of food and then return to our cells to eat, balancing the trays on our laps. I was becoming quite proficient at this task now but I have always hated eating off my lap, it's so common. Awkward as well.

I was walking towards the stairway that led down from the first floor, when I noticed a female screw with a mop of blonde hair standing by the stairway.

I was wearing my blue striped prison shirt and dark grey trouser and blue canvas prison slippers. I liked to wear prison greys because they were comfortable, more comfortable than denims, and they looked smart. My cuffs were buttoned and my shirt tucked into my trousers and I thought that I really looked smart - for a prisoner.

I could hear this female screw screaming at the top of her voice, but I couldn't make out what she was shouting, so I kept walking. As I approached her she was turning a peculiar colour of red and another male screw came running to join her. Her face was now nose to nose with mine and I was being showered with her saliva, which smelt of Tic Tacs.

In the end the male screw had to explain what her problem was with me: "Your fucking shirt! Do it up! Now!"

I heard what the male screw said, but I thought all the buttons on my shirt were buttoned up. She kept screaming at me and I really didn't have a clue what it was about. I looked down and all the buttons on my shirt were fastened. So I looked blankly at her, remaining impassive and said: "Excuse me. Is something wrong?"

She bellowed back "Is something wrong, MA'AM! You arsehole!"

The male screw leaned forward. "Stop acting thick and do your top button up!"

I tried to fasten the top button, but it was missing. "Sorry, I can't because I don't have one." My explanation appeared to calm her down, but the male screw screamed at me: "When being addressed by an officer in Wandsworth you have to stand still and you address me as sir and a woman officer as ma'am!"

"Yes, cur." I collected my lunch and returned to my cell.

The following day during slop out I was standing outside my cell waiting to be locked away when I looked down to see this same female screw getting dragged into a cell by one of the prisoners. He was clearly attempting to rape her because he was shouting in her ear. "I'll make you cry like a baby, bitch! I've got someone I want you to meet!"

While she was being dragged backwards with his arm around her throat, she managed to get to her whistle and give an almighty blow. The sound of heavy footsteps could instantly be heard above her screams, pounding down the wings and getting nearer all the time. It was at this point that I thought it best to shut myself away, so I stepped into my cell and pushed the door closed.

Exercising in the yard was a breathtaking experience for me. It was so dangerous that after two visits I thought it safer to remain in my cell.

I was eventually able to sleep only when Harry had scored a deal. He went to sleep like a baby.

Obtaining drugs in prison was so important to the men. It was all they ever thought of and they would do anything to get them, 'downing' any form of medication that might take them away from the reality of their lives. Certain drugs attracted certain types. Non-drug users were able to mix freely and could be trusted by some drug users. This would only relate to the softer drugs. Once the user had moved up into the harder drugs, they would only mix closely with other members of their sub-culture. They knew that if you were not prepared to share a needle with them, you were not one of them. This acted as a form of safeguard, but in reality it led to hell and death.

When Harry finally woke again he kept on about his barrister.

"What's his name, Harry?"

"He's called David Mullins. I've been told he is the best that you can get, but he only deals with murderers."

"Oh does he? If that's true why is he my barrister as well?"

"Do you know him?"

"Yes, he's my barrister!"

"Do you think he will give me some money if I ask him, so I can buy some drugs?"

"I doubt it, Harry but you can ask."

Harry returned from his legal visit in a very excited state, he said. "He does know you, Con. He said to say "hello" and that he was sorry."

"Is that all?"

"Yeah, he reckons he's stepping down and I've got to find another barrister. He's given me some names to contact."

Wandsworth was the second prison I had been in, and it fell well below what could be classed as humane. In fact it made Exeter look like a holiday camp. It would be an understatement to call Wandsworth Dickensian in attitude; it was openly cruel, which made any inmate reluctant to speak out about its darker secrets of murder, abuse and torture. One was left to suspect foul play in many of the 'suicide' hangings. There are more hangings in our prisons today than there were in Albert Pierrepoint's day, believe me! Screws appeared to be bound together in determination to inflict misery on everyone. There was certainly no chat or banter between screw and inmate and the inmates were clearly treated as the scum of the earth and in need of punishment.

My thoughts drifted back to my own father, who as a staff sergeant in the Military Police tortured young men in a similar way during his service and would bring remnants of this stark regime home to us, his own flesh and blood. There was to be no protection for me here; that was clear. Difficult prisoners were abused and tortured without any thought for them, their circumstances or their families. How Her Majesty could ever put her name to such places beggars belief.

There was a clear concern here of nonexistent staff-prisoner relationships and absolutely no predictable regime for slopping out. No association and insufficient activity made everyone feel isolated and alienated, which could drive anyone insane or to even consider self-harming.

Despite it all, I was determined to keep walking on in the hope that God would help me, somehow.

CHAPTER FOURTEEN

■ ■ ■ ■ ■ ■ ■ ■

BACK TO THE WALL

The month passed painstakingly slowly. Leaving Wandsworth Prison in what looked and felt like an aluminium fridge with a skylight window appeared to be a blessing. I arrived at Maidstone in time for lunch and was met by a gentleman wearing a smart-looking tracksuit. He was polite and seemed to be most caring and helpful. He even had access to my personal file, which he glanced through as we were being processed.

"What a refreshing change from where I have just come, officer" I exclaimed.

His response was immediate; he sounded very surprised. "I'm an inmate, not a screw!"

I was shocked to see a convicted prisoner wearing civilian clothes and having access to what I believed was my private and confidential information.

"Can you wear what you want then?"

He perched himself on the table next to me and said "It's very relaxed here. So let's see what wing you're going on then." and he studied the list on his clip board and said "Prison Number?"

"WL 2639."

He studied the clipboard and said: "Oh dear, you're Buller the copper, aren't you? They've put you on Medway! You really need to get out of there if you can."

I was intrigued. "Why's that then?"

"There are some heavy guys on that wing and if they don't like you they will burn you out. There are three or four cells burnt out every week on Medway. Best get out as soon as you can, I reckon."

I now knew I was almost certainly about to enter the lion's den. So I asked him "Is there any chance of getting on a different wing?"

He winced and said "Not when you're doing a twelve, mate. Sorry. You'll be on Medway for probably two to three years I reckon."

The walk to the wing took me and a fellow traveller, Ian, right over to the other side of the prison. Ian was serving a double life sentence and I didn't want to ask what for. He seemed like a nice chap though. He was a professed Christian and he had brought his own guitar with him. The two of us walked with our escort in silence to our wing.

Medway is a secure wing in that it is always locked up. There is movement in and out of the wing, but this is organised meticulously. A telephone briefing is made to whatever department the prisoner is going to, giving details of all the men leaving and arriving on the wing.

Inmates were given a specific amount of time to reach their destination and when they arrived they were logged in at the other end. Tallies had to match or the whole prison shut down, with 'Bang Up' and then 'the count' was made.

I was unable to have visits because of the distance my visitors would have to travel, and my relationship with Heather was now starting to cool down. I had become aware of this by a change in the style of her letter writing. I had to assume she was now seeing someone else. At the same time she was still trying to keep my hopes up by maintaining contact and visiting me whenever she could.

Sarah had contacted probation informing them that she didn't want any contact between me and my sons, so whenever I approached them to try to make contact they refused to help me. Sarah had married her detective sergeant in London a week after my trial had finished. She had stripped the family home of everything and moved from Devon to live in London.

I kept beating myself up with guilt about my children and truly believed that I would never see them again, at least not as children. Michael, my eldest, was tall, gentle and very sensitive to the feelings of others. Luke was tall also and had inherited my cheeky wit, personality and sense of humour. I often remembered the stories I had told them and how I would include them both in the plots. I always depicted them as generals and officers fighting battles with strange monsters and dangerous animals. I would have loved to have had their assistance and support with this battle.

I often sat quietly in my cell remembering their excited faces, the hugs and the cuddles and all the love they poured out on me and each other. All that was now gone and the only treasures left were my memories of them. Where Sarah was nonplussed about the children, I loved them desperately. They were mine and she knew it!

I often meditated on life, and waiting for a partner to return home from prison is another form of punishment inflicted upon those innocent partners who really need to be helped, not punished. This was another crime the system had inflicted on me and my family. What had my family done to deserve their punishment? How could the victims of all this hatred, pain, loss and grief deal with their shattered lives too, I wondered. What was the answer to it all? I only wish I knew.

Medway was a self-managed wing with its own Probation

Officer, Governor, Principal Officer, Senior Officer and separate kitchen facilities. The prison food was still brought on to the wing from the main kitchens, but if an inmate wanted to prepare his own food he could. All he had to do was buy what he wanted from the canteen and then cook it or bake it himself, pay someone to do it for him or order his 'bitch' to do the work. There were lots of bitches busying themselves on the wing.

I knew I had a problem and I needed to identify the 'main man' on the wing. So I walked into the Probation Office and said: "Hello, I've just arrived."

Mr Phillips smiled politely and said "Welcome to Medway. Have you put in an application to see me?"

"No, I just want to ask a question, if that's OK?"

"Oh, that's fine. What's the question?"

"I need to find out who the 'main man' is on the wing."

Now Mr Phillips looked really confused. "Why?" he asked.

I smiled politely and said "I'd like to meet him."

"What for?"

"To speak to him, of course. Can you just tell me who he is or do we have to do the hundred questions bit?"

"Well, it's very sensitive. It's something that we are not supposed to know about. I'm sure you understand. What's it all about?"

I wasn't going to get a straight answer to my question, so I said: "OK, let me explain. I am an ex-policeman and I have seen all of this on the telly, but I'm sure that you've witnessed this first hand and that makes you one step ahead of me."

I still had his attention. "Go on?" he said.

"If I go and speak to this man, whoever he is, I'll tell him the score, you know, that I am an ex-copper and then we can go into a recess and sort it out."

The probation officer's face turned pale in colour and he said: "Are you for real?"

"Yes. Look, you don't have to tell me his name, just tell me what he's wearing or you can just point to him."

Mr Phillips looked shocked. "I can't! Have you any idea what type of wing you're on? There are men in here who will never get out of prison for the rest of their lives. These men have nothing to lose by killing you! They have killed other inmates on here before, so I know they'll do it."

Although I knew he was probably right, I said: "I don't think so."

"Listen, I'm telling you they will! You can't stay here! I will have to speak to the Governor about this right away. We need to move you to another wing immediately."

Mr Phillips got up to walk over to the door. "Please listen to me, it's really not a problem, just tell me what he's wearing" I said.

Mr Phillips opened the door and turned to face me. "He's over there in a check tracksuit, you know, with different colours, red and green. His name is Terry Stoles. Please don't do this!"

Mr Phillips left his room in a hurry. I followed him on to the wing and saw lots of prisoners moving around. I could still see the man who was wearing the tracksuit that fitted Mr Phillips' description and as I walked towards him I kept a keen eye on those around me. I walked in front of him, blocking his path: "Are you Terry Stoles?"

Terry was about six foot two with short mousey-coloured hair cut short. He weighed about fifteen and a half stone and looked very fit. He spoke with a strong, deep, East London accent. There wasn't a flicker of concern on his face as he spoke. "Yeah, who wants him?"

"I'm Con and I've just come on to the wing. Can we have a chat?"

He stood there expecting me to say more, but I hesitated momentarily. "Yeah, go on then" he said.

"Not here, Terry. In my cell."

Terry smiled and said "Yeah, OK." Then he followed me to my cell. I waited for him to get right in and half closed the door behind me. I wasn't sure where to start. "I've been told that you run the wing. Is that right?"

"Yeah, I've got my hand on what goes on in here, you know, I keep an eye on things. What's the SP?"

"I wanted to tell you face to face that I'm here to do my bird and I'm not looking to run any tricks or do any of the other stuff."

"Fair dos. What's that got to do with me?"

"I want to be straight and upfront with you, Terry, as to who I am."

Terry gave a knowing smile.

"I was a copper thirteen years ago and I left. I'm doing two twelves and a three and all I want is to be left alone. Is that going to be a problem with you?"

"We knew you was a rozza. Reception told us you were on your way over."

I don't know why I was surprised. "They did?"

"Of course they did! At least you've been straight with me. So let me tell you the score as I see it, Con. You won't 'ave no problems with me or any of my boys but I can't speak for the others. The worst thing that'll happen to you on this wing is that you'll get plunged."

I'd heard that there was a swimming pool in the prison. "That's OK Terry, I'm a really good swimmer."

Terry laughed: "You have been out a long time!" He lifted his right arm and motioned as if he had something in his hand, then lunged forward. "Plunged, you idiot! Get it?" He kept indicating a stabbing movement with his hand. "Stabbed! Do you understand? It's a risk that you'll have to take, Con. *Capisce*?"

"I'm Greek and we say *katalaveni*. The Italians say *capisce*! Of course, Terry, I understand. I'll take that risk."

"You've got some arse, Con. I like that."

"You might like my arse but you aren't getting any of it!" We both laughed aloud simultaneously and Terry left my cell.

While having a scout around the wing to see where everything was, I met a guy who was about five feet ten with a skinhead haircut, number zero - in other words he was bald. He seemed friendly, so I introduced myself to him and said: "Hi, I've just come on to the wing and my name's Con. What's it like on here?"

He smiled: "It's cool, my name's Dan. You can wear your own gear and get stuff in no problem, so it's OK. How you doing?"

"I'm doing a twelve, Dan."

Dan looked surprised at my response and said: "Nah, I didn't ask how long you was doing, I said, 'How are you doing?' Anyway, I'm doing eighteen for robbin' banks."

I left Dan and carried on looking around. Eventually I wandered back into my cell and read one of my mum's letters. Suddenly Dan burst into my cell and half closed the door behind him. He was in a panic and checked to see if anyone had watched him come in. He spluttered out: "They're going to kill you! I heard them planning it! You've got to plot up your door!"

That was a new one to me. "What the hell are you on about, Dan? What does 'plot up your door' mean?"

He held a large prison-made tractor bolt in his right hand. "Look" he said. "Dig a hole in the floor and put this in it." He showed me where to dig the hole for the bolt in the floor.

"What does that do? How will that stop them, Dan?"

"When they burst in to get ya, the door will smash against the bolt. It slows them down, Con. It reduces the number of men who can come in at the same time."

"Ah!" I said as I mused over this 'hypothetical' attack.

Dan asked: "Get it? You have a better chance to defend yourself."

"Thanks for the advice, Dan." I took the bolt from his hand and walked over to the door, opened it wide, and threw the bolt out of the door. Hearing it land on the floor outside, I looked Dan straight in the eyes.

"Tell them from me, my door is always open and they can come in whenever they want. It's not me that they'll be wrestling with, it's God."

His eyes opened wide and he looked terrified. "You're fucking mad! You're going to die in here!" Dan turned and ran out on to the landing and disappeared from sight and the rest of the first day passed without incident. I was aware of being pointed at by various men and I guessed that there were rumours being circulated about me.

When I entered the bathhouse I noticed that there was a choice of either a shower or a bath and as it was my first day, I considered that a shower would be the safer option of the two. So I began to remove my prison clothes, shirt first, then my trousers, socks and slippers. As I was undressing I watched two men, one black and the other white, walk in. I stood with my back to them, but I kept a watch on them out of the corner of one eye.

I kept my feet flat on the ground as much as I could. The thick, black layer of body fat that covered the floor seemed to adhere to the soles of my feet. It looked as if a residue of dead human skin had built up on the floor over years through poor cleaning, getting thicker and thicker.

Suddenly both men rushed at me. I saw a flash of something in the black man's hand, a 'jammer' or home-made knife probably, and I knew that I was in trouble. Using my left hand I blocked the hand holding the knife while at the same time I gouged the man's eyes with my right hand. He fell to the floor screaming: "My eyes! You bastard! My eyes! I can't see!"

At that moment the blade fell on to the tiled floor. I leapt and turned using a back roundhouse kick, which hit the other target on the side of his head knocking him unconscious and on to the grimy floor. My landing wasn't in textbook style and I fell heavily on to the floor, grazing my hip and elbow. I collected my soap and towel and walked casually back to my cell. As I passed the riot button I pressed it and the alarm bells started ringing immediately. The looks on the faces of the other prisoners were of amazement.

The main wing was now being scoured by screws, who were trying to find out what had happened. They ran into the shower room and found the two men. There were no witnesses to the incident. Both men were taken over to the hospital wing for treatment and the atmosphere quickly returned to prison normal.

The following day I decided that I had to step up my own security and err on the side of caution wherever I went. So when I was in the queue for breakfast I made sure that I always had my back to the wall. I knew then that I only had to defend the other 180 degrees.

I had to try to get some reprieve from the wing, so I applied to go on Education. I told the screw at the gate I wanted to start my own business when I left prison, so I was engaged on courses in business studies and computer technology. All appeared to be going well for about a week and a pattern was forming of me going to classes every day. The following Monday I returned from my business studies class and the Principal Officer said "I need to speak to you. Come into my office." I followed him into his office and he closed the door behind me. "You're going to have to get off this wing because we've had a letter in the Box. They are going to kill you. You must take these threats seriously."

I was naturally concerned, but tried to play it down. "I don't think they'll kill me, I've done nothing to them" I said.

"Please believe me, this threat is very real. We can't take you off the wing, so you will have to ask to get off."

"I'm quite happy here, really. There are some nice guys on this wing, and we are starting to get along."

He said: "They want to kill you because you are embarrassing them. They're really struggling to do their bird and you don't fit in here. Anyway, it's entirely up to you."

I was, of course, being facetious. The men hated me and my presence on the wing was clearly disturbing them. I knew that. So I said "If one of them wants to put me on the 43s, they're going to have to do it because I'm not running away."

"There are men on this wing who are more than capable of doing that, I assure you. But, if you're sure?"

"Yes, I'm sure. These guys are doing deals, drugs, wearing their own gear, bullying, scheming, ducking and diving but still they struggle to do their bird. I'm an ex-copper doing my bird without any of that nonsense. I know I'm doing it the hard way, so what's their problem with me?"

"It's you being able to do that really pisses them off" he scoffed. "So what's your plan of action?"

I could feel things closing in on me. I knew it wouldn't be long before everything would finally come on top for me and they would probably force my hand.

"The best form of defence is attack" I said. "I'm staying until one of that bunch of idiots takes me out."

The prison day started at 8.10 am for unlock, giving us time to shower and have breakfast and then go to work or classes if you were on education. The morning movement normally stopped for lunch at 12.10 pm, when we queued up for food and then went back to our cells and got banged up. The doors were unlocked again at 1.45 pm and it was back to whatever duties you had been assigned or chosen to do. That ran until 5.15 pm when we returned to the wing for our evening meal and again, bang up. The evening session started with unlock at 6.05 pm and the doors were open until bang up at 7.45 pm. During this time you could attend activities of your choice or association with other inmates, except on a Friday and weekends when the evening session was not operative.

This pattern ran from Monday to Thursday. On Fridays I had put my name down for music classes and I was added to the list to go over to the chapel. At 6 pm that evening there were only three of us waiting by the gate and we were eventually released to walk over to the chapel.

When I arrived the tutor, a gentle, quietly spoken man of about thirty with fairly short blonde hair and an enormous smile, said: "Hi, I'm Gavin. what sort of instrument would you like to learn to play?" He reached out to shake my hand and I said: "I'm Con. I'd really like to learn how to play the trumpet."

Gavin's eyes opened wide in surprise. He said: "I play the trumpet myself! Follow me and I'll find a quiet room for you to practise in." He led me through the chapel to one of the side rooms and pulled out a small case. "Here were are, a trumpet" he said. "Do you read music, Con?"

Feeling a bit sheepish, I said: "I did a long time ago. I'm going to have to learn again, eh?"

Gavin was very reassuring. "That's not a problem. I'll run through it with you and then you can practise."

"Thank you. Can I take it on to the wing and practise?"

"Of course you can! Take it with you when you go back tonight." He gave me some sheet music and wrote out some instructions for me to follow. What a lovely man, I thought. So kind and helpful, how refreshing.

I was determined to practise and that evening, when the screws had put everyone away for the night, I got out my trumpet and gave it a blast. It was difficult for the other inmates to work out where the noise was coming from, and because I hadn't played the trumpet since I was twelve, it didn't sound too good to begin with. When I paused for breath I heard a neighbour shout: "Shut the fuck up!" They kept screaming, but I kept playing and trying to learn until I could play every note through to top C.

I was really pleased with my achievement and it gave me a sense of inner satisfaction. I had started to learn to play the cornet when I had joined Alresford Silver Band and I was rubbish back then as well. My mother would send me off to practise in the woods and I thought, if only these guys would do the same!

The following morning I went off to my computer class as normal. I was trying to get to grips with Lotus 123. As I waited at the gate I noticed that the screws did all the cleaning on the wing. They were frightened of the inmates and would do the basics, like clearing up and serving meals, in order to keep the place feeling stress free as they were also at risk of attack should things kick off.

The gate opened and I walked over to the education block for my computer class and worked away quietly until 9.45 am, when suddenly the door to the computer class burst open. Standing in the doorway were five black prisoners, and they looked very menacing. The tallest man of the group, dressed in a flashy looking tracksuit and new trainers, was screwing his face into a good impression of Rowan Atkinson playing the part of Mr Bean. He pointed at me and shouted: "We've come to kill you, pig!"

I was wondering what to do. I thought the best idea was to ignore them, so I carried on as if they weren't there, but it quickly became apparent that this man wasn't going to leave quietly. He raised his voice louder still and screamed at me: "Can you hear me, pig? You're going to die!"

I looked up at the men standing in between me and the door and said. "I've never met a bunch of arseholes like you lot in all my life! How long have you lot been in prison, for God's sake?"

"That's got nothing to do with it! You should be on the 43s!"

"It has got something to do with it. You must know that you can't kill me in a computer class with a tutor present. Are you stupid? Wait outside! I'll park my computer and come out and then you can kill me outside so there are no witnesses."

The men looked at each other in astonishment. Conceding to my request, they quietly left the room. I parked my computer, switched it off and went over to the tutor. "Excuse me, Mr Arnold, I have some business to attend to outside. Is that OK?" I asked.

The tutor was clearly relieved that his equipment now had a chance of remaining intact. "That's fine, yes, you can go" he said.

I let the door swing shut behind me and turned right into the corridor. The group which had interrupted my class were waiting for me outside the coffee room and I recognised the leader, who was from my wing. Speaking in a light-hearted manner, I said "What's transpiring, guys? What's your problem?"

They were huddled in a small group and I counted seven of them, all dressed alike in tracksuits and trainers. I heard one of the lads say "Leave it, Matt", but Matt had taken a particular dislike to me for some reason. He pointed his finger at me. Trying to sound menacing he snarled: "We haven't got a problem. You have! We're going to kill you!" I got the impression that he was trying to look cool in front of his little gang, but he wasn't convincing anyone.

I focused on Matt's friend and said: "What's your name?"

Matt was straight at me: "Don't give him none of your shit! Let's just kill the pig!"

Matt's fellow gang member said: "No, let's listen to the man first. If we don't like what he says, then we can kill 'im. My name's Perry."

I said: "Nice to meet you Perry, my name's Con."

Matt was getting frustrated. He snapped back: "This ain't no pussy business meeting. Don't listen to him, Perry. He'll try and talk you out of it."

I looked at Matt in a disappointed way and said: "You should really listen to Perry, Matt, he talks a lot of sense. He's a clever guy. Sorry to disappoint you lads but I really don't have a problem, you do. You're the ones struggling to do your bird with me on the wing. Do you realise how stupid you look walking about the prison in your own gear? You're in prison, for Christ's sake! The screws are laughing at you."

They were mortified and their heads dropped to look at their trainers, lost for words. I went on "So don't fuck about! If you're going to kill me, hurry up because I'm in the middle of a computer class".

Perry said: "You're a copper!"

I nodded and said: "I was, thirteen years ago. If you look back over your last thirteen years, did you make any mistakes? I did, so I left. I didn't stay. What about your mistakes?"

Matt stepped forward and said: "That makes no difference, you're still a pig and we're going to kill you!"

I could see that Matt wasn't going to back off. He was now

looking for support from the others, who appeared to be backtracking. So I went on "Do you all feel the same way about me?"

Perry took hold of Matt's elbow and tried to pull him away. "Leave it, Matt" he said. "We ain't got a problem with this man, he's only trying to do 'is bird, the same as us. He's a con now and he ain't no copper no more."

A third man decided to speak up: "Yeah, I don't have no problem with him either." They started to melt away.

Matt was now looking very unhappy. He clearly still wanted to carry out his threat and I could see another inmate to his right considering his position too. The odds had now been reduced in my favour from seven against one to what now looked like being one against one. Matt's arse was clearly going from 'sixpence to half a crown'.

Matt's only option was to flee. He turned quickly and left the building in a hurry, shouting: "I'll get some real brothers who will sort you out big time, pig!"

I looked at the rest of the group expectantly and said "Can I go now?" and they nodded. So I said: "Thank you gentlemen, I think we're done here, don't you?"

I returned to my computer class. As I sat down I looked up to the heavens and said. "You are a faithful God. Thank you."

At the end of the session I was feeling a bit apprehensive about going back on to the wing and as I walked through the gate I felt the presence of evil. It hung like a thick cloud on the wing, but I kept walking. I collected my mail and walked on to the main landing. A white, unshaven, heavily-built balding man walked towards me looking down at the floor, pretending he wasn't looking where he was going. I couldn't see a weapon in his hand so I moved quickly to the left to avoid him, but he hesitated and suddenly threw himself at me. He launched into a barrage of verbal abuse.

"Get out of the way, pig! Watch where you're walking! You think you own the place, fucking pig! Go on then, pig, have a go! Go on!" He started to push me in the chest with both hands and I stood there looking into his eyes, which seemed to annoy him even more: "Well, what are you saying pig? Don't swear at me you bastard! Pig! Pig! Pig! Come on then, if you want to fight me, fight me!"

I stayed silent and looked beyond this man to the other guys who were 'plotted up' ready to get me once the fight had started. I suspected that someone was going to come in with a knife once it all kicked off and I could count six possible assailants in all. A right mixture of dark cruel faces, like a shoal of piranhas, all about to strike at me. I waited for him to make a move but all he kept doing was shouting: "Pig! Pig! Pig! Pig!"

Finally, I smiled and said "I love you brother. God loves you too."

The man in my face looked visibly shocked. He was left unable to speak or move and I sidestepped him and carried on walking to my cell, leaving a grumbling crowd behind me. Their plan had failed, yet again.

As I entered my cell that evening, carrying my meal, I placed my tray on the worktop and Matt ran into my doorway carrying a full bucket of human excrement and urine. He threw it all over me. The contents also spread over the walls of my cell, food, bed and clothing. The stench was crippling and I wanted to puke. I had to strip my cell out immediately and I threw everything out on to the landing. I eventually collected it all together and put it into a plastic rubbish bin in the recess.

Everyone was waiting for me to scream "43s!" but I never did. However, now I was left in my cell without my donkey jacket, jumper, mattress or bed linen. Everything had to be binned.

Fortunately, I kept some extra clothing in a plastic bag under my bed and I showered and changed.

I then began the never-ending job of trying to scrub out my cell, but that still didn't remove the stench. It was unbearable and their behaviour was sub-human, but I still wasn't going to relent to these bastards. It made me even more determined to stay. I showered yet again, cautiously, once I had finished and changed into my last set of fresh clothing and returned to my empty cell.

A screw turned up to see if I wanted to leave the wing and run to 43 gate. He asked: "Is everything OK?" He had been watching everything that had happened. He went on: "Kit change isn't until next Tuesday." He pointed to the recess and said "So put all that lot back in your cell until next Tuesday!"

I said "I can't."

"Why?" he asked. This was the moment they had all been waiting for, for me to cry for help: "I'm a victim. Please help me!"

I said: "I wet the bed and all my gear."

"You did what?" He looked shocked.

I said: "Yes, it was me. I wet the bed. It must have been something I ate."

The screw snapped back: "I don't care, kit change isn't till Tuesday. You're not getting any more gear."

I had no option but to remain calm. "That's fine" I said. "I don't have a problem with that."

I had to sleep with my barred window open because of the smell, with no covers or warm clothes, and it was freezing at night. Relentlessly I persevered with my trumpet playing. I now had learned to play more notes on my trumpet and I was invited into Wolfy's cell for a singalong Christian meet up with him and another inmate. We sang a song I had learned in Exeter Prison: "My shackles are gone, my spirit's free, oh praise the Lord, He lifted me. My sins are forgiven and now I am free. Oh praise the Lord, My shackles are gone, my spirit's free!"

The other prisoners on the wing were getting more and more agitated by my persistence and Matt was still determined to get me off the wing.

I knew this situation couldn't carry on for much longer before I would go crazy. It was safer for me to shower first thing in the morning. One morning I went to the showers as normal. The landing was quiet and I kept my eyes on the door in case of trouble. Three black prisoners walked in together, stripped and then walked into the showers. Time for me to leave, I thought and quickly washed the soap out of my hair. Suddenly the two nearest me turned around and tried to grab hold of me and I struggled free. They were determined to overpower me and I thought, you're not getting the better of me.

I noticed that the third man had a blade in his right hand and a rather nasty grin on his face. I had often thought about what I would do in this scenario and prepared for it by working out in my cell after bang up. This is all about domination and abuse and there's no way you're going to get the better of me, I thought.

They were right in my face and really strong, so I used my right elbow to break the nose of the man on my right with my first strike. I quickly turned to use the recoil to land firmly on the side of the head of the second man with such force that I was thrown forward and landed on the floor, managing to soften the impact by using the palms of my hands and arms as a damper. I swung my legs around to sweep the third man's feet from underneath him and he went down on to the tiles heavily.

I sprung up off the floor by pushing up with my hands and regained my footing, then grabbed my towel and shorts and quickly left the showers, pressing the alarm bell on the way back to my cell. As I dried myself off I could hear the alarm sounding, radios crackling and screws running to discover what had happened. Within a couple of minutes I was dressed and waiting in the queue for breakfast.

The experience in the showers left me in a psychological mess. I was under so much stress that when reading I couldn't remember the last word I had read. I was fast approaching breaking point.

I continued to go to business studies and as I walked out of the wing my senses were confirming my worst fears. I entered the education block and sat quietly in the classroom with my tutor, Ray. I decided to warn him. "Ray, if something goes down in the class today get out quickly and protect yourself first" I said.

Ray said: 'I have worked here for a long time, Con, for God's sake be careful. There are a lot of very dangerous men in here."

I nodded and said: "Yes I know. I'm only trying to do my bird but they won't leave me alone. I think today is going to be my final day."

Ray looked very concerned. "I hope not. Please be careful. I'm a trained psychologist and they will carry out their threats, believe me!"

At this point two men entered the room and sat at a desk opposite me. They were only there for a few moments before they began to get angry and started to shout at me. "You shouldn't be walking the wing. You're provoking the men and disturbing the prison. You should be on the Rule. You're a copper! You're not one of us!"

At precisely this moment the door burst open and Matt raced into the room with a new gang. Matt shouted: "Prepare to die, pig!"

I remained seated and shouted back "You're unbelievable! What's the matter with you all? Don't you listen to anything I say? You can't kill me in front of a member of staff!"

I turned to Ray, who was now shaking like a leaf, and said "Ray, get out now! Get out while you can, because this is going to get ugly."

Ray, a normally passive and softly-spoken civilian member of staff was unable to speak. He just sat in his chair shaking violently. "Ray! Go!" I shouted. Then I turned to the other men and snapped "You guys are really out of order! You're scaring this poor man to death. He doesn't deserve to suffer this crap from you lot. Let him go!"

Matt stepped forward, putting his hand on Ray's shoulder. "No! We want him to stay. We want him to see what we're going to do to the pig!"

Ray, still unable to speak, was gripped by fear. As the men moved forward I stood up quickly and banged both hands on the table, then hurled my chair against the wall behind me. I shouted "I'll take you all on, you bunch of losers! It's not just me you're dealing with but God and He's going to kick your arses for this!"

Matt looked visibly shocked by my declaration and seemed to freeze on the spot. He snapped back: "Who are you, Cool Hand Luke? Why aren't you frightened of us? You're about to die!"

The henchman on Matt's left walked behind Ray and lifted his right fist ready to throw a punch. I remained calm and stared each of them straight in the eyes, one at a time.

"So kill me! You would be really stupid to do that in front of a member of staff but that's why you're in here. Because you're stupid! I thought you knew the score in prison. Not in front of screws or member of staff! Get rid of the tutor and then you can try and kill me!"

Matt shouted back: "You're being unfair!"

"How am I being unfair? I'm just doing my bird and you lot are the ones who are being unfair. Now pack it up!" I looked at the faces of my attackers and said: "One of you will go down with me, believe me, and I don't care which one it is but I will take out at least one of you."

Matt's attitude suddenly changed. Now he was trying to use reason on me. "Please go on the 43s" he said.

"Put me on the numbers, if you think you can. It's easy, look how many of you there are."

"We can't do our bird with you around. You're making us feel uneasy. You don't do any of the things that we do and we don't feel relaxed with you around."

They had really annoyed me now, so I said "I can't believe you lot! You walk around in your own clothes, like you're not in prison! For God's sake, do your bird and let me do mine. You're pathetic!"

Matt was pleading with me. "The whole wing is getting together to kill you. Why aren't you afraid? You're going to die, man."

"I don't think so. I thought you useless bunch of losers were going to kill me. What's suddenly made you change your plan? You should all be ashamed of yourselves!"

Matt said "Why?"

"Why? You blacks scream about discrimination. All that to me is just bullshit! You're the ones who are the racists! Your race has been victimised for centuries and now you're doing the same thing to me. Show ME some respect, man!"

Matt's reply was instant: "Why should we respect you?"

"Are you Muslims?"

The men looked around at each other in what appeared to be a state of shock. "So what if we are?"

"Well, I reckon that you are all Muslims, proclaiming the teaching of Mohammed. I know the president of Sufi International. He's a personal friend of mine. When I tell him what a bunch of arseholes there are here at Maidstone he won't be very impressed!"

"What's his name then, if he's a friend of yours?"

I said: "His name is Sayed."

Matt said: "How do you know him?"

"I told you, he's a friend."

The whole area suddenly erupted into an ugly scene of violence and screws poured into the room. They grabbed me and I was carted off screaming to the segregation block. "Don't Block me! They should be nicked, not me!" I screamed. but I didn't stand a chance. I was immediately placed in isolation.

The duty officer was polite but insistent. "You've got no option, you have to go on the 43s. Sign here."

I was furious. "If they won't let me do my bird on the wing, I'll do it on my own in the block! I'm not going on the 43s!"

"We'll see." He left and an hour later the number two Governor came into my cell, a tall and attractive woman with thick, wavy, shoulder length chestnut hair and a warm smile. She spoke quietly. "What's going on? You're making yourself very unpopular."

Was this woman truly a governor? She was in a job that commanded respect, but her motherly manner and calm voice were reassuring. It gave me the confidence that she would indeed deal with the situation I was now in. She was about the same age as me and appeared to show me considerable respect, even though she knew nothing about me.

"I'm not looking to be rated in the popularity charts, Ma'am, I wouldn't stand a chance of winning" I told her.

She smiled and spoke softly "I am so sorry that this has happened to you. I really don't know what to do with you. Are you prepared to ask to go on the 43s?"

"No, ma'am! I want to do my bird on the wing with the others. Just put me back on the wing and everything will be fine."

"I can't do that, I'm afraid. You will be a casualty, believe me. I need to speak to the Home Office." She left, closing the door slowly behind her.

The following day the number one governor came in to see me. He was a completely different kettle of fish.

"What's all this about?" He said with a scolding tone.

He reminded me of an impatient, semi-retired headmaster, so I reassured him by saying: "There isn't a problem, just put me back on the wing."

He pulled on the tails of his double vented wool suit and then straightened what looked like his old school tie in a rather formal way. "We can't do that. You will have to go on the 43s."

I tried to look through his poor choice of chequered weave and said: "Listen. I'm not a nonce, a ponce or a grass. There has just been a misunderstanding, that's all. Put me back on the wing."

He looked peeved and said: "We can't put you back on the wing!"

So I said: "Well, I'll do all my bird in the seg then!"

He snorted and said: "You're just a proud man, that's all. You'll have to go on the Rule." He turned on his heels and left me alone to enjoy my solitude.

I was preparing myself for re-entry on to the wing by building up my exercise routine in the block with floor exercises. I was at the peak of fitness and ready for whatever the System had to throw at me.

Each day I was allowed certain privileges, by law. I could wash, take an hour's exercise and even boil a kettle during my ten-minute tea break, while I was out of my cell. I was being kept in isolation under Good Order and Conduct, in that I was disturbing prison life. How bloody ridiculous!

While I was out of my cell no other prisoners were allowed to be around me. No one from any part of the prison was allowed to visit the unit apart from the block cleaner.

One evening I heard a screw shout from the other side of my door: "Slop out!" The door opened and the screw said: "Time for a shower if you want one?"

I quite fancied a shower, so I said: "Thank you."

I noticed that the landing was empty and the screw had quickly disappeared down the stairs. The poor lighting in the corridor, which I had to cross to get to the showers, was so dark that I was unable to see the wall at the far end.

I felt uneasy and alarm bells were ringing in my unconscious mind. Something was wrong and I couldn't understand what it was.

I thought I heard a movement as I entered the shower room, so I made a noise as if I was taking my clothes off and turned the shower on. Then I hid behind the wall which led to the urinals and kept watch. I could see two men silently and slowly approaching the shower cubicle. One of them was Matt and he was carrying a knife, which I assumed he was going to plunge into me. They came right into the shower room. I realised that my fellow inmates on Medway were not going to let me walk away unscathed.

I suddenly broke my cover and ran out from my hiding place to surprise the two men. I ran at them from the side and Matt and his fellow assassin fled the scene. I chased them to the top of the stairs that led down to the door. As I stopped on the third step from the top I watched the screw unlock the door for them and they were gone.

I left the shower running and returned to my cell, leaving my door half open. I watched through the crack in the door as the screw walked slowly up the stairs. He entered the shower room and looked around for my dead body. It clearly wasn't in there, so he turned the shower off and walked slowly to my cell door. As he put his face around the door, assuming that my body was inside, my face shot out from behind the door. I was very angry because I knew that I had been set up and he was part of their plan. I looked the screw in the face and said: "You put me in the Seg and you separated me from the other men. You are supposed to have me in isolation. Don't you ever do that to me again!"

The screw was speechless. He nodded and locked me back in my cell.

The following day, I had to go to the hospital for an X-ray. The fight in the shower room had aggravated the old injury to my back in the police van and the pain was excruciating. I was diagnosed as having spondylitis. The thought of serving twelve years inside prison in such conditions was daunting.

CHAPTER FIFTEEN

■ ■ ■ ■ ■ ■ ■ ■

SWEET FRESH AIR

The silence in the segregation block was broken by the sound of footsteps pounding up the concrete stairs outside my cell. Suddenly my door clunked and the observation panel opened.

"You're on your way Con, so get yourself ready!"

I sat up in my cell and began going through my exercise routine. When I had finished I rang my bell so that I could be let out to have a shower. I was now extremely cautious when leaving my cell. I turned to look at the screw and said: "What's going on?"

"You're being shipped out this afternoon."

"Where to?"

He appeared to be excited - at the prospect of some overtime, I assumed. "We don't know yet" he said. "Have you got any property left on the wing?"

I said: "Only prison clothing, letters and grief."

The screw smiled. He appeared to be helpful, but I didn't feel I could or should trust him, so when he said: "I'll go over and get them for you." I immediately responded "No, that's OK. I'll go and get them myself. I want them bastards to know that I'm not frightened of them, so I'll get my own property if that's all right with you." He nodded approvingly.

After lunch I was escorted from the Seg back to Medway and

the screw unlocked the gate and we walked on to the wing. There were looks of disbelief from the troublemakers and of respect from Terry and his gang and 'Wolfy' and a few of the other Christian men I had got to know during my short visit. As we walked on to the landing, which was now full of inmates, I thought it was like something out of a Clint Eastwood movie.

As I led the screw to my cell door and waited for him to open it, the other cons stood watching me in silence. I made sure I held my head high. As the door swung open the smell was unmistakeable. Sewage!

I held my breath and reached under the frame of the bed and pulled out the dark grey cardboard prison box that held my papers. "My God, they're still here!" I thought in amazement. I pulled the knotted HMP plastic bag full of my personal letters out of the box, deciding to leave the rest of my clothing. I said to the screw "I'll leave the cleaners to sort the rest out", knowing full well that it would be a screw that would take care of things as there was no wing cleaner. No one wanted that job and the screws were reluctant to ask anyone to clean up after another con as most of them were doing life sentences or heavy sentences for more serious crime.

The atmosphere was much the same as before with washing lines stretching overhead from one side of the wing to the other, full of a mixture of damp faded shirts, tracksuits, socks, trousers, underpants, vests and trainers tied on by laces swinging in the draft from the vented windows that stretched high up into the boarded apex of the roof. The scene was reminiscent of a back-street slum area in New York City. How anything could dry out in this pungent and stark display of fallen humanity belied belief. The entire building and its putrid atmosphere were fermenting in a cesspit of unregenerate foolish pride, now stripped bare before my eyes like a rock being lifted from a secret grave to reveal all manner of crawling things hidden beneath, scrambling for protection from the light of the sun.

I shuddered for a moment. How had I survived for a month in this place? I could have taken my last breath in this sewer. But treating me in this despicable way had only been the catalyst to lift me up and promote me ahead of time. So, I thought that maybe, just maybe, I should be grateful for the pain and anguish they had inflicted on me. I pondered on that thought for barely a moment and rebuked it: 'Nah'.

I walked towards the notice board with a strange, faint feeling of being detached from my own consciousness. I turned to observe their faces once more, more closely this time. They were scrutinising my every move. I knew it was me looking at them, but at the same time it felt as if it wasn't really me staring back at them but whoever it was who had the power to use my eyes to observe this. I reassured myself – "Costa, it's just stress. Get your arse out of here, now!"

As I moved through the wing I could see that some of their faces reflected a deep regret, but I only noticed this in a few who were on the periphery of my vision. The others were displaying their feelings with overt displays of rage, ego, denial and pride for their predicament which had cast this huge shroud of gloom over them all. I was sure this gloom extended into their families, their victims and their victims' families.

I pinned a poster I had made earlier on to their notice board. It had been drawn and written in my own hand and was of a large Celtic cross with the inscription:

'I have been crucified with Christ; it is no longer I who live, but Christ who lives in me; and the life which I now live in the flesh, I live

by faith in the Son of God, who loved me and gave Himself for me'. (Galatians 2:20)

Gripping my personal papers in the palm of my right hand, I walked up to the screw and said "I'm done here". Then I wandered over to the gate and waited for him to catch me up. As he approached me he said "Are you sure you've got everything you want from here, Buller?"

There was nothing more I wanted from this place. "Yes" I said. "Thank you for letting me get my things. I really appreciate this. I did have some unfinished business on the wing to attend to."

He sounded surprised and said "Yeah? I reckon you'll be glad to be leaving this place behind."

I answered quietly: "That's a fact I can't deny."

The officer opened the gate and we walked in silence to a waiting van. He cuffed me and put me in the back, then climbed in the back with me and said "You won't be any trouble will you?"

I looked down at my feet and said "I can hardly run in canvas prison slippers, can I?"

"I'll take that as a no, then." He smiled warmly.

As we pulled out of the main gate I noticed that there were two screws in the front of the van. So I said "How many prisoners are we picking up on the way?"

The screw who was sat opposite me said "There's no one else. This trip is just for you."

"Me? Why do I need three prison officers to take me to another prison? If you'd have given me a rail ticket I would have just turned up at the gate on my own."

"Not according to your records." He nodded to the front of the van and said "We've got an armed escort up at the front because we've been told the van is likely to be a target."

I was shocked by his remark. "Target? Who would want to break me out?" I asked.

He laughed and said: "Not break you out, dumb nut!"

"What then?"

"Wipe you out!"

I thought for a moment, trying to grasp what he was saying. "I don't think so."

"The Governor thinks you're at risk, so that's why we can't tell you where you're going."

The driver pulled through the gates and on to the road and we drove off into a future that had now become even more uncertain. The whole scenario was reminiscent of a script unfolding in a movie. I felt convinced that I was being sent on some sort of divine passage; it was surreal.

The van headed towards the West Country and I felt a deep relief as I moved further and further west. I knew I had been set up in the shower and I should really be dead right now, but I felt very much alive. "Thank you, Lord" I said to myself. "Please keep me safe."

I had hoped that one day I would see the policemen who had lied to put me inside walk in through the front gates of the prison, but I knew they were untouchable by anyone outside their group. They had made it that way and they were bound together in their deceit.

By the time we had passed Andover on the A303 and had travelled about ninety miles, I was starting to feel uncomfortable. So I asked "Any chance of a leak?"

The screw called back to me "We're not supposed to stop for you on this one, but if you're desperate we will." He radioed to the car ahead. "He needs a leak. Yeah, there's one just ahead. OK, we'll pull in there."

I said "Thank you."

The screw sat in the back with me, trying to make polite conversation. "The con wants a natural break and we could do with one as well, so your wish is our command" he said.

Both vehicles signalled left and we pulled off the A303 at Popham Service Area. The screw sitting in the front outlined the terms.

"We'll trust you to walk across the car park and into the toilets on your own, but remember, I play rugby, and if you try to run I will bring you down hard and then the three of us will give you a bloody good kicking. Do you understand?"

I said: "I understand."

"Don't hang around either, because if any of your old colleagues turn up you might get shot."

I nodded and said "I'm only wearing prison slippers. Why would I want to run away from you guys? I feel so much safer in your company." and I raised my right foot for them to see my slipper.

The driver said: "Where's your shoes?"

"The prison can't find any that fit me. I'm size 12."

The driver said: "Go on then. Straight there and straight back."

I left the van and they followed behind and I walked to the toilets and back without incident and quickly sat back in the van. The screw was about to put my handcuffs back on when he realised it would be pointless. So he called to the driver and said: "We don't need these, do we?" He lifted the cuffs up for him to see.

The driver called back "Nah, I don't think so."

The screw tucked the cuffs away in his pocket and the van pulled out of the service station. We continued all the way down to Newton Abbot and then into Channings Wood Prison. As we pulled up outside the main gate, the screw opposite me spoke. "We'd better put these on or we'll get into trouble. You don't mind do you?"

I was surprised that he asked for permission. "No, not at all" I said. "I really appreciate what you've done for me. Thank you." They put the handcuffs back on me.

We drove in through the main gate and I was walked through to the reception block. The duty officer looked like a man who enjoyed his food. He was tall and stocky, balding and wore a handlebar moustache. He stared hard at me and said: "I know you!"

I'd never seen him before in my life, so I said "I don't think so."

"I'm sure it's you. I know all about your case. You were stitched up by the Flying Squad."

I said: "Word certainly does travel quickly in Devon." He started to search for all of my personal belongings and looked confused and asked: "Where's all your gear?"

I said "I don't have any."

"I can't let you in unless you have at least one set of clothes."

I was surprised by his statement. "I'm not going anywhere to wear personal clothes" I replied. "I'm a prisoner and I wear prison clothing."

"You might have to go to court!"

"Court? Oh, I see. Don't worry, I'll get some sent in tomorrow."

"You'd better."

After documenting, photographing and directing me to the induction wing, I walked up to a double set of large iron gates. The reception officer unlocked one of them and stood back and waited for me to leave.

"Go on then, what are you waiting for?"

"Are you going to just let me walk out on my own?"

"This is Channings Wood, not Maidstone, son. This is a C Cat prison. So off you go!"

I moved forward nervously and stepped out into what felt very much like the unknown. I could smell freshly cut grass, which was such a pleasant change from what I had been used to. Seagulls! I could hear garden birds singing, and my heart lifted.

I had to find the induction wing in order to drop off all my gear and I walked along a narrow path that led me into the main body of the prison. I immediately recognised the short, stocky, balding young man waiting patiently ahead of me. His cheeky little face and enormous grin was unmistakeable.

"Simon! What happened? I thought your boss was getting you out?"

"Nah. No chance! They dropped me in it and I got five years for kidnap. When I got convicted I came straight to this dump from Exeter. This place is a shit hole, Costa and I'm going to escape. Come with me?"

I looked around at all the lush green grass and thought he must be mad. "This is heaven in comparison to where I came from, Simon. Go where?"

Simon looked deadly serious "Albania."

"Albania! What the hell am I going to do in Albania, Simon!"

"It's out of here, Costa. You have to get out of here!"

"Simon, listen! I have been sent here by God and He has something really special that He wants me to do for Him here!"

Simon was now looking at me as if I'd gone mad. "Like what, Costa?"

"I don't know, Simon."

"Well, don't worry about that for now. Come with me." Simon walked with me to the induction wing and I found my cell and dropped off all my letters and a bedroll. The two of us walked to Simon's cell on Exe Wing and I kept seeing people I recognised along the way. Much to my surprise, quite a few of them seemed pleased to see me.

Simon's cell was neat and tidy and the walls were covered with pictures of pretty young ladies. I said "Simon, who put this lot up?"

"Do you like my girls?" He spun around on his right heel and opened his arms as if he wanted to embrace them! "These are all mine! I put them all up when I got here. They're beautiful aren't they? Mine, they're all mine!" and he started to laugh loudly, reaching out with his hands again and slapping his thighs. I fell silent, not knowing quite what to say. I stopped at his door and said.

"Simon, I'm sorry but I can't come into your cell. These girls have all got mothers! You can bring me back once they've all left."

Simon looked shocked by my reply and was quick to respond "Don't you like my girls?" and he began to laugh nervously.

"I don't want to look at your pictures, Simon. If you really want me to come into your cell you will need to take them down. I really don't want to see them."

Simon followed me out of Exe wing, realising that I was uncomfortable with his collage of girls spread across his walls. He continued with his guided tour of the prison. It wasn't long before the word got out that Con was back on tour. Inmates I had met at Exeter and had got on well with appeared eager to see me again and arrived at my cell door to shake my hand. I was constantly stopped as I walked through the prison grounds by men I had helped with their depositions. I was pleased to be around so many men I knew.

In the cell opposite me was a large Scotsman called Jock. I noticed that every time I looked in his direction he'd growl at me and pull an ugly face. "I must do something about this guy or he'll end up causing me a problem here" I thought. I made a mental note to pick him up on his manners as a matter of urgency.

After my cell was opened the following morning, I noticed that it was left open until lunchtime, unless I decided to close it myself. If I did so I had to call a screw to open it up again for me. The afternoons operated in the same way. At teatime the doors were locked and I was left to relax after eating my food. In the evenings the doors were again left open until nine.

There were two television rooms I could use and a pool table on each block. I was fascinated at first, but I realised that when you watched television you became more conscious of time and what was happening in the outside world. I preferred to get involved in some other activity so the time passed more quickly.

'Bang up' was easier for me to cope with, and I knew that when the door was shut I was safe as the other inmates were also locked away. But this new situation brought another danger for me. If someone wanted to attack me, they had all day to form a plan and execute it. Although I knew quite a lot of the inmates, I was still subjected to verbal abuse and threats of violence and I was taunted relentlessly every day.

Jock was troubling me, so I waited for the right moment to strike and went straight into Jock's cell, pushing the door open as I went inside and half closing it behind me. Jock panicked, because this was how the PP9 beatings were executed. For the first time I could actually see fear in his eyes. I gave him a hard stare and said "Have you got a problem with me?"

"No!" He had a strong, rough Glaswegian accent and I noticed food stains and sweat marks under his armpits. His stinking condition accentuated his red beard and large frame.

So I went on the offensive "I don't like the way you're looking at me. You came from Maidstone, didn't you?"

Jock was flapping and twiddling with his beard and said: "So?"

"I had problems at Maidstone and if they're going to follow me down here I want to sort them out now! Right? So do I have a problem with you?"

"No, mate! I don't have any problems with you! I thought you did with me, that's all."

"Why?"

"I was on Medway six weeks ago and it scared the shit out of me. I asked to go to another wing!"

"I was on Medway."

"Medway! Oh boy! They cut a bloke open in the showers when I was there. He came out of the recess holding his guts in his hands. It was awful! Violent! It was unbelievable in that place and I couldn't stay in there no more. If they didn't like you, they'd burn you out. They'd use petrol! Petrol, for Christ's sake!"

"What was the guy's name, Jock?"

"I don't know, but they made a right mess of him."

"Yeah, I heard they did that to people they didn't like. Sorry if I misunderstood you, Jock."

I reached out and shook his hand and Jock became a good friend to me. Jock used his menacing appearance as his self defence mechanism. It frightened the weaker lads and they kept clear of him.

As I left Jock's cell I reflected that prison was all about bullshit, drugs, fear, ignorance, laziness, lack of self respect and forgetfulness. I suddenly remembered something my mother had told me. "If you lose your money, you've lost nothing. If you lose your self- respect, you've lost something. If you lose your faith you've lost everything!" I was determined to work on these areas by self-correcting myself. I promised myself: "I won't take drugs.

That's easy. I won't allow myself to be intimidated by anyone. That's a really hard one but I'll study and try and reduce my own ignorance. If I act quickly on that, it will mean that I won't be being lazy or forgetful. Easy!"

During my induction week three men escaped by climbing over the wall, but they were recaptured very quickly. One broke his leg from the fall on the other side and the other two were caught running across the fields.

I played chess with Jock regularly on a giant chess board painted in white on tarmac on the recreation area near the prison clothing exchange. The pieces were about a meter tall. It was really funny watching Jock carrying his chess pieces from square to square and getting more and more angry as he did so because he kept losing.

I was expected to find work in the prison within the first week, so I decided to get on to a business course with Simon, which extended over a twelve-week period. Simon still maintained that he wanted to escape and he frequently visited my cell for a second opinion on his plans for the breakout. "Where is the best place to get over the fence, Costa?" and "What route should I take to get out of the area, Costa?" Being familiar with the prison layout I inevitably ended up spotting the flaws in his plan, little things he had overlooked.

Simon seemed to like my company and he acted as most young men might do in these circumstances. He clearly enjoyed the ambience I had created in my cell by dismantling an old calendar of the Greek Islands and sticking the pictures up individually on the wall with toothpaste. I hung my calendar of Peter Rabbit over the light switch. Yes! I had finally gained control over light and I turned it on and off by pressing the picture in the right place on the calendar to operate the button underneath.

Getting my own light switch gave me a wonderful feeling that I had now got some control over my own life. As the months passed, instead of turning over the out-of-date pictures of Peter Rabbit, I carefully released them from the wire and glued them to any available space I had left on the wall.

I ate my meals at my small desk in my cell, and this was quickly becoming a social event. It seemed that every time I turned around I had another person sitting on the edge of my bed, until it was full. Further arrivals chose to stand up to eat their meals just inside my door. I grumbled "Don't you lot know that there's a canteen in this prison?" They just laughed, thinking I was being light hearted.

Jock, who was sitting nearest the window and was, at my request, now eating his madras curry with a plastic fork instead of his fingers, grunted "Good one, Con! Ha ha ha. You love us all, really."

I tried to look serious "Who the hell told you that, you Scottish reprobate!"

Still chewing a mouthful of curry, Jock said in his usual coarse Glaswegian accent "Well, we love you, you old baldy Sassenach!"

"There's no English in me, bird brain! I'm half Greek, a quarter Irish and a quarter Scottish."

Jock's face shone like the sun. He gave a huge grin and shouted "Daddy!" My bed started to shake with all the laughter that erupted.

Jimmy, another character, was about 48 and five foot ten with greasy mousy-coloured hair and tattoos all the way up both arms. He had "Hate" on the right fist, a skull and cross bones up the forearm and "Love" on the left fist with a coloured drawing of a crucifix up his left arm. When he spoke he irritatingly sucked at his moustache with his tongue, which confounded and muffled his Cardiff accent. He was a self-appointed lay preacher with a bad temper and when he laughed his badly-fitted left upper central incisor, which was capped in gold, immediately became the focal point, but no one had the heart to tell him. He had the habit of talking as he ate and inevitably salivated food tended to spray out wildly in all directions. I braced myself as he opened his mouth to speak. "Good one, Jock. You found the old bastard before I found mine! He pissed off years ago!"

Craig, who was next in line, said "Is that true?"

I tilted my head slightly and said "Yes Craig, I'm a quarter Scottish."

Craig was about 28 and had a warm smile and short-cropped hair (number two length all over). He had a stocky muscular body and spoke with a soft Cheshire accent. "No you daft sod!" he said. "Are you really his dad?" The whole cell erupted once again with more riotous laughter, and the door swung open gently to reveal the duty officer, who stuck his head into the cell and took a deep whiff, suspecting, one presumes, that we were all 'off our faces' on drugs.

He spoke suspiciously in a Devonshire accent. "What are all you lot up to then?" he asked. This brought about even more laughter. Craig shouted out "Hey, boss, Jock's found his dad! He's only just found out that he was sat on his dad's bed all along! Ha ha ha!"

"Keep it down lads." He carefully noted all the faces as he looked around the cell and said: "What are you lot on?" He looked at Jock and said "If you're not careful you'll shrink your papadom!"

He smiled, suspecting something, closed the door again slowly and left us to eat our meal. Simon was third in line from the window and he suddenly interrupted the laughter. "I wish you were my Dad, Costa. I wouldn't mind. My Dad was an arsehole. He's dead now though."

Jimmy, said "Wake up you lot and smell the coffee! You're in fucking prison! This ain't no fucking holiday camp! You're all laughing like you're havin' a bleedin' party night out or something! Pull yourselves together and act like prisoners!"

Determined to keep control of the situation, I interrupted. "Prison? No one told me I was in PRISON, for God sake! My God! I don't believe it! Are you lot prisoners?"

As quick as a flash Jock was back into the conversation "Of course we are you stupid baldy bastard! We're all fucking prisoners! And he tugged at his rotting sweat shirt. "Look! Look! What the fuck do you call this then?"

Craig laughed and said "I'd say it's a filthy, dirty T-shirt in need a good wash, you dirty bastard!"

More choruses of laugher erupted from my cell and I said "No one told me that I'd have to mix with prisoners! I was told that this was a holiday camp! How the hell did you lot get in? My God! Prisoners! In my chalet! Someone notify the press immediately! I hope you lot wiped your feet before you came in?" More laughter.

The door swung open again and Kevin, a lofty under-nourished, self-confessed white witch from North Devon, was standing in the door frame struggling to get in. He asked: "Can I come in?"

Jimmy called out "Look! It's Christopher Lee!" More laughter. "Come in and tell us one of your scary stories? Ha ha ha. Has anyone ever told you that you look just like 'im?"

Kevin just smiled. "All the time, Jimmy." Looking at me he said "How you doing, Con?"

"A twelve, Kevin."

Kevin frowned "I know you're doing a twelve! I asked *how* are you doing, not how *long* are you doing! Anyway, that's one mother of a sentence. I couldn't do a twelve!"

"Me neither, tell me about it, Kevin. How long are you doing, Jimmy?"

Jimmy was busy looking at my pictures on the wall. "Me? A nine. It's a long story, Con. Don't ask me about it! Anyway, why haven't you got any pictures of naked girls on your wall like we have?"

I pointed to the only two photographs on my noticeboard, of Michael and Luke. "My sons are visiting me this week and the Pope said he might drop in for a chat, so I won't have that sort of girl in my chalet" I said.

"Chalet?" Kevin had missed the earlier jokes.

"It's a long story, Kevin. This bunch of reprobates have come around to give me a quote for installing a double glazed patio door." I pointed to the window and indicated that it would be extended to the ground. "I can't work out which side to fix and which should slide open. What do you think? Left to right or right to left?"

Kevin smiled and said "It should open right to left of course. You might as well do it properly or not at all."

I could hear the screw banging doors in the background and said "That's exactly what I thought. I'm glad you came around, Kevin. Anyway, this isn't a bus shelter, so off you go you lot. Haven't you got homes to go to?"

As the group left my cell the duty officer arrived and I said "Thank you officer. I shan't be needing you any more this afternoon, so you can pop off home if you like, but I'll be expecting to see you in extra early tomorrow. Don't forget to clean the car like you promised. Anyway, I've got a bit of a draught coming in through this door, so I'll close it if you don't mind?" I gently pushed it shut.

I heard his reply: "Fuck off, Buller!"

I had a small collection of photographs and introduced various members of my family to my pinboard as the weeks passed. I would treat them as if they were visiting me in real life, taking them down again as they 'left' and then bringing in more recent faces. I liked to imagine I was having a meal with them and I would chat away with them and imitate their voices in reply. Harmless fun really. My conversations sounded so real that some of the inmates wandered into my cell to see who I was talking to! I would invite Simon around to my cell saying: "My son Michael is coming for dinner tonight, would you like to meet him again?"

When Simon arrived I would welcome him and take his coat from him and we would all sit around the photograph and talk as if he was really there. You need a good imagination to cope with the monotony of prison life, and Simon was happy to play his part in my small farce.

I was given a Greek flag by Panayiotis just before he was released after serving seven years for killing his mother-in-law in a rage. I placed it in my window and would dream of being back on holiday on my favourite Greek Island, Corfu. I had often felt like using anger on my own mother-in-law at times, but quickly found the strength to dismiss the idea. I had often thought Panayiotis' mother-in-law must have really pissed him off. He had married an English girl and her mother kept interfering, apparently. I suppose that's why I could relate to him, because I had married in the same way.

The cell windows in Channings Wood were a lot larger than any other prison I had seen and offered a good view into the grounds. The vertical slotted bars were wide enough to get an arm through, so I was able to reach out to feel the wind blow through my hand and throw food to my spiky little friends. I had a favourite, Herbie the hedgehog. He was no ordinary hedgehog, I hasten to add. He loved music, cheese and good company. Me! When Herbie looked up at me it was as if he knew that I was trapped and he appeared to have some empathy for my predicament. I loved Herbie for that tenderness and sensitivity.

CHAPTER SIXTEEN

■■■■■■■

DEAR JOHN

Late one afternoon when I was sitting in my cell after coming back from an emotional visit with Heather, there was a gentle knock on the door and Simon pushed it open to see if I was at home.

"Simon! Come in."

Simon placed a clear plastic jug of steaming water on the green worktop and said. "I thought you might need a coffee."

Simon was a nosey little sod and he was keen on finding out how my visit had gone earlier. "Sure, I'll just finish this letter off and you can make the coffee. You know where everything is, don't you?"

He opened my small cupboard, helped himself to powdered milk, sugar and coffee and pulled open a packet of my Hobnob biscuits. Then he jumped on to my seven-foot bed and started munching away noisily and waited for me to finish writing.

"How did the visit go?" Simon was so predictable. Sweet really. Simon always turned up to find out my latest news and what letters I'd had and wanted to know how my visits had gone. He already knew I was expecting this one with Heather to be particularly difficult.

"It was a short one, Simon."

"Short? How short?"

"About three minutes short."

"Well, how was she?"

"Doing very well it would seem, Simon."

"Oh yeah? What's she up to then? If it only lasted three minutes, it has to be bad news?"

"You knew there was a problem, Simon. Heather has got herself a new boyfriend. She dropped in to give me a verbal 'Dear John' and burst into tears and then fled the building."

"No! Bitch!"

"Yeah! She's got some bottle, I'll give her that, Simon. At least she came in to tell me to my face. I respect her for that."

Simon was momentarily lost for words and we both stared out of the window. "Why couldn't she just keep on writing? The bitch!"

"I could tell from her letters that there was something going on a while ago, Simon. Way back when I first got arrested. You know, in Exeter."

"It's still not on though, Costa."

"It's life, Simon. It's harder for the women, I reckon. They have to cope with life outside prison and all the stresses of work, bills and the temptation of all the other men around them, especially at work. That's how she met this new guy."

"I'd be gutted if it was me. Are you all right?"

"Prison's a terrific leveller, Simon. If you prepare yourself mentally and say "I'm going to lose everything in the end" it can't get in to hurt you. Anything that's still standing when you get out has got to be a bonus. Know what I mean?"

"No! I don't want to lose anything."

I thought back to my meeting with Heather in the visits hall, as Simon grabbed another Hobnob and passed me my coffee. Heather was about five foot six and had coloured her hair blonde and curled it tightly. It was held back with a headband. She walked briskly over to my table with a long, cold, sallow face void of any genuine emotion. She put her elbows on the table and leaned forward, then spluttered it all out. "I can't take any more! We've got to have to break from each other. Maybe we can get back together when you're out."

In my last letter to Heather I had said that if she did have someone, I would prefer to know now rather than to find out when I was released. "I don't want you to live a lie just because you might think that you are keeping up my morale. Don't do that to me."

So I asked "Who is he, Heather?"

"There isn't anyone, honest!"

I sat quietly as she twiddled her fingers nervously. I knew her well enough to see that she was being ripped apart by this secret, so I said: "Is he sitting in the car waiting for you?"

Her head lifted quickly and she looked me straight in the eyes, searching for signs of what I might know. Realising that she had already betrayed herself by her reactions, she knew it was pointless to continue with this pretence. "Yes, he brought me down because I was upset."

"I know you're upset, Heather. I really understand and I want to thank you for supporting me the way you have. You have been brilliant and I love you for it. I've known for quite a while you know, I could tell from your letters."

"How long?"

"About two years."

"You're not stupid, are you? I'm sorry Costa, it's just that this has all gone on for so long and it's hard for me to cope on my own out there. Maybe we can meet up when you get out?"

"Maybe, but I doubt it."

"Who is he?"

"He's just a guy from work. He doesn't really mean anything to me." Suddenly Heather burst into floods of tears. "I knew you'd take it well. I'm the one who's cracking up and it should be you!"

Heather's betrayal was now revealed. She jumped to her feet, sending her chair crashing back on to the floor. In a rather theatrical display of disloyalty and shame, one hand covering her mouth, she raced out of the hall sobbing uncontrollably.

Was this it? Had she finally found the strength to abandon me here?

Moments passed, slowly, until I came to a realisation that I had indeed been extracted from the life we once shared and I was now left feeling wounded, fragile, miniscule and exposed to all the dangers that awaited me in this dark place. Heather had been my anchor and now she had cut the rope that secured me to her, leaving me to be caught up helplessly in the ebb and flow of prison life, bobbing among the other visitors who were still clinging on to their own shattered relationships with their loved ones. They were struggling too, hoping and dreaming of the time when they would finally be reunited.

Getting a verbal 'Dear John' is hard to describe. Numb is a good word. I was aware of heads turning cautiously to study my demise and expressions of dread on faces. I'd done the same in one of my earlier visits and wondered if I would be next. The two screws, who were reading nonchalantly behind a desk at the front of the visits hall, raised their eyes to study my bearing. The visit thus far had lasted all of three minutes and I sat quietly hoping that Heather might return, but as I glanced out of the window I saw her, still in tears, climb into an old blue Ford Fiesta which had pulled up alongside her. Then she disappeared from sight.

I genuinely wished her well and said to myself "Have a good

life, Heather". It was sad and I felt empty, but, in reality you can't expect a young woman to put her life on hold while her boyfriend serves a twelve-year prison sentence. I was relieved to know that she had at least found some happiness through all of this pandemonium.

The screw on my right decided to get up from behind the desk and walked to my table. "You can't sit here without a visitor, Buller" he said. "Make your way back to your wing!"

Calling on all my strength, I managed to stand slowly, turned and walked through the door into the security area. "Open your mouth!" I was ordered. I reacted instinctively by opening my mouth wide. "Drop your trousers!" I loosened the clasp on my prison greys and my trouser dropped to my ankles. "Drop your pants to your knees and bend forward!" There was no point in resisting. "Right, get dressed again!" As I pulled my pants and trousers back into place he searched my prison issue sweater and the collar and cuffs of my shirt.

"Kick your shoes off!" I stepped out of my old prison-issue slippers and he stepped forward and kicked them towards the door and barked: "Where's your shoes?" Tired and emotionally exhausted from my visit I tried to remain composed, but my trembling voice betrayed my grief:

"I don't have any. The stores don't stock size twelve, so I guess people with big feet don't commit crime."

He looked stern and snapped back: "Don't get smart with me, arsehole. Get some sent in then!"

I left the visits hall without saying another word to anyone and walked slowly back to my cell.

CHAPTER SEVENTEEN

■ ■ ■ ■ ■ ■ ■ ■

FATHER ANSCAR

The morning ended painfully, I had received three letters, two 'normal' post and one from Maidstone Prison; I read that one first. Wolfy had finally decided to put pen to paper and updated me on matters relating to Terry Stoles and to give me a message: "Hello, Con, How's the trumpet playing going? Ha ha ha. They're not missing you here! In fact you pissed them right off big time! Just a bit of advice, don't come back! I've moved on to Weald 'cos they're renovating Medway and the nonces are moving in, so things are good here now. Reggie Kray was asking after you and when I told him I was writing to you, to tell you about Terry getting plunged, he told me to say: "You've got some balls!" He was sorry he missed you and he reckons: "Respect is due!"

There was a tap at the door – Simon. He gave me a big smile. I said "Come in, me old cocker" and he perched himself on the end of my bed and searched my table top for information.

"Well, how many letters did you get today?"

"Three, but I've only opened the first one so far. It's from Wolfy in Maidstone."

"What's he want then?"

I was upset and really wanted to change the subject, so I said: "Just updating me on his move, that's all". I decided to ask Simon a question. "Do you know who the guy is next door?" Even though I was on the end of the block I still pointed towards his cell.

Simon laughed "That'll be Dig 'em up Dave. Why?"

I pushed my letters away from me and turned to talk directly to Simon: "He howls like a wolf in the middle of the night! That's weird!"

"He's into necrophilia. That's why they call him Dig 'em up Dave."

He stopped laughing and sat on my bed with a silly grin on his face.

I said: "Well? What's so funny?"

He looked at me inquisitively and said "Do you know what necrophilia is?"

"I can't say that I do, but I really don't think I want you to explain it to me, thank you."

"They have sex."

"No, enough!"

"There's a right bunch of weirdos on this wing, Costa, present company excepted of course." More laughter and Simon quickly raised his hands in defence.

I said: "Very funny."

Simon decided to fill me in with more detail: "He's a mate of Freddie the Freezer."

"Freddie the Freezer?"

"Yeah, Freddie the Freezer. He's got a face like an old olive tree, weathered and twisted, you know? They're both doing life for murder."

"Shouldn't they be on the 43s?"

"Everyone's too frightened of them to put them over there. They're always together and they're tooled up."

"Nice."

Simon went on: "Freddie is serving life for murdering his wife."

"Don't Simon, I can tell where this is going and I don't want to hear any more. Make a coffee."

"No, listen to this. Freddie..."

I was right on to him. "Simon! Pack it up. That's enough!"

Since meeting Simon again at Channings Wood, he seemed to be getting less crude and we had become good friends. As we sat drinking our coffee, Simon asked: "Forget Christianity. Why don't you become a Muslim and you can hang out with my crowd? We get special food brought in for us." I was surprised by his invitation. "I don't really understand that much about your faith, Simon" I said.

"Have you read the Koran?"

"No, have you?"

He smiled. "Not all of it but it's near enough the same as the bible. Read it and you'll see there isn't much difference really."

"I'll get a copy from the library."

"If you're going to read the Koran, it's only fair that I read the bible. That way we'll know more about each other's faith."

I knew that Simon was dyslexic and thought it best to offer him some constructive advice. "You can't just start reading the whole bible from start to finish, Simon. It would be like walking into a library and reading every book in turn from left to right. Just read the gospel of St John to start with."

"OK. That's easy, I've read that already but I'll read it again."

Simon prayed separately with other Muslim believers and I decided to start my own regular praying vigil. I really wanted to know more about why I had been sent to Channings Wood. So I looked heavenward and said to God: 'I want to find out what Your purpose is for me in this place. Why did You send me here?' I carried on attending all the Christian religious services and the more I attended the more I realised how little I knew about my faith and the more confused I got. I applied to do an Open University theology degree and in readiness I started asking myself questions about things which I found odd and wanted to know the answer to, such as: "Why are there so many different Christian religions?"

Father Anscar, a Catholic 'Monk' priest, had started working at the prison and was ministering to the men and taking Catholic mass once a week. So I started asking him lots of questions. He was a tall, slim, balding, humble and kindly old man of about seventy and he shuffled around the prison comforting and helping the inmates. That was all he wanted to do. Once he brought a novice in with him, Father Dominic, and in conversation I said: "Father Anscar is such a lovely man. He'll do anything he can to help the men." Father Dominic said: "If Father Anscar had his way, he would give everything away and there wouldn't be anything left at Buckfast Abbey!" I loved that quality of this very special man of God.

Father Anscar's posture befitted his vocation and age. As he walked through the prison visiting his flock, hunched slightly forward and meek, one would automatically identify him as being a monastic, even though he was without a habit. He instilled calm in everyone and nodded and stopped to listen to the men as he walked through the grounds, though he spoke with a nervous stutter.

I asked Father Anscar lots of questions about Christianity and he encouraged me to read about church history in order to discover for myself the answers to my many questions. One afternoon he approached me full of joy and said: "I have a book for you, Con." He passed me a small object wrapped in brown paper; by his demeanour it appeared to be treasure of some kind.

I thanked him and slowly and carefully removed the brown paper from a book called *The Sayings of the Desert Fathers*. "Thank you, Father Anscar, I will return it to you as soon as I have read it."

Father Anscar nodded and walked through into the chapel. He sat two rows back from the altar in silence as I sat in the back row and started reading my new book. A deep peace fell upon us. After about twenty minutes I went and sat next to him; he looked as if he was asleep and I whispered: "Thank you for the book, Father Anscar." He raised his right index finger to his lips and said "Pray".

Thinking that he wanted me to repeat some prayers, I said: "Oh Father, Lord of heaven." Father Anscar raised his finger to his lips and still keeping his eyes closed said "Quietly", so I lowered my voice to a whisper and carried on: "and earth, I..." But he put his finger to his lips again, with all patience and said "Silently". I found this really strange and I thought: "Why did he ask me to pray and then quieten me? How can I pray to God without using words?" Father Anscar never did explain, he just let me discover the answers for myself.

One evening I knocked on his door. There was no answer and I opened it slowly. He appeared to be asleep. He was sitting in his chair with his elbows on the desk and his head in his hands. The room was silent. I whispered "I've brought you some coffee and biscuits, Father Anscar." I always made him a large pot of coffee as he seemed to enjoy holding his mug while listening to anyone who might happen to come along to talk to him. Having a jug meant that he could share his drink, so I always put a few extra cups on his tray for that purpose.

"Sit down, Con. Let's have coffee together." He motioned towards the low green plastic easy chair and he asked "How's the reading going?" I unscrewed the central stopper, poured myself a coffee and lowered myself into the chair beside him. The light was now starting to fade through the small skylight window and the room reminded me of how the light fell away in my cell at night.

Neither of us attempted to reach for the light-switch and our heartfelt conversation seemed to encompass a rich, deep feeling of inner peace. "Really well, Father Anscar! I'm reading the Desert Fathers as you suggested. I've also read something of the Great Schism in the church. How sad that this should happen."

He coughed lightly and whispered. "This is indeed a very sad situation."

He lowered his head, tilted it slightly to one side and fell silent, retrospective and with his eyes now closed. One would have thought he was asleep. He appeared to be encompassed in an extraordinary peace. As the light dimmed in the room his fading outline became a silhouette against the wall. We were enveloped in silence, a peaceful unity, lamenting as a father would for his lost son. I was humbled. I had never had the privilege to share in or witness this depth of humility before and I was drawn into its unfathomable depths.

As soon as I spoke I regretted breaking our silence, even though my words were spoken softly. "Yes, Father Anscar, it is."

"This is where your answers lie, Con. You can go deeper if you wish, that's up to you. It's your journey." He whispered in a resonance so deep and soothing that it brought immense comfort to my soul. I was at peace with myself and in my mind's eye I could see a small child sharing a treasured moment with its father. It was a moment of such purity that could only be compared to the waxing of a candle in the heat of the flame, a treasure so pure that the moment was etched in my mind for ever.

There was a knock at the door and I was forced to leave. I quietly left my chair, turned on the light and as I opened the door I greeted a fellow inmate who wanted to talk with Father Anscar. I left the solitude of the room and returned to attend my work.

The more I read the more I hungered to know more. At the same time I began to discover the answer to some of the mysteries of my own life.

With a Greek Mother and a Protestant Irish Father, I still couldn't understand why I had been baptised into the Orthodox Church in Malta. I realised that this must have been initiated by my mother. After moving to Britain when I was nine years old, I was then sent along to a Church of England School and attended St Peter's Church in Alresford, which was initiated, most definitely, by my father!

In the 60s the root to my own faith, which is Orthodoxy, was no longer visible in the western world and when I had asked my own father for an explanation, he had told me that they were the same thing, only running in parallel. This situation was really very confusing to me and while at Channings Wood I applied to take an Open University degree in theology. While I waited for the result of my application, I thought that I might as well find out as much as I could about Christianity before the course started. I remembered looking around the Chapel library and thinking I needed to start at the beginning and try to imagine that I knew nothing - not a lie, because, basically, all I knew about Christianity was a few stories I had read in the bible. So I looked through the various denominational books in the library that were on display outside the Chaplain's office and I took a handful back to my cell to study.

I carried on reading the books Father Anscar had recommended and then went on to those I had picked up in the library in the Chapel. It left me wondering why there were no books on the early Church. I needed to ask for help. So I wandered over to the main library and spoke to Jessica, the Head Librarian. She was a tall middle-aged woman who liked to wear low-cut frilly blouses, silk patterned on-the-knee skirts and strong perfume. Larry, the orderly, who lived in the 43 Unit, was following Jessica around like a vacuum cleaner feeding off her cheap perfume. I knew he was a rapist and Jessica seemed to get some sort of kick from the attention. Weird, I thought.

"Hi Jessica, can you get hold of any books on the early church?" I asked her.

After searching on her library system, she announced: "I've got lots of material on the Reformation, but that's about as early as I can get I'm afraid."

Now, I really hadn't got a clue what she was talking about and I could see that she was about to discover my secret - this guy's an idiot.

"I want a book about Christianity that dates from around AD 35. What date was the Reformation?"

Now I had her stumped. "I've no idea!" With that Jessica started to search her records frantically.

"Why not? Can't you just look it up?"

"I've never been asked that question before. I'm looking it up for you now."

"I can't believe no one has asked you that before, Jessica!"

"I can't either. Here we are! The Reformation was in 1517. The Protestant Reformation was the 16th-century schism within Western Christianity initiated by Martin Luther, John Calvin and other early Protestants. It was sparked by the 1517 posting of Luther's 95-point Thesis. The efforts of the self-described "reformers", who objected to the doctrines, rituals, and ecclesiastical structure of the Roman Catholic Church, which led to the creation of new national Protestant churches. So it's as I said, in 1517."

I made a quick mental calculation. "That's good, Jessica, I really appreciate that, but what happened to the other one thousand four hundred and eighty two years?"

"What do you mean?"

"I mean, I can barely remember what I had for lunch yesterday, so how on earth can the 'Reformers' of 1517 have had any idea about what happened in AD 35?"

"All you need to know is in the bible."

"OK, when was the bible put together? Did Jesus have printers at hand back then?" As soon as I'd said that I regretted it because I now felt really stupid.

"I don't know! This is something that you're interested in, not me!"

"Can't you look it up?"

"No! Get a bible off the shelf, you look it up."

So I wandered over to the 'Religion' section and started to look through the bibles on display. I thought: "Stroppy bitch! Why is it that when people get asked a question that they don't know or understand, they get all stroppy? Why can't she just say: 'I'm really sorry but I have no idea?'"

The library screw then called out: "Finish choosing your books now, the library's closing." So I wandered over to Jessica and asked her: "What period was it when Jesus walked on the earth?"

She looked astonished and said: "I don't know. I didn't think there was a period at that time."

"The Romans were there though, weren't they?"

"I suppose so."

"Well, I reckon it was the Byzantine period. So do you have any books from that period?"

"No!"

"Do you have any books on art, mosaics or illustrations from that period?"

"I'll have a look and if I find anything I'll order it up for you."

"Thank you Jessica."

The screw looked agitated and clearly wanted to go home. "Piss off Buller, go and annoy someone else with all your stupid bloody questions!" he snapped.

"Thanks Mr Harris, you don't 'alf remind me of my dad, he was a screw in the army."

"Watch it, Buller, you're asking to get nicked. Now piss off if you know what's good for you!"

I wandered out of the library and popped into the chapel on my way back to the wing. There I met an Anglican priest called Gordon. He was looking very fresh and full of life. "Can I have a word with you, Gordon?" I asked him.

"Yes, what's it about?" he replied. We walked into the office together.

"I've been over to the library and I'm looking for a bit of information."

Gordon seemed very interested now and asked "What do you want to know, Con?"

"Well, let's say that I've had a chat with someone or I read something somewhere and I suddenly decide that I want to become a Christian?"

"Right. What do you want to know?"

"Well, I'd need to be baptised, right?"

He smiled knowingly and said: "Yes, if you've not been baptised already."

This was a serious question because it was starting to baffle me now. So I asked: "Well, which Christian church do I join?"

He proudly announced: "The Anglican Church of course. Let me have a look at your record. Ah, I see, you're Orthodox, so you're already a Christian!"

He was missing my point, so I went on: "That wasn't the question, Gordon. "If I wanted to become a Christian, which Christian church do I join? Let's say I was talking to a man on the wing and he said: "I want to be a Christian just like you." What church do I send him along to? How does all that work? You've just said that I'm Orthodox, which isn't Anglican, so how can it be the same church?"

"Well, he just goes along to his nearest church and if he feels comfortable there he joins."

"So what are you saying? Are we all one church going along together?"

"Yes, love is the most important thing. Without love you don't have anything."

"That's funny because my dad said the very same thing, but something that confuses me is this; when the Creed is being said in church we all say: "We believe in one holy, catholic and apostolic church, right?"

He nodded. "Yes."

So I asked: "Well, which one is it? There has to be a One Church! Is it the Anglican Church, Catholic Church, Baptist Church, Pentecostal Church, Mormon Church, Quaker's or Jehovah Witnesses? They all sound different to me."

He now looked uncomfortable. "I've got a meeting in a minute and I can't talk for much longer. Just love your neighbour and Jesus and you'll be fine."

Now ignorance was demonstratively my greatest weakness and the following day I went back to see Jessica. She now appeared to know something more about this subject and seemed keen to help me. "The English Reformation happened in the 16th century when the Church of England broke away from the authority of the Pope and the Roman Catholic Church" she told me.

I thought for a moment. "So the English Church was originally Catholic?"

Jessica smiled sarcastically. "That's right." She seemed amused by my ignorance of Church history, which at this point I found overwhelming, as was the thought of setting about trying to catch up on so much history.

I felt the urge to close my eyes prior to asking the next question "So why did they separate?" I looked at Jessica in anticipation of a profound account of this part of history, which had clearly passed me by. "I can't help you there, but it's not really important because everything starts from the Reformation."

I was puzzled. "And that was from the 16th century onwards?"

"Yes."

"But I want to start at the beginning and move forward from there."

"We don't have any books to cover the earlier period of Christianity I'm afraid, there's only the Bible."

I walked across and picked up a Bible from the shelf and said "Why?"

"Like I said before, it all starts from the Reformation."

I opened the Bible and quickly flicked through the pages. "How can it, Jessica? Jesus was doing His miracles in AD 33, right?"

"Yes."

"Matthew wrote his gospel between AD 50-70, Mark wrote his gospel between AD 65-70 and Luke wrote his between AD 70-80. Then John, according to this, wrote his gospel around AD 96. So how can it all start in the 16th century? What about the bit in the middle? There's fifteen hundred years missing? That's the bit I'm interested in and I need to know about. How can I find out about what happened in between, Jessica?"

"I've no idea. If you can get hold of the names of the books that you want I will see if I can find them for you?"

"So the gospel of John goes up to around AD 96, so what period in time stretches on from there?" I asked her.

Jessica quickly typed something into her library system. "You were right, it's the Byzantine Period."

"Well, do you have any books on the Byzantine period?"

"No, sorry."

"What about Byzantine art?"

"I haven't found anything yet but I'll see what I can find out for you. If I find something, do you want me to order it up for you?"

"Yes please. Thank you, Jessica. This is getting really interesting. I would like to know why there is this huge gap. Haven't you ever wondered why?"

"I've never thought about it before, Con."

"I'm reading a book about the desert fathers at the moment and it's really interesting. It's the sort of book that refers to the early Church that I'm interested in."

"Right, I'll see what I can dig up."

Now my work was starting in earnest and I was right, ignorance was my greatest hurdle at this point and I had already promised Simon that I would read the Koran from cover to cover. So I collected a copy and began reading it in earnest in exactly the same way that I had advised Simon not to read the bible! I felt like a medieval detective delving into the past.

When I had finished reading the Koran I really wasn't any the wiser. So I convened a meeting with Simon in my cell one Saturday afternoon in order to discuss our findings. He was just as excited as I was to discover what we had both uncovered.

Simon came, as usual, with his plastic jug full of steaming hot water. The only difference this time was that he also brought his own 'makings' for the coffee. I started by asking him the first question: "What did you get from reading the gospel of John?"

Simon was straight back to me, as he had clearly read the scripture and wanted to tell me all about it. "The bit I would like to know more about is being 'born again' and Nicodemus couldn't get his head around that either! So all you have to do is get baptised and say a prayer and that's it, you're born again!"

"That's good, Simon. I'm really pleased you read it through. What I've been trying to do is find out where the church is. Say I want to become a Christian in prison and I go up to a Chaplain and say "I want to be a Christian". He'll say something like "OK, that's cool. Pray here, say this, say that." Then what?

Simon looked worried "What do you mean, what?"

"Well, Simon, does that mean that I am a Methodist or am I a Catholic or am I a Baptist or a Jehovah's Witness or what?"

Simon was now finding this too much information to take on board. "That's why it's so easy being a Muslim!"

"Let me explain what I've been checking through."

"Go on then, Costa."

"Well, from what I can see there is only supposed to be one Church. It says so in the statement of faith which is called the Nicene Creed, which was composed in part and adopted at the First Council of Nicaea in AD 325 and revised with additions by the First Council of Constantinople in AD 381. It is a creed that summarises the "One Church" right back in early Christianity. So I went looking for it, this "One Church", and it did my head in. This was before Muhammad, he was born in AD 570 in the Arabian city of Mecca. I read that he was orphaned at an early age and brought up under the care of his uncle Abu Talib. He later worked mostly as a merchant, as well as a shepherd, and was first married by the age of 25. Being in the habit of periodically retreating to a cave in the surrounding mountains for several nights of meditation and prayer, he later reported that it was there, at the age of 40, that he received his first revelation from God. Three years after this event Muhammad started preaching these revelations publicly, proclaiming that "God is One", that complete "surrender" to Him is the only way acceptable to God, and that he himself was a prophet and messenger of God, in the same vein as other Islamic prophets. So this 'one Church' was some time before Muhammad, right?"

"Yes, Costa, Jesus was a prophet too."

"So I searched for this early church and I read about the Lutheran Church. I found that this church was started by a monk called Martin Luther who had left the Catholic Church in 1517. So I asked myself "Why did Martin Luther leave?" and "Why has Father Anscar stayed?" Most peculiar, Simon. So I remembered what my Dad had said "They're all one church running along together in parallel." My Dad had called me a stupid bastard for not knowing that!

"So I read on about the Church of England and that church only went back to King Henry VIII. It was started in 1534 because he didn't agree with the Pope and he wanted a divorce with the right to remarry. That meant the Church my Dad sent me to started in 1534!

"One thing that I know for certain, Simon, is that Jesus started His ministry in AD 33, and that was well before 1534. So what's going on here? If I'm going to find out what really happened I need to go back further. At the same time I have to ask myself how on earth can I concentrate on praying when all I'm doing is reading and talking about Christianity. There has to be more to it than reading, talking, listening to speeches, singing hymns and songs and jumping up and down and clapping my bloody hands!

"I've started to forget about my set prayer times because I'm spending too much time with other things, Simon. I have to concentrate on some sort of prayer rule. I've got to make some sort of a plan about all this. So I reckon I need to concentrate on three areas. I'm determined to find the answers I need. So I'm focusing on ignorance, laziness and forgetfulness. All the different Christian religions I have looked at seemed to have a root that went back to the Catholic Church. So I had a look into Catholicism and I started to read about its origin. I also read about a Catholic monk called Thomas Merton. Then I went back to the book of the Desert Fathers. These books were really hard to get in prison.

"I read that the Catholic Church once shared the same rich apostolic and doctrinal heritage as the Orthodox Church for the first one thousand years of its history and that, until the first millennium they were one and the same church. Unfortunately, in 1054, the Pope of Rome broke away from the other four Apostolic Patriarchates (which include Constantinople, Alexandria, Antioch and Jerusalem), by tampering with the Original Creed of the Church and then the pope considered himself to be infallible and the Chief Priest on the Earth.

"This means that the Roman Catholic Church is really only a thousand years old! Now if they've tampered with the Creed, what else have they tampered with, Simon?"

Simon had clearly had enough of my ranting and all the information that I had gleaned was just too much for him to take on board.

"Religion's a load of bollocks! It's about controlling and killing people! I've had enough, Costa. You can carry on if you want to but don't you realise that God is already working through you in here? I can see that, it's obvious!"

"Do you think so, Simon?"

"Yes. The men follow you around like sheep and come to you to pray on them. Why would they do that if they didn't believe that you were a man of God?"

"I haven't considered that before."

"You breath God. You don't stop talking about God and you thirst for God. I've never met anyone like you before."

"Hmm..."

"You must be doing something right, how have you managed to survive in here being an ex copper and all that without God's help?"

"He's definitely protecting me, Simon."

"Keep going on with your journey, Costa."

"I will, Simon. I've got to find the truth."

Now this was getting more and more interesting and I kept on reading. I discovered that the Orthodox Church, whose meaning is 'Right Glory', had to be investigated further. I read that Orthodoxy was not a Religion but a way of life in Right Glory. Whatever that meant. The only Glory that I had witnessed so far was evangelical Christians jumping up and down clapping their hands and proclaiming God's glory in praise, worship and thanks, shouting "Hallelujah!" It was good entertainment, though it was a bit freaky to start with. I'd also read in one of my books that Orthodoxy had also been described as the 'straight way' to God.

After doing so much reading and being a man of action, I decided to take no risks. I would start praying East and West, which meant more prayer. I managed to get hold of an Orthodox Prayer Book and started praying for the unity of the Church by praying using the Common Book of Prayer first and then the Orthodox prayer book. I tried to imagine that I had one foot resting in the Western World and the other in Eastern Europe, which to be quite honest was a bit of a weird feeling. Now, if God was going to talk to anyone, He was surely going to talk to me!

I realised that I was fighting, initially, against three evils and believed I was making a little progress with them. My ignorance was being beaten into submission through all the reading I was doing and my laziness was being treated by rising at 5 am and praying with the Common Book of Prayer and then my Orthodox Prayer Book and then my own prayers for my family and friends. When my cell was opened at 8.10 am I was already 'all prayed up', so I quickly showered, had my breakfast and made my way up to the Chapel to pray with the Anglican Prison Chaplain.

I kept praying for unity in the Church and I incorporated fasting as part of my daily life. I was now praying for five to six hours a day, from when I got up at five in the morning until I finished my prayers at around midnight. In my constant search for the truth it seemed that the more I prayed the more the men seemed to be drawn to attack me verbally and physically, and when I walked through the wing I felt like I was 'running the gauntlet'. However there were some who appeared to be drawn to me by some invisible force. They told me that they felt secure and at peace in my company. When they said that I thought of Father Anscar.

I lay on my bed, turned inward and started to empty myself again in front of the small wooden cross my sister had given me. I tried to imagine the cross in my mind's eye, calling to Him from within and pleaded, "I need You. I want to come back to You. I am not worth anything without You. I lost my happiness when I lost You. I lost my life when I lost You. My life is without meaning without You. My life is without taste without You."

So I carried on pouring myself at God's feet. "Oh God, I want to come back to you but my enemies are stronger than me. There are so many men in here who tell me there is no help for me in You. So rescue me! Lead me back to You!" But still I felt nothing and I couldn't receive or feel anything from Him.

Now I could easily have given up at this point and said "There isn't a God!" Now my battle was against laziness and forgetfulness, so instead of slackening off, I stepped things up and began to pray ceaselessly. I told Him "I lost my power when I moved away from

You and I need you to give me a special power, from You, and give me special help to come back to you." The more I prayed the more I began to get followed around the prison by other inmates who were eager to be around me.

I spent a lot of time in my cell flicking things that I kept remembering about my past up to God and saying "Here's another one, and another one, and another one." I kept on praying to God and at the same time I kept asking the chaplains, "How do I find my way back to God?" But they looked at me like I was stupid, until eventually I just got on my knees in my cell and, in my mind's eye, threw myself under His feet and called to Him "I won't leave You without getting a blessing! You have to help me get back to You! If You consider me as one of Your children, help me! You didn't only forgive my sins – but You have to save me from the love of sin. I can't come back to You as long as sin is taking over my heart! Take away the love of sin from my heart – I can't get rid of sin and come back to You! You must first come and show me and make me leave the love of sin. If I was able to get rid of sin on my own I would have been able to come back to you earlier. I want you to make me get rid of sin – I need You to give me strength!"

It was success in prayer that led me to succeed in repentance. Whoever thinks that there's a way for repentance other than prayer they are deceived by the evil one, because through prayers you get power to come back to God.

I forced myself in prayer rather than in any other work, because it was through prayer that the wall between me and God was removed and I was able to come back to Him once more.

I was amazed at how many obstacles I threw up to distract me from prayer, because I really didn't know how to truly pray. I would prefer to theologize, meditate, read, talk and serve the needs of others in the Chapel rather than pray in my cell (my heart) alone.

(To be one man, alone, with his God, forever in prayer. Ceaselessly!) Consequently I spent time in prayer. I had previously leapt at the opportunity to attend religious meetings rather than to pray as I should and I opened myself up to so many distractions.

This was the reason I failed in my relationship with God for so many years. I had no spiritual power or real relationship with God. No true relationship. I had to learn how to come back to God and how to take from Him. You see, I thought I was doing well by spending time with God showing Him how much I loved Him and trying to do lots of good deeds in the hope that He would reward me, His faithful servant, but, in truth, God was always there, wanting me to take from Him. He had already done everything that was needed! I was just blind and I couldn't see.

Once I had learned to pray and feel I was taking power from God, I knew I had succeeded in prayer. When I prayed and took blessings from God, I knew that I had succeeded in my prayers and when I prayed and repented of all my sins He let me know that I had succeeded in my prayers.

It wasn't long before our numbers grew and we would meet after work behind the gym in an area I called Apostles' Corner. I tried to answer the men's questions and told them stories about life. I would sit and draw in the dirt, explaining to those who were interested the things I had read about. Like me, the men had no idea that this split in the Church had taken place and that it was now divided.

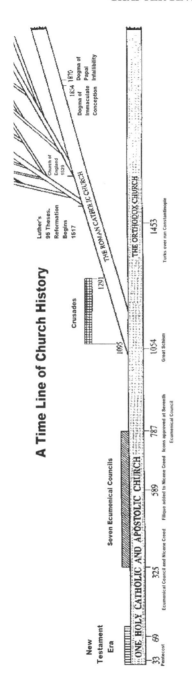

Drawing of split in Church drawn for men in dust and dirt in Apostles Corner.

CHAPTER EIGHTEEN

■ ■ ■ ■ ■ ■ ■ ■

"YOUR MUM'S DEAD!"

One night I had returned from the chapel and was locked away in my cell. I had just completed my prayers and was sitting cross-legged on the bed reading when I heard the sound of marching feet approaching. Suddenly my cell door flew open and three screws stood in my doorway.

"Is your name Buller?" said one.

"Yes?"

Without any further explanation he barked out: "Your Mum's dead!"

They turned on their heels and went to close the door but I managed to stop them by putting my foot in the way. "What do you mean, my mum's dead?" I get three letters a week from her! I got one this morning! How can she be dead?"

The senior officer said "Don't make this difficult for us, boy, we've done all we need to do. Your Mum's dead!"

"Yeah?"

"Yeah, your Mum's dead!"

"You guys are unbelievable. You walk into my cell at eleven o'clock at night and say "Your mum's dead!" No wonder so many men are found hanging in the morning! How do I know it's true?"

I somehow managed to remain calm. "I want to ring my father to confirm this. Can I use a telephone, please?"

"No, you're not entitled to use the phone. It's late."

I started to walk into the corridor toward the wing office and the men followed me, not knowing what to do. I stood by the locked door of the wing office.

"Open the door. I want to call my father to confirm this."

The senior officer opened the door and rang through to the gatehouse. "Hello, yeah, we've told him but he refuses to believe us. He wants to ring his dad!" The officer quickly passed the telephone over to me and I telephoned my father.

"Dad! What's going on? The screws reckon that Mum's died. Is this true?"

My father sounded frail. "I'm afraid so, son. She died suddenly in Greece."

"Sorry Dad, I'll call you tomorrow. Are you OK?"

"Yeah, goodbye son."

The senior officer looked smug. "See, I told you it was true!"

"Thank you. Yes, she is DEAD!" I emphasised the 'DEAD' even though it made me feel sick inside.

They walked me back to my cell and locked the door behind me. With the sound of their retreating footsteps, I knelt on the floor beside my bed to pray.

The following morning, Zak, a fellow inmate, called in to see if I was OK. Zak, a transvestite, was around five foot eleven, with beautiful long brown hair that fell straight down his back to his waist. His classical dark good looks, tender nature and sensitive eyes were overwhelming. He had told me that he was serving a life sentence for GBH for defending himself against an attacker. He held a knife to his throat and inadvertently drew blood and he was convicted and given a life sentence.

"Are you OK Con? I heard the telephone call come on to the wing about your Mum last night."

"What time was that?"

"Eight thirty. I thought it was best to leave it to the morning to see if you were OK. Are you?"

"They never told me until eleven o'clock, Zak!"

"Bastards! The whole wing knew about it before you did then."

"Zak, I'm glad you never mentioned it last night. How can they have left it for so long before they told me?"

"I expect they wanted to go home as it was near the end of their shift."

"You're a good friend Zak. Thanks, I'll be fine."

Zak respected my sexual and spiritual beliefs and never once tried to alter the balance of our friendship by acting inappropriately.

The following day my father came to visit me and the prison visits hall was packed. As I walked into the massive hall, after a body search, I quickly scanned the room for my dad among the sea of stressed faces. I suddenly saw my sister waving her arms at the far end of the hall and began to walk towards her, dodging legs, pushchairs, couples kissing and children scouring the hall for some form of entertainment, totally overwhelmed by the bizarre atmosphere.

Coral leapt at me and gave me an enormous hug. I turned to look at my father, who had recently had his right leg amputated from the knee down. He remained seated and he just nodded.

Coral was trying to hold her tears back. "Costa, how are you?"

"What happened to Mum?"

Coral now began to sob, holding on to me tightly. It seemed that the tighter she pulled on my waist the more she wept and finally she released me.

I turned to my father. "Dad. How are you coping?"

"Not so good, Son, I've got a problem with the circulation in my left leg now. I have to go into hospital tomorrow for an operation."

"What happened to Mum? I had a letter from her yesterday and then they told me that she was dead!"

Coral was trying to control the flow of tears, weeping into handfuls of tissues, which seemed to aggravate her already swollen eyes. We all sat down at the table to talk, holding hands.

My father spoke slowly and softly, in a hoarse, tired tone. "She died suddenly in Greece. That's all we know. Heart attack, probably."

"Are you going to bring her home?"

"No, Sophie has already buried her in the monastery in Killini. They have to bury them quickly out there because of the heat." Sophie, my younger sister, lives with her husband on the island of Zakinthos.

The visit seemed to end quickly with a shout from one of the three screws on duty. He was sat behind a refectory table near the entrance door.

"Finish your visits!"

Richard, my father, shuddered and lowered his gaze on to the floor as Coral sat leaning forward over the table towards me with an incredulous look on her face. "It can't be over yet! We've only just got here. What does he mean, "Finish your visits!"

After an emotional farewell Coral and my dad walked to the sliding door, turned and waved to say goodbye while I joined the queue of men waiting for body searches before leaving the visit hall.

I was on a business studies course and we had all been asked to talk on any subject of our choosing for ten minutes. I chose "Life". When I stood up to talk to the group, Mr Gerard prompted me. "You'll need your notes, Con" he said.

I smiled. "I think I know enough about life to talk without any notes!" and there was a ripple of laughter from the group. "I just need the blackboard and a piece of chalk, if that's OK?"

Mr Gerard, a rather intense man with an enormous stomach and a tanned, wrinkled face, sucked heavily on his unfiltered Woodbine cigarette:"The floor is yours, Con. Tell us all about Life."

I took a deep breath and began. "For those people who don't know me, my name is Constantine Buller. I'm 39 years old. I've previously worked in the police and I've been a broker and a management consultant. I am currently serving a total of 27 years, with a concurrent sentence of 12 years. I am going to talk today about Life." I drew a single horizontal line across the board.

How has my Baptismal gown been stained?
Cleaning my heart and mind...

GOOD THINGS / PASSIONS

1 2 3 4 5 6 7 8 9 10 11 12 13 14 15 16 17 18 19 20 21 22—▶

Birth

BAD THINGS / PASSIONS

I drew a zero at the far left of my line. "When a child is conceived it has a soul. Ideally every child should be conceived in a caring, loving relationship that has been taken to God and blessed in marriage, but, because of man and woman's sinful nature, children are conceived in other ways according to their own will, situation and circumstances. This has led to the murder of untold numbers of innocent children through abortion.

"The environment in which every child enters the world will affect its development for the rest of its natural life. This horizontal line represents an example of a single life. The dot on the far left is conception and the line goes along in years to eighteen, when we are expected to take legal responsibility for our own lives. This isn't something we can take or leave, it is mandatory." I then wrote in the ages from one to eighteen across the top of the line equally spaced them apart.

"Hopefully, we get born into a caring loving family and we have a mum and a dad who take care of us, watch out for us and feeds us. So when we reach the age of eighteen we are properly prepared to make the leap across from our childhood years into the adult world." I then drew a pit at the end of the line of childhood years and a ledge on the other side and drew in a small gate and wrote "Adult World" over it.

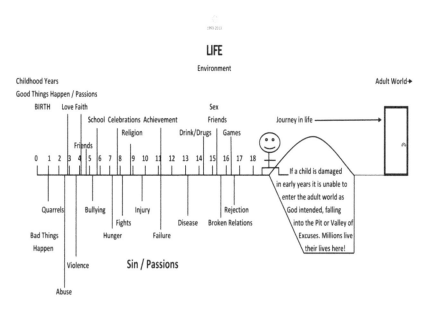

"If all goes well and we have a good life and get to the end of our childhood years, which doesn't necessarily mean eighteen, by the way, we jump across this valley and reach the other side and gain entry into the adult world. So, we should have been properly prepared to make the right choices in life, for a job; a partner, family, home, social groups etc, and we should have a good life. Then, as we walk down the various paths open to us in life we should be able to make good choices for ourselves and the ones we love in life. Lets draw some of these choices in the adult world:

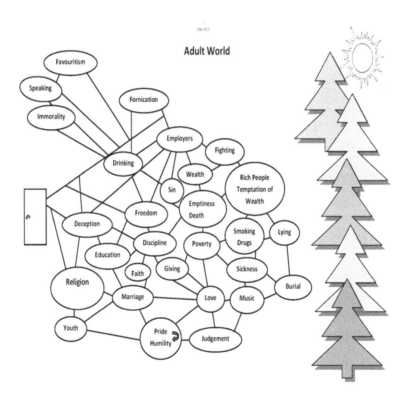

"Unfortunately, when we are growing up, good and bad things happen to us. Things are not always pleasant and it really isn't always our fault because our parents can get it wrong too. They make bad decisions and treat us in bad ways. Some of these ways are very bad for us indeed.

"Now, as you can see, I have gone back to the childhood years and drawn from age one through to eighteen and I'll put "Good Times" on the top and "Bad Times" on the bottom. Good times are things like: birthdays, holidays, starting school, making a friend, going to a party. They get listed on the top as 'good things' and I wrote them in.

"The bad things that happen to us we will list under the line according to the year they happened. Now when I was five I put too much butter on my bread, so my Dad put a whole half pound pack of butter between two pieces of bread and made me eat the sandwich. It was his way of pointing out that being greedy, by putting too much butter between two pieces of bread, was wrong. Well, it made me sick and I then learned how to beg for forgiveness, because he made me carry on eating until I had finished the lot. So that goes under the marker for five years and as bad. Now according to how good or bad you thought that something was, it is a good idea to draw a line relating to the severity of it, so that one was a pretty long line. Can anyone think of any other bad things that can happen to people?"

The group started to come up with suggestions and I wrote them on the board in relation to what they told me. We carried on working with the good and bad incidents in life until I had a fairly full childhood years section and then I moved on.

"OK, so all these bad things and good things have happened to people. When we go to jump across into the adult world we realise that something has gone wrong. We are not ready to make the jump and when we try, we fall into an area, which I call the

'Valley of Excuses'. We've all heard them: "I've been stitched up" or "I was grassed up" or "I can't read very well" or "I just can't get a job."

"They have tried to jump across the valley but they have fallen and are now trapped in the 'Valley of Excuses' and they can often stay there for all their lives; because when you are down there, if you try to climb up the hill to get into the adult world, it is just too steep and you keep falling back in. A bit like you keep seeing the same old characters coming in and out of prison.

"Let's say we do manage to climb up into the adult world and we walk through the gate. We then enter the forest of life, where, as we walk down the various paths offered to each one of us, we hear people telling us what they think the answer is to life. "Get up the gym, the answer is in fitness" or "Have a puff on this, it will make you feel better" or "Have another drink and be happy!" or "You need God, go and pray here!""

We then started to come up with ideas, and drew a whole list of examples in the group of what others perceived as the answer to life.

"That's good, so we now have a pretty good idea of what we are talking about in relation to our understanding of 'life' but when we look up, we see the light of the Sun shining through the trees and we know that there must be something more. We can see the rays of light to prove it, but how do we find the answer to this puzzle.

"In order to discover this we need to go back into ourselves and to find our way back to the point where we jumped into the adult world and then walk back and repair the damage.

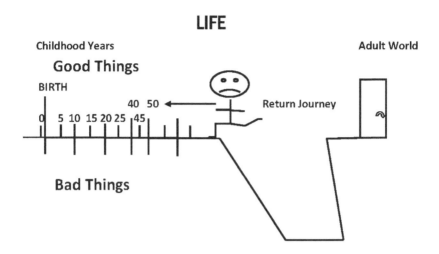

Once we have done that we can then make that jump into the adult world again, and this time make a successful jump and then work our way through to the light behind the trees. Doing this will give us a better chance of making it through the adult world, but if we could just go back into ourselves that bit further we will discover something really special. We will actually find the Sun (Son) and return to being able to walk with God in paradise, today. We don't have to wait until we die, because He is within us, in the here and now! We will then discover a new language, that will lead us through all the trees that life puts in our way and give us true Joy."

I then showed them how to achieve this on my drawing on the board. When I finished ten minutes later the whole group jumped up and started clapping. Every member of the group came to me afterwards and asked if I would help them do the same. As there was nowhere private for me to talk to the men, I asked the Chaplain for a room to listen and pray with them and he agreed that I could use a room in the chapel and help them on their journey. Our group grew larger all the time. The horrendous life accounts of some of these men could fill a book – a book filled with pain and sadness.

I wanted the men to feel better about themselves, so I would cut their hair for nothing. This helped many of the weaker inmates who were depressed and struggling with prison life. It was through the act of giving that I was overwhelmed by how much was given back to me freely, with love.

I was even invited by my Muslim friends to eat with them during Ramadan. I could see no reason, with God's love, to refuse to sit and eat with my friends. The verbal abuse and threats kept being poured out on me every day, but in faith I walked the wings without any physical harm being done to me.

While praying in my cell one afternoon I heard a tap on my door and I called out "Come in!"

It was Arthur, the number one prison Chaplain. "Can I come in?"

The cell was dimly lit but clean and tidy and I said "Yes, of course. Make yourself at home." He smiled nervously.

"We've been praying in the chapel and we believe that God is directing us to ask you if you will be our Chaplain's orderly. The job holds much responsibility and we would like to know if you will take on the job."

I was very surprised and said "Are you sure? Are you really sure that it's God who is directing you?"

Arthur smiled sympathetically. "Yes, we are sure."

I immediately replied "Arthur, you must have made a mistake. I'm the last one to ask to do this job because I am hated by most of the men in here. They hate me with such venom. I'll be a burden to you all."

"Well, we think that God wants you to work in the Chapel."

"How can I argue with Him. I'll do it of course."

CHAPTER NINETEEN

■ ■ ■ ■ ■ ■ ■ ■

FATHER OF LIGHTS

One night I was praying in my cell and had been in a continuous state of prayer for about three hours. My cell was small, no bigger than a bus shelter, with a steel door on the end, and my pictures of Greece were now covering every available space on the walls. I still switched my light off by pressing on my calendar. I had just finished by saying: "Father, God, I am so stupid. Please show me what it is that you want me to do for you? You have to make it really simple for me to understand." I then stood up and pressed on my calendar to turn the light off and noted that it was exactly eleven o'clock. I took my watch off and placed it beside my bed. The security lights outside warmed my cell with an orange light which allowed me to see dimly.

I climbed into my bed and pulled the canvas cover up to my chest and as soon as I closed my eyes I heard a clear audible male voice say: "Open your eyes."

As I was in a single cell, I was shocked to hear someone speak to me inside the cell with the door locked and I immediately opened my eyes. I saw a bright light above my small cupboard the size of a table tennis ball. It was black in the centre and around its circumference was a bright sparkling light, which looked similar to arcing electricity. It was brighter than sparkling diamonds under a bright light.

The hole got larger and larger and I felt a surge of incredible power enter me through my feet and move up through my body, completely paralysing me. I was unable to move and, with my conscious mind frozen, my body started to lift off the bed. I was elevated into the centre of my cell and then I started to move through the bars in the window and the hole was now becoming big enough for me to pass through. I went out of the window and reached a point where my feet were the only parts of my body left in the cell. Then I stopped and began to move towards the hole above my cupboard.

As I looked down my body and into the hole I could see the outline of a man with a beard arced in electricity. He was looking at me as He moved through space. I kept moving closer and closer to him and all around Him was this incredible energy of what appeared to be the bright shining stars in the night sky.

I believed that I was going to go through this hole, but for some reason unknown to me, I was moved back to a point above my bed and slowly lowered back to where my journey had started. The cell was filled with a whirl of holy presence, which gently subsided allowing me to eventually stand. I put my hand up to the window I had just passed through, but now it had returned to its original state - solid. I checked my watch and the time was now five minutes past eleven.

It took me some time to go to sleep that night. In the morning I got dressed and walked up to the chapel with another orderly called Barry. There was normally only one orderly, but the chaplains had employed Barry to help support me while I ministered to the men who kept asking me for help to find God. When I reached out to switch the lights on in the chapel the switching unit gave me an electric shock. At the same time there was a loud bang and the unit caught fire. The flames lapped out from behind the panel some four or five inches and covered my hand.

I barked at Barry "Quick! Go and tell the screws over in the gym that the chapel's on fire!" Barry ran out of the chapel and across to the gym and two prison electricians arrived quickly to examine the damage. By this time the flames had died down but the unit was still smoking heavily. Both electricians were mystified by what had happened and were unable to give a logical account of what had taken place, as the latest electrical equipment had recently been installed. All the senior electrician could say was that there was no way any power surge had come out from the mains side of the unit. The only alternative was a surge of power going into the light switch from an external source.

I decided to ask the chaplains one by one what they thought had happened to me. I explained how I had been lifted off the bed and was taken through the bars on the window. "What was the significance of this hole and the person I saw etched in electricity moving through space, Arthur?" I asked him.

Arthur smiled and said "It's very rare, I think God paid you a visit."

So I asked the same question of them all and they were mystified. I asked Father Anscar, and he couldn't help either. So I said "Surely the Abbot in the Monastery will explain what this is?" Father Anscar agreed to ask him and to see if he would visit me. He was true to his word and about a week later the Abbot came to see me in the chapel. I explained what had happened to me again.

The Abbot responded to my explanation of events."I used to be a scientist and I know the brain generates electricity, so I think it was electricity that caused this to happen" he said.

I wasn't at all convinced. I had deliberately omitted to tell him or anyone the extraordinary phenomenon that I had discovered. I could now lie on my bed and pray and float up into the middle of my cell whenever I wanted to. What was happening to me?

Then Father Anscar became unwell and Father John came in to take the Mass. When I walked into the foyer of the Chapel, Father John was moving from one office to another in front of me. Without a word spoken by either of us, in my mind's eye, I could see into his mind and I sensed him panic. He quickly looked over to me and we made eye contact, and his look was one of disbelief. I could clearly see what he was thinking and he could do the same with me!

I had up to this point been silently repeating the Jesus Prayer: "Lord Jesus Christ, Son of God, have mercy on me, a sinner." Father John was clearly panicking and looking around for somewhere to hide, but any attempt to secrete himself would have been futile and he realised this. So we both stood there looking at each other without needing to speak a word, while knowing everything we were both thinking.

I finally broke the silence. "You know, don't you? Why has this been hidden?"

Father John stayed silent. He quickly looked away, like a thief who had just been caught, and made himself busy getting on with his work in the prison. I was left to do the same. Now I knew there was something going on and it was being hidden. Why? I had to assume that this was a deliberate act of concealment, not just from me but from everyone!

I resigned myself to finding out more. I had to find out more about this secret language. I had stumbled across this mystery in my search for the truth and suddenly it all made sense. There is a noetic unity of mind when one is perfectly in tune with nature, like two cows standing in a field. They are at one with each other and do not need to communicate, like the mysteries of the horse whisperer who is at one with his animal. They just knew and understood without needing to say a word. There's no need for speech!

I started to vacuum the chapel floor, thinking "That's how Noah managed to get all the animals on to the ark!" This 'knowing' was fascinating! I wondered why this secret language had been so carefully hidden from us all. Now I knew that there was another level of spirituality above nature and this was the reason I could elevate in my cell. I had to somehow explore this higher realm in a deeper way.

Later that day, Vicky, a Welsh-speaking female screw who was about five feet tall with bleached blonde hair, was walking along the corridor slamming doors. She did this whenever she was working and she loved to 'bang the men away' at night. As Vicky approached my door she grabbed the handle and tried to slam the door, but I had jammed my foot in the frame. This clearly annoyed her and she shouted: "Get your foot out of the way! Now!"

I looked her straight in the eye. "You clearly enjoy exerting power over men."

Vicky snapped back. "Do you want to be nicked before I go home?"

I moved closer to the gap in the door frame. "Let me just tell you something and I want you to remember this. Every time you close this door, you are closing it on an innocent man."

She was straight back in my face: "They all say that."

"One day you'll learn that I have cleared my name and I just want you to know now that I have forgiven you for what you are doing to me."

My remark had clearly hit home and she said: "Stop it!"

"I am innocent. You can close the door now."

She stood in the doorway, unable to lift her arm to reach the handle of the door.

"You close it then!" she snapped.

"I have already forgiven you. You close it!"

Vicky walked away, leaving me to close the door myself. Each night when Vicky walked past my cell after that, she made sure she left me to close my own door.

More and more men kept approaching me for spiritual help and prayers. They could see the truth in the things I told them and in my faith. One weekend Simon and a group of inmates asked if I would baptise them. This was a first for me and I didn't know what to do, so I took them up to see the Chaplain. I knocked on the door and I recognised Arthur's voice - "Come in!"

I opened the door. "I've got some men here and they are asking for me to baptise them, so I've brought them up to you."

The Chaplain looked shocked. "I can't baptise them! They will have to wait until they get out of prison and then go and see their local priest."

The only thing I could think of saying was "Where does it say that in the Bible? I thought they did it right away in a river."

"That was 2000 years ago!"

"I see. Are you going to tell them that then? If you are I'll send them in." He nodded and five inmates walked into the Chaplain's office.

The Chaplain stood up to explain "We just don't have the facilities here to baptise people I'm afraid. You'll have to wait until you get out and ask your local priest. Sorry."

All five men then walked out without saying a word and waited for me to join them. I was puzzled. "What happened to the piece in scripture when the jailer asks to be baptised then?" I said to the Chaplain.

He looked irritated. "It's different today" he said.

"Not as far as I can see. It's quite clear – 'And he took them the same hour of the night and washed their stripes. And immediately he and all his family were baptised.' In my book, 'and immediately' means straight away!"

"Not here. Sorry."

"Maybe not in the chapel. I understand your position must be difficult, Arthur. They have asked me to baptise them if you refuse. Will you baptise them in the bath on the wing?"

The Chaplain snapped back "If I start baptising men in the bath on the wing everyone is going to think I'm insane!"

I was shocked by his response. "Are you serious?"

"No! It's not happening in this prison!"

"Well they have asked me and I can't see any reason in scripture to refuse them baptism. So I feel duty bound to go ahead and give them what they want."

"That's up to you, but this can't reflect upon me. Sorry."

Later that evening a young man of about twenty-two years walked into my cell as I was about to start my meal. He was around five foot ten, slim, unshaven, with dark brown curly long hair, and he was smirking in a rather bizarre way. I looked deep into his brown, almost black watery eyes and I could see that he was full of pain and sadness.

"Do you mind if I eat my meal with you?" he said.

"Pull up a bed." It was the only place where he could sit. He slowly lowered his body on to the green canvas cover and with his plastic fork he began to pick at his food in an uninterested way.

"You a copper then?" he asked.

"Yeah, they dropped me in by parachute three years ago to find out who was smuggling the 'blow' into Channings Wood. I've finally managed to suss out who it is."

He laughed aloud and his whole face beamed a cheesy grin from ear to ear. "Who is it then?"

"I reckon it's you and you've jammed it in between the cheeks of your arse!"

His laughter was such that his bread roll fell off his plate and on to the floor and he said: "Yeah, how did you know?"

"It's the way you swing your legs when you walk. Can I call it in and go home now? Case solved."

Still laughing, he said: "You're a funny copper."

"What's your name then?"

"Why?"

"Well, look at it this way, when I file my MI5 report tonight, what am I going to tell them? "I don't know the guy's name but he walks like John Wayne." I'd be a laughing stock!"

His laughter increased as did his grin. "You'd grass me up then?"

"No question about it!"

"It's Robin."

"Hi Robin, I'm Con and you're nicked!" and we laughed at the joke together.

Robin became a regular lunchtime visitor, and then started inviting himself in for all his meals. He would just push the door open, walk in and sit on the edge of the bed. Quite often he would sit there and eat his meal without saying a word, and I could tell he enjoyed my company. I never questioned or challenged him, just listened to him if he spoke and then answered any of his questions.

After about a month, Robin came into my cell as usual. He was quiet and deep in thought, but something was clearly troubling him. Suddenly he found the courage to speak out. "I'm going to die."

"Well the mortality rate is 100%, Robin, did someone lie to you about that?" I began to wonder what he was going to tell me. Was he sick? I just let him handle the situation.

"No, I'm going to die soon."

"Yeah?"

"Yeah."

"How do you feel about that, Robin?"

"I'm frightened." His eyes began to fill with tears and he stopped pushing food into his mouth.

"How much time do you have, Robin?"

"Not long. You'll probably throw me out when you find out what I've got."

"Yeah? It's heavy shit then?"

"Yeah."

"Do you want to talk about it?"

"Nah."

"That's cool. Can I have your bread roll before you go?" The mood lifted as Robin laughed for the first time that day.

"Yeah. I'm not going to die that quick though!"

"I meant I'd like it before it falls on the floor, if that's all right?'

"Oh, right."

"If you keep talking it's going to go stale, so as quick as you like!" I cupped my hand in anticipation of catching it. "Come on! I could starve to death before you keel over!"

Robin appeared to find my dry wit and dark humour quite refreshing. "I'd have liked a dad like you."

"Yeah?"

"Yeah. I never knew my dad."

"I don't think my two sons would agree with you there. They've got to be well pissed off with me."

"No?"

"Yes. Life can be shit sometimes, Robin and we don't always know the answers or reasons why. My own sons are probably wondering what they did wrong, but they didn't do anything wrong. They were casualties in all this crap and that makes me feel bad, but I still love them even though I don't see them or hear from them. I hang on to my memories and think of them every day. Maybe your dad does that for you?"

"Yeah, maybe. I'm HIV positive."

"Right. I thought it was something serious!"

Robin looked annoyed as he turned his head towards me. "That's enough shit, isn't it?"

"Look at it this way, Robin, no one's given me a date yet. At least you know that it's very soon! The real question that you should be asking yourself is "Am I ready to go yet?""

"No, I'm too fucking young to die!"

"I can relate to that."

"What the fuck do you know about it?"

"My third son died in my arms and he was only a baby. I tried to bring him back but it was too late. I suppose he would have been more annoyed than you if he thought about it like you do. At least you had twenty odd years of life, eh?"

"Yeah, sorry."

"That's OK Robin, losing him screwed my head up for about five years. I know where he is now though, so I'm cool with it now. Can I ask you a question?"

"What?"

"Why do you need to take drugs?"

Robin laughed: "They take me away from this place. I go where no one can touch me. I'm off me face, stupid."

"You have to come back, though?"

"Yeah, that's the crappy bit about it but you just go and get more."

"But you have to buy it, Robin, that means it must be false, no?"

"It means I have to score another deal, that's all."

"Where I go, Robin, it's free but it costs you everything. It's far better and I don't have to rob houses to go there. Thanks for being straight with me."

Robin stood up and sauntered to the door, leaving me alone to ponder his dilemma.

There was a young lad on my wing called Lenny who was about twenty, medium height and really thin and bony. He had tattooed three teardrops on his right cheek and a falling teardrop below them. Lenny had told me that he had done this when he was bored, and I could tell that he had a terrible passion for 'blow' and tobacco. He'd 'swoop' the wing picking up butt ends off the floor when he was short of money. Being an addict, that meant he was 'swooping' constantly. Shortly after Robin left my cell he returned to tell me that Lenny was in for a PP9'ing and he had fled to the Block for protection.

"Can you have a word with the Vicar and send him some fags, Con?"

"I'll have a word with Arthur later."

"Thanks, Lenny's in debt but tell 'im that the lads have sorted his debt out and he can come back on the wing. OK? Can you do that?"

I wandered over to the Chapel to have a word with the duty minister and explained the situation. "Sorry, there's nothing I can do to help I'm afraid" he said.

"Can I go over there and talk to him?"

"You're not allowed in the Seg. Sorry."

"Well, I'm going to try and see if I can get in."

You don't have a chance, Con. If I get a call from the Duty Officer I will have to deny all knowledge I'm afraid."

"That's OK." I wandered over to the corner of the Chapel and prayed quietly. Then I picked up a bible, wandered over to the Seg and rang the bell. The grumpy duty officer came to the door: "What do you want?"

"Pastoral visit for Date." (That was his last name.)

"Oh, right!" The screw unlocked the gate and let me through and opened Lenny's cell: "I'll put you in the adjudication room. Hang on, you can go into the Governor's office. Give me a shout when you're done."

"Thank you officer, you are very kind."

He closed the door and left us alone and then went back to his office to make himself a cup of tea.

"Hello, Lenny, I've brought you some cigarettes and a comic. Are you alright?"

"Bored but this is great. Thank you."

I reached into my pocket and pulled out half a dozen Mars bars and some sweets and started to explain what Robin had told me. "So you can come out of here, Lenny. You're not going to get PP9'd for being in debt. The lads have settled it for you."

"That's great news."

"Listen, Lenny, if you want me to help you sort yourself out, you're going to have to make a conscious effort to move away from your old habits. Can you do that?"

"Not at the moment, Con. It's just too much."

"That's OK. Listen, when you think you have had enough and you can't take any more, let me know and I will help you. OK?"

"Thanks, Con."

"Is there anything else I can get for you? I can't get you drugs obviously but at least you have something to chew on. The blokes are really worried about you, Lenny. Get your arse out of here as soon as you can, eh?"

"Tomorrow, Con."

"Good man. Anything else, Lenny?"

"Pray for me, Con."

"Would you like me to pray for you now?"

"Would you?"

"What do you want me to pray for, Lenny?"

"Me Mum, Con, she's been really sick for years."

"I'll pray for you as well, Lenny. Close your eyes and try and see a cross in your mind and then lay all your worries at the foot of that cross. Can you see a cross, Lenny?"

"I can, Con!"

"Good. "O God, our help and assistance, You are just and merciful and hear all our prayers of Your people; look down on Lenny, a miserable sinner, have mercy on him and get him away from all his troubles that are attacking him, which You know he deserves to suffer for. He believes and acknowledges, O Lord, that all trials of this life are given by You for punishment when we drift away from You and disobey Your commandments; deal not with Lenny over his wrongdoing but according to Your amazing mercies, for Lenny is the work of Your hands and You know all Lenny's weaknesses. Give him, we beg of You, give him divine helping grace and endow Lenny with patience and strength to endure his difficulties with complete submission, to Your will. You know his misery and the misery of Lenny's Mum and family and friends and to You, Lenny's only hope and refuge to which he flees today for relief and comfort, trusting in Your infinite love and compassion and in time, when You know best, You will deliver Lenny and his Mum from this trouble and turn distress into comfort, when he will rejoice in Your mercy, when he will praise Your holy name, O Father, Son and Holy Spirit, now and ever and unto the ages of the ages. Amen."

Poor Lenny was now sobbing and I noticed in the corner of my eye that the screw was watching us pray. I raised my hand to indicate that we had finished and he walked Lenny back to his cell and locked him away. He walked back to me and we walked to the gate together. The screw was shaking his head like he had just woken from a dream. "Who are you?"

"I'm the Chaplain's orderly."

"You're a con?"

"That's right. I really appreciate you letting me pray with my flock." As I turned to walk through the gate he slapped his forehead with the palm of his hand and locked the gate.

When I walked back into the chapel, the Chaplain was rather surprised. "Did they let you in?"

"Yes and I prayed with Lenny. He should be out tomorrow."

"That's unbelievable!"

I walked back to the wing and knocked on Robin's door. "Hi Robin, the Chaplain wouldn't go and see Lenny so I went instead."

"You're joking. They won't let you in there!"

"Lenny's coming out tomorrow and I told him what you said and prayed with him. So he's good and you can stop worrying about him."

They let you in 'cos you're a copper, eh?"

"I keep telling you, Robin. MI5! Anyway, I've got to go now and file my report before they leave their office tonight."

Robin giggled: "You're a really funny man. I like you, Con, you're a laugh."

"I love you too, Robin."

When I arrived in the chapel the following morning, Arthur had already started the prayers but he stopped and looked up to smile at me.

CHAPTER TWENTY

▰ ▰ ▰ ▰ ▰ ▰ ▰

THE POOL IN THE WOOD

The men kept coming to me and asking me questions about their problems. Simon came into my cell one Sunday afternoon. "Can you to tell me a story about life? I've been asked to prepare one for a workshop tomorrow."

I wanted to be sure that he was being serious, so I said "Like what, a bedtime story?"

"Yes, exactly! A bedtime story. Go on, make one up. Please?"

"OK Simon. I'll tell you an ancient story which means a lot to me. It has a lot of hidden and profound meaning and it relates to our passage through life."

Simon looked really excited and sprang to his feet. "I'll make the coffee and you can tell me it when I get back."

As soon as Simon came back with a steaming jug of water, he opened my cupboard and started to make the coffee. Then Robin arrived.

"Simon reckons you're going to tell us a story. Can I come in and listen to it as well?"

I smiled. "There must be rubbish on in the TV room this afternoon for you lot to be wanting me to tell you a story. Yeah, OK. Simon is making us a coffee at the moment. Take a seat."

Robin jumped on to my bed like a small boy just before being told a story at bed time and my heart melted for him. Just then a rather stinky Jock popped his head around the door. "Simon said you were going to tell us a story. Can I listen? I'll be really quiet!"

"Yeah, the more the merrier, park your bum on my magic bed. I hope you brought your mug with you, Jock?"

With a big silly grin on his face, Jock pulled his plastic mug from behind his back and shouted "Yeah!" He tapped it with his plastic spoon and smacked his lips together.

"You're all going to have to be really good or I'll cut the story short. Agreed?"

They all responded together and my mind flashed back to my story times with Michael and Luke. "OK, so let's begin. Once upon a time in a kingdom far, far, far away, there was a castle and a king and queen lived there. In this kingdom the people did not fight, nor did they do anything dangerous, and the kingdom was huge. They did, however, get bored easily, so the Queen encouraged them to play nice games and to write and play music and just to have fun. For this she praised and rewarded them well.

"One day some of the King's knights wanted to do something really exciting; dangerous even. So they asked the King if they could go hunting in the forest at the edge of the kingdom. The King was not happy with the thought of his knights going into the forest because it was dangerous in there, so he asked the Queen for permission and she was furious. "No way, it's far too dangerous!" she snapped. The King tried to reason with her. "Just agree to three of my bravest knights going and I will say no more" he said. The Queen eventually agreed to his request and after much deliberation, excitement and preparation, three of the King's bravest knights went hunting into the woods. They were just so excited to be doing something so dangerous.

"The King rode with them to the edge of the kingdom and watched them bravely disappear into the forest, then he rode back to his castle. The day passed slowly and the King grew more and more worried about his knights as they failed to return from the forest and he discussed this with his Queen; she too was exceptionally worried for the missing knights.

"As the sun was starting to fall in the sky the Queen ordered that three more knights be sent into the woods to search for the missing men. They were to report back to her as soon as they were able. The King gathered three more knights together and instructed them to search for the missing knights. They too had set off in great excitement and the King and Queen watched as they entered the forest with great interest. These knights were never seen again either. The King and Queen waited and waited for them to return, but they were never heard of again.

"The King was now in despair and he spoke with the Queen regarding the matter. She was not amused. This time they sent out twenty brave knights to search for the missing knights and to bring them all home safely. They too failed to return. Oh dearie, dearie me!

"Well, the Queen was now frantic. She told the King, in no uncertain terms, to decree that no one was ever to go into the woods again. Whoever went in the forest was sure to be killed. The Royal Family would not entertain any requests for permission ever again.

"Now a sort of strange peace fell upon the Kingdom and after a while the Queen gave birth to a son. They really loved their son and the King was always playing with him in the castle. Everything appeared to be well and everyone was very happy indeed. The King and the Queen were so very happy together and their people played on and amused themselves without a care in the world.

"The decree went on for years, until one day a young knight rode in from another kingdom. He approached the castle and shouted for the King. "I want to fight your bravest knight!" he said.

Jock interrupted my train of thought: That's me! I'm always looking for trouble!" and he laughed aloud.

I quickly took control of the situation and said "Jock, if you're going to interrupt, I will have to ask you to leave!"

Jock whined like a scolded dog and said "Sorry. Carry on, I'll be a good boy."

"Anyway, the King left his son and went to see what all the noise was about. The young knight threw out a challenge when he saw the King. "I want to fight your bravest knight!" he screamed. The King was horrified, "Oh" he said "We're a peaceful people and we don't do things like that in this Kingdom."

"The young knight was shocked. "Well," he said, "if no one will fight me, give me something dangerous to do. Yes, that's it! I want to do something dangerous!"

"The King said: "You just don't understand. We don't fight, nor do we do dangerous things in this kingdom. Why not join the others in song?" The young knight was even more shocked. "Well, I really want to do something dangerous to prove how brave a knight I am!"

"The King thought for a moment and said: "The only dangerous thing around here is the forest. The Queen and I have forbidden anyone to go in there and certain death will befall anyone who goes against our decree. I have lost twenty-six of my bravest knights in that forest!"

"The young knight thought briefly and said: "Ah! That sounds just like the sort of thing I've been looking for." He then rode off in the direction of the forest. And his little dog following him close behind.

"As he approached the forest the boy bravely rode in, his little dog following behind. After travelling for some time he came to a pool in the middle of the forest. As he rode past a hand suddenly came out of the water and grabbed hold of his dog. Then the hand and the dog disappeared under the water!

"The young knight didn't get upset, because he realised that he was in the right place. "Ah!" he said, "I must be in the right place, but this task is too much for one man with a small bucket. I must return to the castle and get some help."

"So the young knight returned to the castle. He asked the King for six men and seven buckets and the King gave him what he asked for and they returned to the forest. He led them to the pool and the young knight ordered that it be emptied. They all worked long and hard for many days and eventually they emptied the pool. Lying at the bottom of the pool was a very small child and a hairy old man. He set the child free and the young knight ordered that the hairy old man be apprehended. He was tied up and taken back to the castle.

"The Queen was well pleased. She ordered that a cage be built and the hairy old man be put in it for everyone to see. She ordered the King to forbid anyone to open the locked cage and he left the golden key in the safe keeping of the Queen. She hid it under her pillow and everyone went back to singing, drinking, dancing and having fun.

"The people were happy now because the mystery of the forest had been solved and the kingdom quickly got back to normal. The King and Queen's son started to grow up quickly and on his eighth birthday the King gave him a beautiful golden ball as a present. He was thrilled with his ball and played with it for hours. This activity occupied him for most of the time.

"But then one day, as he was playing, the golden ball rolled away from him and entered the old man's cage. The King's son was horrified and ran away because he knew that if anyone went near the cage they would surely die. As time passed the King's son began to miss his golden ball more and more. One day he became brave enough to approach the cage. He said to the hairy old man: "Can I have my ball back please?"

"The hairy old man smiled, as he was well pleased with the boys bravery and said: "You must do something for me." The King's son was keen to listen and said "Yes, what is it I have to do for you?"

"The hairy old man stood up and went to the boy and said, "If you open the cage I will give you back your golden ball."

"The King's son was horrified. He ran away, because he was sure that he would be killed if he released the old man. Some considerable time passed and the King's son grew stronger and more daring. He approached the cage again. This time he was more assertive and snapped: "Give me my ball back!"

"The hairy old man smiled more broadly still. "You must release me before I give you your golden ball! One favour deserves another" He said.

The boy replied: "I can't do that, the King won't let me!" and again he ran away.

"More time passed and the King's son became more determined to get his golden ball back. When his parents were out, he went back to the hairy old man's cage. Once again he asked for his golden ball back.

Again the hairy old man said: "You must release me before I give you back your golden ball."

"The King's son thought carefully and said "I do not have the key to let you out."

"The hairy old man smiled broadly, because he knew that the

boy had no idea where the King had hidden the key. He said: "The golden key is hidden under your mother's pillow."

"The King's son was filled with dread, for he knew that his mother would never give him the key if he were to ask for it. He knew that in order to retrieve the key he would have to steal it. With that he ran away to the castle, crept into his mother's bedroom and looked under her pillow. He found the golden key! He ran down the castle steps to the cage, but in his haste to unlock it he cut his finger.

"The old man was fully clad in black. The only part of his body that could be seen was his face, which was covered with a long unkempt beard. He stooped to exit the cage and his long flowing black cloak fell to cover his ankles. He bowed gracefully with his right palm open on his chest, but as he began to leave he could hear the boy sobbing. The old man stopped, turned to face the boy and said quietly: "You have your ball, what is it that you want now?"

The King's son wiped away his tears and said: "If you leave me here they are sure to kill me!" He knew full well that it was forbidden to speak to or release the hairy old man and the punishment would be very severe.

The old man said: "Well, what do you want to do?" He thought briefly and said: "Go with you!"

"The old man said "You do know that if you come with me you can never return here?" The King's son nodded his head in agreement and the old man lifted him on to his shoulders, covered him with his cloak and ran with him into the forest.

"When the King and Queen returned they immediately noticed the empty cage. They searched and called for their son, but there was no answer. They soon guessed what had happened and great grief and mourning fell upon the Royal Family. Ah!"

Jock was unable to keep his mouth shut "The bastard! Is that the end?"

"Not yet, Jock. We've drunk a lot of coffee, who needs to go to the loo?"

All three of my guests left quickly to use their own toilets and were back in an instant, seated on the bed and waiting for the rest of the story.

"When the hairy old man had reached the forest he put the boy down and said: "You will never see your parents again. I will keep you with me and if you do all I ask, things will go well for you. I have much treasure, worth more than any Kingdom on the earth.""

"After walking some distance under the protection of his black cloak, the old man stopped and they both rested beside a beautiful crystal clear pool which was fed by a gentle shimmering waterfall.

"The following day the hairy old man said to the boy, "I must go away for the day. If you want me to take care of you, you will have to do something for me. Guard the crystal pool and be sure that nothing, under any circumstances, falls into it. If anything goes into the pool it will wrong the pool, and that will be very bad".

"The boy agreed, as he thought that his task was a simple one. While the hairy old man was away the boy lay by the pool and soon became bored. As he started to relax, he became aware of his injured finger. It was now throbbing quite badly with pain. "No one will know if I cool it in the pool" he thought, so he leaned over the edge and dipped his finger into the cool water. But as soon as his finger touched the water, it turned to gold. He pulled it out quickly and tried to wash it, but the gold would not wash off. The boy was in quite a panic, as he knew that the old man was soon to return.

"When the old man returned he said to the boy, "Has anything happened with the pool today that I should know about?"

"The boy held his finger behind his back and decided to lie: "No, nothing at all!"

"The hairy old man looked at him and said "You are lying! Your finger hurt and you tried to cool it in the pool and it turned to gold."

"The boy was shocked that the hairy old man knew what had happened. He said "I will correct it this time, but if you wrong the crystal pool again, it will be very serious indeed!"

"The boy promised faithfully that he would not do anything wrong ever again.

"The following day the old man said to the boy "I must go away for the day. Do you promise that you will look after the crystal pool and under no circumstances let anything fall into the water?" The boy did not need to think twice as he wanted to please the hairy old man. "Oh yes, I promise!" he said and so the hairy old man went off for the day.

"The day passed slowly and the boy soon grew bored again and he wondered if he could see his reflection in the crystal pool. He got close to the edge and was very careful not to lean over too far. However, a single hair fell from his head into the water. As soon as it touched, he caught it, but it was too late; the hair had turned to gold.

The boy was sure that the hairy old man would never notice that a single hair had wronged the pool, so he hid it in his pocket.

"When the hairy old man returned, he knew what had happened. He asked the boy the same question: "Did anything happen today?" Again the boy decided to lie and said: "No, nothing!"

"The old man was very angry. He said "You are a liar! A single hair fell from your head into the crystal pool. As it touched the water you caught it and it turned to gold.""

"The boy was amazed. He pleaded with the old man for one final chance. The man agreed, but now he gave a stern warning. "If this happens a third time, you will not be able to stay here any longer" he said. The boy promised faithfully that he would not do anything wrong ever again.

"On the third day the hairy old man left the boy once again by the crystal pool. After a while he wondered whether he could see his reflection in the water and he had the desire to look straight into his own eyes. He went right up to the edge and leaned over further and further.

"Just as he saw his reflection in the water a lock of his hair fell forward. He pulled his head back quickly, but it was too late. Every hair on his head was like the array of pure gold. He didn't know what to do and he started to panic. His hair shone like the sun itself and he took a scarf from his pocket and tied it around his head to hide his shame.

"It was not long before the hairy old man returned. He was furious, because again he knew what had happened. The boy tried to make an excuse, but the hairy old man would not listen. "You will have to leave! You cannot stay here!" he said. "I will give you one gift. If ever you should be in real trouble, come to the edge of the forest and call my name three times."

"So that night the boy left. After two days of walking he came to the edge of the forest.

"When he came out of the forest he found himself in another kingdom. He took a muddy path through the hills and after walking for some hours he came to a large city. He tried to find some work but no one would employ him because he had no trade. By this time he was hungry and tired and his whole body ached.

"As a last resort he went to the King's castle, which was beyond the city. He knocked at the kitchen door and the cook answered and let him into the kitchen. She took pity on him and fed him and gave him something to drink.

"The young boy told the cook how he came to be in the Kingdom and what had happened to him. As he was about to leave the cook offered him a job, working with her in the kitchen. He was delighted and promised to be a good helper to her.

"The days passed happily and the cook kept the young boy busy carrying wood and water and raking the cinders. She grew to like him more and more and they became good friends. He always wore his scarf and never would be seen without it wrapped around his head, because he was so ashamed of the wrong he had done and of the colour of his hair.

"The cook would take the King's food up to his quarters, as was the custom. Then one day the cook was unwell. She had prepared the King's meal, but she was unable to climb the stairs to take the food to him. She asked the young boy if he would take the food to the King for her.

As he went into the royal chambers, the King let out a mighty roar. "Why have you got your head covered before your King? No one covers their head before me! You must take off your tarbush!"

"The young boy was terrified and quickly thought of an excuse. "I have a sore place on my head" he said. The King was furious and called the cook. She managed to climb the stairs to see the King and he ordered her to explain. The young boy still refused to remove his scarf, so the King ordered him to go from his kingdom and to never return.

"Now the cook felt sorry for the young boy and asked the gardener if she could swap him for his son, who could help her. So the young boy started working in the gardens. He worked hard to try and impress the head gardener.

"One sunny day, when the young boy was working on his own, he became so hot that he removed his scarf. He used the scarf to wipe away the beads of sweat from his brow and to cool his head. As he did this, the sun caught his golden hair and set it alight with incredible colour and the light reflected into the bedroom of the King's daughter.

"The King's daughter was sitting bored in her room. When she saw this beautiful light reflecting into her room, she quickly went to the window, where she caught a brief glimpse at the young boy and his golden hair. She was truly intrigued by this boy.

"The Princess then ordered her servant to get the young boy to pick some flowers for her. The message went through the house to the head gardener and he ordered the boy to pick some flowers for the Princess and to take them to her. So the young boy picked some wild flowers for her and was walking back to the castle when an angry head gardener stopped him. "Why have you picked wild flowers for the Princess? You must go and pick her flowers from the King's garden!"

"The young boy looked surprised and said "The Princess will like wild flowers more, as they have a stronger fragrance." He then continued to walk past the head gardener and entered the castle. He went up to the Princess's bedroom and knocked on her door. The Princess opened her door and saw the young boy wearing his headscarf standing there before her."

Jock barked in "What a woofter!"

"Jock! You have already been warned" I said. Then I continued. "The Princess invited the boy into her room and she took the wild flowers from him. She was thrilled with them. Then she said: "Remove your scarf and rest a while.""

"Oh, no, I can't do that. I have the mange!" said the boy.

"The Princess gave the boy some gold coins and he left and

returned to his work in the garden. The young boy didn't know the value of gold, so he gave the coins to the head gardener for his children to play with.

"Now the Princess could only think of the young boy and would dream about his beautiful golden hair. The following day the same thing happened, but this time, when the Princess gave him the gold coins, she pulled at his scarf and it fell from his head and all his golden hair fell to his shoulders. The Princess stood watching in amazement. The boy really was speechless! He quickly put his scarf back on and immediately left her room.

"Some time had now passed and the King was drawn into a war with a neighbouring kingdom. All the King's knights immediately prepared for battle and this created a lot of excitement. The King was unsure of winning the war as his enemies were more powerful, for they retained a large army.

"The young boy asked the head gardener if he could go to war, but he was told that he was too young. However, he was determined. He went to the stables where the knights and the horses were. He pleaded with the knights to let him have a horse and armour to go to war, as he really wanted to be able to fight with them.

"The knights laughed at him and they refused to give him the opportunity to fight. After some joking, they said they would leave him with a horse that he could ride into battle with, if he really wanted to fight for the King. When they had left the boy was to go to the stables to collect his horse and armour. The young boy was obviously thrilled at being given this opportunity."

Jock was back into the story. "Yeah! Fight the bastards!" he roared.

"OK, Jock! The knights rode off into battle and the very excited young boy raced to the stables to see what horse he had been left. It turned out that he had been left with a wooden sword and shield and a horse with only three good legs! But he was still determined to go into battle, so he rode the three-legged horse through the streets. All the women laughed at the sight of him. He rode the horse to the edge of the forest and in desperation he called out for the hairy old man three times, as he had been told: "Old Man! Old Man Old Man" He called from his heart.

"At once the hairy old man came to the edge of the forest and said: "Yes, what do you want?"

"I want to go into battle because the King is at war and his enemies are stronger than him. The knights have left me with a three-legged horse and a wooden sword and shield. Can you help me with this?"

"The hairy old man smiled and asked "Is that all you want?"

"Yes, that's all I need!" said the young boy. So the hairy old man said: "As you have not been greedy, I will give you this request, and more!"

"The old man left and quickly returned with a beautiful black horse which was very powerful. There was also a set of black armour, which the boy put on immediately, and he took the powerful sword and shield. He really felt powerful now and confident.

"Suddenly four hairy old men came out of the forest on horseback and the King's son rode with them into battle. When he saw where the battle was raging, he lifted his sword high and cried "Attack!"

"The King was on the brink of defeat, but when he looked up and saw the men riding into battle he felt new hope and was greatly encouraged. The King's son and his four hairy men slaughtered the enemy and chased the deserters, killing every single one of them.

"The King's son returned to the edge of the forest and called the hairy old man again three times. When he appeared he gave him back the four hairy men, his horse and armour in exchange for his own and returned to the garden, where he told the head gardener of his victory. The head gardener felt that this fine young man was making it all up, but at the same time he listened and praised him for his courage.

"Now when the King returned from battle he told his story to the Queen. He explained about the victory and how four hairy men in black cloaks and shields and a black knight who led them into battle on a powerful black horse had saved them. The Queen listened intently and was very grateful to have the King home again.

"As the days passed, the King became really curious. He wanted to know who had saved him and his kingdom from defeat, as no one had come forward and claimed the victory. The Princess was suspicious and asked the whereabouts of the boy in the garden on the day in question. The head gardener confirmed that the boy had been away that day and had returned in a very excited state, speaking of fighting a great battle.

"The King called for a tournament to be held and every knight in the kingdom was to be present. Now, the King's son really did want to attend the tournament, but the other knights again gave him the same lame horse. The King's son rode the horse to the edge of the forest and again called out to the hairy old man. "Old Man! Old Man! Old Man!" Within a moment the hairy old man was there.

He looked at the boy and said "Yes, what is it you want now?"

"The King is having a tournament and I must go! Can I borrow a horse and armour again?"

"The hairy old man said "Is that all you want?"

"The boy thought briefly and said "Yes, that's all I need."

"The hairy old man said "As that is all you have asked for, I will give you your request, and more!" He left for a moment and returned with a beautiful gleaming chestnut horse and blood red armour, a red lance and a powerful matching sword and shield. He also gave him two hairy men, similarly dressed, to ride with him to the castle as an escort. The old man watched the King's son ride off to the tournament. He was very proud of him indeed.

"The tournament was spectacular and the brave knight fought all day long and won every event. At the end of the day, the King called all the knights together and said, "Whoever catches the Golden Ball will have the hand of my daughter, the Princess, in marriage." This caused great excitement! The Princess could see all the knights gathered together in their full armour and she watched as her father threw the Golden Ball.

"The Golden Ball immediately fell into the hands of the young knight, the King's son, who at once turned his horse and rode away across the fields. He reached the forest and gave back the horse and men and all his armour in exchange for his lame horse. Then he returned to the garden and resumed his work as if nothing had happened. The King's son saw no use in the Golden Ball, so he gave it to the Head Gardener to give to his children to play with.

"The King was very annoyed that the young man had ridden away without claiming the Princess, so he called his closest knights together to consider what action he should take. It was agreed that they should watch the movement of this knight very closely the next day and should he try to leave, as before, he should be apprehended and brought before the King.

"At the beginning of the second day, the young knight rode his crippled horse to the edge of the forest and called for the hairy old man, who again enquired of him what he wanted. He repeated his request for a horse to go to the second day of the tournament.

The old man asked him "Is that all you want?"

The young knight said: "Yes. That is all I need."

"As that is all you have asked for, I will give you more!"

"This time the hairy old man gave him a beautiful white horse and a suit of white armour, a matching lance, sword and shield and two hairy men to ride as an escort to the castle. Again they rode off and again the hairy old man was well pleased with the King's son. He rode bravely into the castle grounds and all the people were in awe of his splendour.

"The second day of the tournament passed well and the young knight won all of his matches. Again, at the end of the day, the King called all the knights together and repeated his pledge regarding the Golden Ball. The Princess was really excited now and she waited with great anticipation. When the great moment came, the king threw the ball and again the young knight caught it. It seemed to fall straight into his hand.

"He turned his horse and started to ride away. The King's knights were trying to follow, but they were quickly lost. The young knight once again went back to the forest and returned the horse and men and his armour was exchanged for his own. Then he rode back to the garden and carried on as normal. The King's son saw no use in the Golden Ball, so he gave it to the Head Gardener to give to his children to play with.

"The Princess was now getting very suspicious. She asked the head gardener where the young boy had been on the days of the tournament. He confirmed that he had been away from his place of work on those days.

"The King called all his knights together and this time he was furious. He gave strict instructions that if on the third and final day of the tournament it should happen again, the young knight should be pursued and wounded in order to assist in identifying him.

"On the third day of the tournament the boy rose early and went to the edge of the forest with his crippled horse to call for the hairy old man. Once more he came to him. He repeated his request for a horse and this time he was given a beautiful and incredibly powerful black horse, together with a set of black armour with a long flowing black robe, black lance, sword, shield, breastplate and helmet. He also gave him two hairy men who were dressed in similar attire. They looked glorious and at the same time sombre as they entered the castle to gasps of surprise.

"Again the tournament went well and the young knight won all of his matches. At the end of the day the King called all the knights together. This time his men were ready and waiting. When the Golden Ball was thrown it fell into the young knight's hand and he immediately turned his horse around. Together with his men they started to gallop at speed towards the gate to the drawbridge.

"The King's men were directly behind them. They dashed across the fields until the King's strongest knight drew close enough to pierce the young knight's left leg with his lance. He reeled back in pain and his helmet fell to the ground.

"The knights were amazed. All they could see was a flowing mass of beautiful long golden hair which shone like the sun. The King's son returned to the edge of the forest and returned the horse and men and took back his old armour and carried on as normal. Again he saw no use in the golden ball, so again he gave it to the Head Gardener to give to his children to play with.

"The King's knights reported what they had done and seen and the King listened intently, as did the Princess. She immediately thought of the boy in the garden, so she told her father of this boy. He thought carefully and said "We must challenge him!"

So the King and the Princess went into the garden and approached the boy, who had only just returned from the edge of the forest. The boy admitted that it was he who had rescued the King in the great battle and he was also the same boy who had been in the tournaments.

The King immediately embraced him and gave him half of his kingdom and the hand of his daughter in marriage. They married in great splendour and lived happily ever after.

"The end!"

The three men sat on my bed were speechless for some time and then Jock said "I liked your story, Con. Thank you."

Simon was looking rather puzzled and rubbed the back of his head:

"Why can't we have a happy ending? My life's shit!"

Jock looked really sad now and his eyes had a faraway look. "My life's shite, Con. Absolute shite!" The other two nodded in agreement quietly.

Simon decided to speak out, trying to grasp what I had been talking about. "So all we need to do is go and get some help, empty the pond and find a hairy old man, don't get bored or do things wrong or you will end up looking like some blonde tart and you'll have to ride a wonky horse!"

Everyone started laughing hilariously until the sound of keys and a screw shouting out in the hallway broke into our rather humorous conversation. "Back to your own cells now! It's bang up! Let the pied piper get some rest! Rats, mice, cockroaches, fleas, bugs, flies, ants and wasps; in your own cells before I get cross!" They all quietly filed out of my cell holding their empty plastic mugs and as I closed the door behind them I heard him bark: "Move it! Move it!"

I turned to lie on my bed and thought "They're still like young boys". I lay flat on my back, slowly crossed myself, invoking the power of the Holy Trinity and resumed the repetition of the Jesus Prayer: "Lord Jesus Christ, Son of God, have mercy on me a sinner." I was clearing my mind of all images and reasoning to bask in the flow of His Holy Spirit, which welled up inside me and spilled up from my heart to flow like a tap and run down my face and over my ears and on to the green canvas cover that covered my bed. Heaven. Union with Him in silence sublime.

CHAPTER TWENTY ONE

■ ■ ■ ■ ■ ■ ■ ■

ROBIN

On the Wednesday evening Robin walked into my cell, sat on the bed and began to eat his roast chicken dinner with a plastic spoon. The smell of his food was quite overwhelming and it quickly filled the cell. He kept pushing his long black hair back away from his face and tucking long matted strands behind his ears as he quickly fed himself. The curtain was closed but there was still a diffused dull amber light which broke through the striped pattern of the curtains that stretched across my small window. The dim light made Robin's irises look almost black and this seemed to emphasise his inner grief.

With a mouthful of food churning around in his open mouth and his spoon sticking up out of his clenched fist he said: "Are you eating today, Hairy Old Man?"

He had listened and I smiled and said: "Not today."

"Why?"

"I don't feel like eating anything today, Robin."

"You never ate anything yesterday or the day before! I'd die if I went without my food for just one meal! Are you ill?"

"I'm fine, Robin. Really."

"I reckon you're fasting for some reason. So why do you fast, Hairy Old Man?" There was a lengthy silence in the cell and

Robin spoke again "If you don't want your food, can I have it?"

"If you need it, take it."

"You'll have to get it for me 'cos the screw has already ticked me off the list."

"I'll go and get it for you, Robin." and I got up and left the cell.

"When I returned Robin had finished his meal, so we switched plates. Dropping his chicken bones in the bin, I washed his plate, dried it up and put it on the bed and sat down to keep him company while he carried on eating.

He still looked puzzled and said: "Go on, why?"

I didn't want to expound on the reasons for fasting and I had gone to great lengths to conceal my fast. I said: "Why what?"

"Why do you fast, Old Man? Things are bad enough in prison without starving yourself."

This was a good question and I had tried to conceal certain elements of my spiritual life from the inmates. This one was very personal, but it was a good question that warranted an answer. I fell silent again, bringing mind to heart.

Robin grew impatient and wanted an answer and he wasn't going to give up and so he broke the silence. "I won't say anything to anyone else and the screws won't find out if you're on hunger strike? I've been watching you, that's all."

"I fast to remind my physical body that my spiritual body has greater power over it and that it must be obedient in all things or my spiritual body will crush it!"

"That sounds scary! Crush is a heavy word to use." The room fell silent again. "You're the real thing, ain't ya?"

"I don't understand, Robin?"

"You're not a phoney, I can see that. I've never met anyone like you before."

"Neither have I, Robin, I haven't met anyone like you either. You'd be a charming son for any Dad to have. I'm here for you if you ever feel like talking?"

"Nah, I'm just bad and you wouldn't want me as a son. If I bit you you'd die as well! Then you'd understand how I'm feelin'."

"Did someone bite you to get what you have?"

"No, I got it from sharing a needle."

"Oh, right. Is that what makes you so angry?"

Robin's mind wandered off for a moment before he spoke again. "Suppose. I'm too young to die! It's all right for you, you've had a life."

"I'm already dead. You just need to climb up that mountain again, Robin."

"What bloody mountain?"

"The one inside you. I met a monk a long time ago and he went to Mount Athos in search of the truth. He wasn't satisfied with half or three quarters, he wanted union with God, today! He was my priest when I was about twelve years old and he told me a story of an old man he knew."

"Is this another one of your stories? I like your stories."

"Thank you, that's the nicest thing anyone has ever said to me in a very long time. I like telling you my son's stories."

"Go on then! Tell me the story, Hairy Old Man."

"You don't need to go to Mount Athos to climb the mountain he was searching for, Robin; even though Mount Athos is a really holy place. You just need to turn inward."

"Inward?"

"Yes, go inside yourself and face the pain and what you've done. That's not an easy call, because not all of what's in there is down to you."

"That's the pond in the forest in your last story, isn't it?"

"I suppose so."

Robin thought for a moment. "So why did all the knights take the piss out of the boy then, you know, giving him a bullshit horse and stuff to fight with? That wasn't right, was it?"

"He wasn't deterred though, was he?"

"Robin was interested and was trying to work things out. "Yeah, but he wasn't going to win in a proper battle, was he?"

I moved forward towards Robin. "He believed in himself and knew that the hairy old man would help him, because he promised him, didn't he?"

Robin smiled "Yeah, he gave him some kick arse gear, didn't he."

"That's right Robin, but that was because he only asked for what he needed and nothing more and then the hairy old man gave him more."

"Yeah, I see that. It's still complicated though."

"Maybe."

"What about this story, then?"

"Ah, the story! Well, it's more of a conversation really. It's about an old man who is being asked about the same thing, fasting and life, you know?"

"An old man like you?" Robin laughed quietly, smiled and waited a few moments, and pointing expectantly at me with his plastic spoon. "And?"

I opened my folder of poems and pulled out the relevant one:
"OK, Robin. *The old man's son approaches him and asks:*
"Old man. Why do you fast?"
He said: "Beloved boy, I fast to know what it is I lack.
For day by day I sit in abundance, and
all is well before me;
I want not, I suffer not, and I

lack but that for which I invent a need.
But my heart is empty of true joy,
filled, yet overflowing with dry waters.
There is no room left for love.
I have no needs, and so my needs are never met,
no longings, and so my desires are never fulfilled.
Where all the fruits of the earth could dwell, I have
filled the house with dust and clouds;
It is full, so I am content -
But it is empty, and so I weep.

"Thus I fast, beloved, to know the
dust in which I dwell.
I take not from that which I might take,
for in its absence I am left empty,
and what is empty stands ready to be filled.
I turn from what I love, for my love is barren,
and by it I curse the earth.
I turn from what I love, that I may purify my loving,
and move from curse to blessing.

"From my abundance I turn to want,
as the soldier leaves the comfort of home,
of family and love,
to know the barrenness of war.
For it is only among the fight, in the
torture of loss, in the fire of battle,
that lies are lost and the blind man clearly sees.
In hunger of body and mind, I see
the vanity of food,
for I have loved food as food,

and have never been fed.
In weary, waking vigil I see
the vanity of sleep,
for I have embraced sleep as desire,
and have never found rest.
In sorrow, with eyes of tears I see
the vanity of pleasure,
for I have treasured happiness above all,
and have never known joy.

"I fast, beloved child, to crush the wall that is myself;
For I am not who I am, just as these passions
are not treasures of gold but of clay.
I fast to die, for it is not the living who are
raised, but the dead.
I fast to crucify my desires, for He who was
crucified was He who lived,
and He who conquered,
and He who lives forever."

Robin looked most uncomfortable. "So I'll get raised from the dead if I fast? That sounds like bullshit to me!"

I was finding it very difficult to explain the unexplainable to Robin "All of this is just too much for you to understand right now, Robin, but if you clean your heart and mind, as He asks us to do, God will finally bless us with union with Him today and save us. It's never too late to take action and start that journey, but it does mean a lot of hard work initially. You can't just say a quick prayer and "Bosh!" it's done. It would be like me asking to be a Christian and someone throwing a white sheet over my head and saying "That's it, now you're a Christian! Praise the Lord!"

I would look white on the outside but inside I would still be the old me and have all the rubbish of my old life laying inside me."

Robin looked at me in disbelief . "That might be right but I like my food too much to fast!"

"That's just your body calling, Robin. You need to strengthen your spiritual body and let it rule your carnal body and not the other way around.

Robin started laughing "Life's too tempting to let go and I want to hang on in there. Have a look at this." He passed me a personal letter and I opened it and read it quietly. When I had finished, I checked the name and address.

"Who's Becky?"

"She's a friend of my mates missus. She started to write to me a few months back."

"Has she visited you yet?"

"A couple of times."

"Have you told her?"

"What?"

"Have you told her what you told me?"

"Ain't none of her business really."

"It is if she is going to do what she's saying in her letter."

"That's up to her."

"Don't you think you should tell her; you know, be honest with her?"

"What's the point?"

"She's got a little girl. How old is she?"

"Two, her names Gemma."

"The point is, if you don't tell her and you let her do what she's describing, you're signing her death warrant. Little Gemma is going to be without a mum!" Robin shrugged his shoulders and puckered his lips in a non caring way. "Doesn't that bother you?"

"Like I said, it's up to her. I'm not making her do that."

"Do you want me to tell her for you?"

"Nah. I'll just see what happens."

"If you don't tell her and she has sex with you without protection you are going to kill her! What about her little girl, Robin?"

Robin shrugged his shoulders again. "Like I said, that's her problem."

"Come on Robin, you can't do that to the girl, surely?"

"Why not?"

"Because it's wrong. You're better than that; just tell her and she'll be cool about it, you'll see."

"I don't care, I'm not telling her!"

"But you're seeing her next week and she's booked a hotel room for your day release! You have to tell her!"

"It's got nuffink to do with you, so leave it."

"But you've told me about it. That means you've involved me now."

"Just forget about it, I shouldn't have told you!"

"But you have. I can't just sit back and say "Good one, Robin, that'll learn 'er" can I? That's a burden you're putting on my conscience now."

That's no big deal."

"It is for me, I've dragged through all my old life and I've cleaned my heart. I don't want a thought like that resting in there. You've made me part of this situation now! I don't even know Becky but I care about her wellbeing and Gemma's, why don't you?"

"I care about them."

"If you did, if you really cared about them, you'd tell her, Robin."

"No! Mind your own business. Just tell me where this heart is."

"It's a mystery, Robin. Here you have to rule over three destructive powers, Ignorance, forgetfulness and laziness. When you think that you are ready and want to move forward and attack these three evils, just let me know."

Pointing to his human heart he said: "So if the heart that you speak of isn't here, where is it?"

"I will try to reveal this to you in words, Robin, but because you are lost in the land of slavery, you may not be able to see across the wilderness to the promised land which lies beyond just words, while you are singing hymns in church and attending meetings. You have to wage war against the three evils, as I mentioned earlier."

"I don't go to church and I wouldn't want to sing or listen to a preacher giving it large. So where is the ascetic heart, Hairy Old Man?"

"Man has cut himself off from God through sin and disobedience for the passions and pleasures of this carnal world, but deep within him he craves for union with God. He fell away from God because of his own intellect, you know the story of Adam and Eve. He thought he knew better, a bit like the boy at the crystal waterfall. He was disobedient.

"So man needs to give back to God what he stole in the beginning, his reasoning and images of his own fancy, in truth all reasoning, images and fantasies and then man can come back to God as a small child. This is when man goes into the wilderness, clears out all his baggage and waits for God to part the waters in his mind so that he can cross on to the other side where he is gifted with union with God, who speaks to you through your conscience and intuition. When man achieves this, which is very difficult, he opens up his mind through illumination. In the Orthodox Church we call this Theoria. The Kingdom of Heaven is within you, Robin, but you are blind and just can't see this at the moment.

"The spiritual heart of man is hidden in a mystery between the intelligence (mind) and intuition and conscience, which is where God is trying to talk to you! He's waiting to give to you his promise."

Robin climbed off my bed slowly and said: "So the pool in the forest is what? My soul?"

"Yes, very good Robin! The wise man goes back to get help because he is wise and brave and he knew that he couldn't clear out all the dross on his own, which would be like him using one little bucket. Once he got help the pool got cleared out really quickly. Like I said before, if you want someone to talk to, just let me know."

"Where would I start?"

"Receiving Jesus Christ is an internal struggle, Robin. When the mind descends into deep heart, which is located between your intellect and conscience, through God's grace you will be regenerated to unite with Him and this will heal the original fall of Adam, together with all you have done, to put you back in the garden. Death to passion and sin in order to attain union with God. TODAY!"

I opened one of my five bibles and turned to read from St John Chapter 1 verse 12:

"But as many as receive Him, to them He gave the right to become children of God, to those who believe in His name: who were born, not of blood, nor of the will of the flesh, nor of the will of man, but of God." God, through grace and His Son, opened the door for man to regenerate himself in order to re unite himself to God and through obedience, having purified his mind, body and soul, receives His Body and Blood and becomes a created god, the second Adam.

"We must present the pure bride, our souls, to the Bridegroom, Christ, pure and clean or we will continue to wait and suffer by the pool. How can the Bridegroom come? Robin, just ask yourself four questions:

Should I:
   a) wait until I die in the condition of the fallen 1st Adam
   b) remain by the pool, drifting in and out of Grace
   c) purify my soul to receive the Bridegroom today
      while I still have time
   d) just say, "it's all too much, I'll wait for Judgement"?

If you make the right choice, you will then come to learn the true fear of God, which is to have found the Bridegroom and attained this union with Him. Then any thought of life without this Communion is terrifying."

Robin pulled open my door and walked out of my cell deep in thought. I went over, gently pushed it shut and lay on my bed. By invocation: "In the name of the Father, and of the Son, and of the Holy Spirit" I kept repeating the 'Prayer of the Heart' until I had taken this inner calling into my mind's eye. "Lord Jesus Christ, Son of God, have mercy on me, a sinner." I kept repeatedly calling to Him for mercy from deep within me with this prayer, and I gently held Robin up in my mind's eye as my mind descended into nothingness, abandoning all reasoning and images to rise up and wax with Him in an envelope of pure prayer; prayer of the heart; in blessed silence; in union with Him in a mystery that defies all human perception or explanation acceptable to human understanding.

After praying, I wrote a letter to Becky and told her of

Robin's plight and that he didn't know how to tell her about his problem. I returned to pray once more in the hope that I had done the right thing.

An echo of a distant voice calling my name pulled me back to fallen humanity and I slowly raised my head, wiped my warm, sweet tears away from my face. The door opened slowly. "Simon?"

"Can I come in?"

I raised my hand and gave him a welcome salute, and he sat on the edge of my bed. "Is everything OK, Simon?"

"I want to ask a favour."

"What sort of favour?"

"I've been wanting to ask you this for a while. Will you baptise me?"

"As a Christian?"

"Yes, of course a Christian! Will you baptise me?"

"Arthur's not happy about baptising people in prison. He's already said no to you and the others."

"I want it done on the wing. You know, in the bath."

"In the bath?"

"Yes, dumb nuts!"

"I'd have to run it past Arthur first."

"So ask him. I don't want to be no Anglican, I want you to baptise me. God's using you in here and I want to start a new life, like you said. Start again."

"I'll talk to him again and see if he will let me do it for you, bro."

I washed my face and put on my new, highly-polished Doc Marten boots. "Let's get some air and we can talk about it" I said.

We walked past the wing office and I nodded to Mr Pitts, who was reading through someone's parole report by the look of it.

We walked out of Clyde Wing, past the main office and up towards the chapel. The garden boys were busy cutting the grass. We walked past the education block and turned left, taking the outer road to the football fields. The sky was clear and the air warm and as we stood talking by the gate we watched the men screaming obscenities to each other as they played against a visiting football team.

Wandering back to our corner behind the gym, which we knew so well, we sat on the grass to talk and were soon joined by Kevin.

"What's this then, another meeting of the God Squad? Don't you lot realise that you're on the wrong side?"

"What are you on about, Kevin?"

"Come on, Con, get real! Christianity is rubbish. It's delusion. I'm a white witch and you lot have got it so wrong. You're on the wrong side, guys."

Simon looked agitated and waited for me to reply. "You told us that already! We're having a private conversation here, Kevin, if you don't mind."

"Yeah. So bugger off, Kevin! Jump on your broom and fly away."

"Don't tell me to bugger off! You're a bloody Muslim, so why do you want to hang out with a Christian and a copper to boot? That ain't right, surely?"

"I'm getting baptised next week, so we'll soon be brothers. So what's your problem, arsehole?"

"Ooh! Tetchy or what? Some Christian you're going to be! I'm telling you the truth, you're wasting your time. You're on the wrong side."

"Kevin, if you want me to drop in to have a chat I will, but we're in the middle of a private conversation here."

"Yeah, drop in if you want to. I'll put the kettle on. See you later."

Kevin wandered off in the direction of the library swinging his legs in a circular motion, thoughtfully.

"Tosser!"

"He's all right, Simon. He's just lost, that's all."

"So you're going to have a word with Arthur for me then?"

"I'll see what he says."

"Well let's ask him now. He's over there. Look! He's walking up from Severn Block towards us. I'll ask him."

Before I could say another word, Simon was marching across the grass towards Arthur, so I tagged along behind. Simon called out loudly: "Arthur! I want to get baptised."

Arthur looked cornered and I could see he was searching for a way out of the situation. "It's very complicated, Simon. You'll have to wait until you get out and then you can speak to your priest."

"I don't have a priest."

"Well you'll need to find one and join a community and then you can get baptised."

"I've asked Costa and he's said that if you let him, he'll baptise me on the wing."

"If he's prepared to do that for you I don't have a problem with it but I don't have the facilities for baptising people in the prison." Arthur didn't looked amused.

"That's it then! Simon snapped immediately. I want to fast first and we can do it in a bath. Brilliant! Thanks Costa."

We thanked Arthur and turned to walk back down to the wing. Simon was ecstatic. As we passed inmates walking in the opposite direction, he stopped them and announced his news.

"I want to do this right, Costa. I want to go under the water three times, like you told us how it should be done. What was that Canon thing?"

"Apostolic Canon 50, Simon."

"Yeah, that one."

"Canons 49 and 50 were made at the first Council of Nicaea in 325. When the creed was compiled by the Church. I'll organise the baptism for Sunday afternoon, bro."

"Great. That gives me time to fast. Right?"

"I'll fast with you, Simon."

"Would you do that for me, Costa?"

"Of course. We need to be prayed up, but you don't have to go completely without food, Simon."

"You do, so I want to do exactly what you do!"

"It's harsh, Simon."

"I want this new life badly, bro. I can do this. I really need to do this right!"

"We'll start from nine o'clock Sunday night up until Thursday morning. The Apostles fast starts on Monday, so it will fit in well."

"That's amazing. I shall remember this Monday for the rest of my life!"

"It's the start of your preparations, Simon. It's Sunday the 3rd of July 1994 that you need to remember, bro. That's when your new life begins."

"Yeah. A new life!"

That night, as I lay on my bed in prayer, I held Kevin up in my mind's eye just before my mind descended into my heart and he was gone.

The following morning as I was unlocked, Kevin was standing outside my door. He was fuming and frothing at the mouth. "You were in my cell last night, you bastard! You freaked me out!"

"It wasn't me, Kevin."

"It was definitely you! What do you think you're doing? That's really dangerous shit and you're not supposed to be messing around like that!"

The screw turned to study us more closely: "Pack it up you two! Go and get your breakfast."

I tried to pass Kevin, but he kept putting himself in my way. "Excuse me Kevin, I want to get my breakfast because I need to get up to the chapel" I managed to get past him, but he kept chasing after me screaming: "You bastard! You bastard. He was in my cell last night!"

I walked up to the servery, collected my meal and walked through the kitchen so as to get back to my cell. Kevin jumped on top of the hot plates screaming: "You're dead, man! You're fucking dead!"

I kept walking and went straight back to my cell. A few minutes later Kevin was back.

"Kevin, I really don't need this. It wasn't me in your cell last night."

"Who was it then?"

"You don't want to know, Kevin."

"Go on. I'll calm down, tell me who it was?"

"It was God, Kevin. I prayed for you last night at the time you say you saw me."

"Bollocks!"

I rinsed my plate out in the sink, pulled my cell door closed and left Kevin in the corridor scratching his head. Then I went to morning prayer.

Later that afternoon Kevin walked into the chapel while I was making a coffee for Father Anscar. He seemed calmer now and wanted to talk. "I'm sorry, Con, I was out of order. I really thought that it was you in my cell."

"That's OK, Kevin. Listen, these things happen, give me a hug." We embraced and I made him a cup of tea. "I love witches, Kevin. White ones as well."

"That's why I'm here, Con. Will you baptise me too on Sunday?"

"What will your head Warlock say?"

"I don't care, what I saw last night is more powerful than anything I have ever seen in all my life, Con. I was terrified! Now if that was God, I definitely want to be on his side."

"You'll need some special prayers, Kevin. Have you got a cross?"

"No."

"Don't worry, I'll make you one with some old matches and a bit of wood glue."

"Thanks."

"It's going to be really hard for you Kevin, they're going to fight to keep you in. You know that, don't you? Don't worry, I'll help you through it all."

"Thank you so much."

"You're welcome to join our fast in preparation for Sunday if you want, just let me know by the end of the week." Kevin gave me a warm smile and left.

Simon and Kevin were true to their word and during our fasting period they shot around the prison as if they were on fire. I then started getting more and more men asking me if I would do the same for them. I kept using the office in the Chapel to talk and pray with the men and in my spare time I cut their hair and gave them cups of tea.

On the Saturday afternoon I was in my cell having a cup of tea with Jock, Simon and Jimmy when Robin wandered in. He looked really troubled and snapped at Jock. "Jock, you dirty bastard, you look like the village idiot peering through a hedge with that beard of yours!"

Jock just smiled, but Robin snapped at Jimmy: "Piss off Jim! Nobody likes you."

Jim reacted very quickly to Robin's remark and went nose to nose with him:

"You know your problem, boy. You've got a big mouth and a bad attitude. Bugger off!"

Before I stepped in to calm things down Robin got really angry and suddenly Robin's faced darkened and went a weird colour and out of his face appeared a horrible-looking demon with horns. We all saw it and our jaws dropped at its sight. Robin turned on his heel and left my cell.

"Did you see that, Con? Did you see the horns? This boy's got serious spiritual problems."

"I saw it, Jim, but you really shouldn't snap at the lad like that. Not in my cell anyway. He's not a bad lad really."

"Yeah, I suppose so. I'll apologise to him when I see him next, Con.

"Thanks, Jim."

The following day Kevin came to visit me with a present. "I've made you a little oil lamp and I've got some sewing machine oil to keep it burning for you at night."

"Thanks Kevin, that's really kind of you."

"You won't be sent back to buy more now, will you?"

"Ah, I see. Thank you."

On Sunday afternoon about fifteen men gathered in the bathroom on Severn wing to watch me baptise Simon and Kevin and there was water everywhere. All but one of the other men requested the same and I started to line up more for the following Sunday. We walked out of the wing singing and clapping and as we walked past the screws' office they all looked surprised.

Once everyone had changed we met up in the Chapel. I made them all hot drinks and we broke open several packets of chocolate biscuits in celebration.

The following week we baptised twelve men, and more and more men were asking questions about God.

The demand for baptism was now becoming an issue. The Chaplains had a meeting and agreed to offer this service to the men. By popular request a large tank was brought into the chapel to carry out full immersion baptisms. Arthur looked very proud of himself for organising this first event.

I brought the refreshments into their planning meeting and Arthur gave me a rather cheesy grin: "You can tell the men that we can offer full baptisms now, Con."

"That's really good, Arthur. How many times are they going under the water?"

"They don't need to go right under, and it's just once."

The Baptist minister chirped in: "That's all you need and I'm working out how it's going to be done, so everything's covered. There isn't any strict ruling on this."

"Oh. What about Canon forty-nine and fifty?"

They all looked around at each other totally bewildered. "Go on then, Con, enlighten us, if you know so much. We're only the ministers here."

"No, don't worry, I'm sure you have it all under control."

"I thought so. You haven't got a clue what you are on about."

"I do actually, the 49th Apostolic Canon is: "If any Bishop or Priest baptize anyone not into the Father and the Son and the Holy Spirit in accordance with the Lord's ordinance, but into three beginning less beings or into three sons or into three comforters, let him be deposed." And the 50th Apostolic Canon is: "If any Bishop or Priest does not perform three immersions (baptisms) in making one baptism, but only a single immersion (baptism) that given into the death of the Lord, let him be deposed. For the Lord did not say, Baptize into my death, but, "Go you and make disciples of all nations, baptizing them in the name of the Father, and of the Son, and of the Holy Spirit." That's Matthew 28:19 I believe."

Arthur tried to smile through my prompt: "I think that between us we have all we need, thank you, Con."

"Through faith, revelation, tradition, the bible, the liturgy, the councils, the fathers, the saints (prior to 1054), the canons, church art and God's grace, we have all we need." I wandered over to the door on my way out and smiled. "Good day, gentlemen."

The baptisms went ahead. I made sure that I had a visit on that day and the flame that had sparked a revival in the men was slowly snuffed out. They knew the truth, through my testimony.

I never mentioned the letter to Robin. When he returned from his day out he wandered into my cell with a very large smile on his face. "You shouldn't have written to Becky, Con."

"You left me with no option, Robin. Are we still good?"

"You're an interfering hairy old man. I should be angry but I'm not. I didn't know how to tell her and that's why I showed you the letter. It was too big to go in my bucket."

"Ah, I see. How was Becky?"

"She was brilliant about it all. I couldn't believe it. I'm going to live with her when I get out."

"Oh right. That's good, isn't it?"

"Yeah, thanks hairy old man."

I stood up and gave Robin a big hug. I passed him my plastic jug and sent him off to get some water so that we could make some tea.

Becky had been amazing. She had written to me and thanked me for letting her know, at least she knew exactly what she needed to do in order to protect herself in regard to Robin's condition. I knew my writing to her was against all the rules of counselling, but it had to be done. It had to be!

CHAPTER TWENTY TWO

■■■■■■■■

PAROLE BOARD INTERVIEW

After nearly four years in prison, I received a notice confirming that I had a Parole Board Hearing, to be held in the Governor's office in the Block. My meeting was with just one man, who introduced himself by saying: "My name is Mr Jones. I'm from the Parole Board in London and I have been asked to interview you. How are you?"

I was flabbergasted. "How am I? Let me tell you something, Mr Jones. I've been in prison for nearly four years. I've been attacked by gangs who have tried to kill me. I've almost been raped and killed in the showers. I've been screamed at every day because everyone hates me for the job I did sixteen years ago and now, you walk in here to see me after waiting for nearly four years and then ask me: "How are you!" Where the hell have you been for the last four years! Where were you when I needed you! Where were you when I was being attacked?"

Mr Jones flicked at what appeared to be a small piece of wool from his thigh with the back of his right hand and he looked rather disinterested. "You won't change your mind about what happened then?"

"About what?" The room fell silent for a moment while I took a closer look at the man sitting opposite me.

Mr Jones, who was about 68 years old, looked rather surprised by my remark. He moved uncomfortably in his chair. He was wearing a dark blue pinstriped suit, white shirt and a silk tie displaying the colours of the Black Watch, with slanted medium sized stripes of red, dark green and dark blue. I knew this because my father wore one much the same. He politely crossed his legs, which drew my attention to his black, mirror-effect, highly polished shoes. This warned me that he was from a military background. His hair was grey and cut neat and short. It was either creamed or waxed into place and my guess, due to the light aroma, was that he had used Brylcreem. His accent was Home Counties and he remained calm. He spoke softly and clearly:

"About parole."

"I'm not eligible for parole, because I won't admit to the offences!"

"What about reporting if you were released?"

"I won't be released because I won't report, and if I were released, no, I wouldn't report!"

With his index finger on his right hand he reached into his top button, just above his tie, and pulled it forward in order to make his collar more comfortable. "We would almost certainly require you to report. It just wouldn't happen if you refused."

"Why should I report? I've not done anything wrong! I am innocent of the charges, so why should you expect me to?"

"Will you take any form of supervision?"

"I really don't see why I should! I used to be a policeman in two forces! You may have imprisoned my body, but not my spirit. When you've finished playing your silly games with my body, just let me know, because I'm not really bothered and I don't want to play your silly mind games!"

"You're making things very difficult for yourself. If you admit the offence you will be released a lot quicker."

"Watch my lips, Mr Jones, I AM INNOCENT! I will never admit to doing something that was never going to happen. If you know anything about SO 11 and criminal intelligence or the Flying Squad or the Crime Squads in London, you'll know that they are groomed from the start of their life on CID. They knew straight away that I wasn't one of their ilk and that meant I didn't fit in. I wanted to do the job the right way, which is the hard way, but not the Flying Squad, because they know that they can get away with it. So they cheat, bend the rules and play a different game altogether from the one I had sworn to Queen and Country to do. I was a bloody good copper and I loved doing the job and I did do the job the right way!"

"That may be the case, but this isn't relevant now."

"It is relevant! How long is this government going to let them carry on acting the way they do? It's corruption and it's widespread and it's been going on since the 70s. Drinking endlessly all day and night, forging duty rosters, working with professional criminals, taking bribes, dealing drugs, breaking into cars, burglary, stealing money from jobs and stitching people up! They should be in here, not me!"

"This isn't going to get us anywhere, Mr Buller."

"They broke into my bloody office just before they arrested me and they broke into my farmhouse as well, stealing my computer and planting evidence, who the hell do they think they are? How dare they!"

"I doubt that very much. Let's calm things down."

"Well you started it by asking me how I was! I'll shorten my answer for you. I'm pretty pissed off as it happens and so would you be given the same circumstances."

He closed my file and said: "OK, I don't think that we are getting anywhere with this interview."

I was so angry that my whole body was shaking and I barked at him: "Well don't ask people how they are unless you really want to hear what they have to say in response! All this won't stop when I'm finally released you know. I've already been told that, so what's the point?"

"What do you mean?"

"I reported everything I knew immediately to my brother, he's a DI on CIB2. I told him I suspected something and we had already agreed to meet up to discuss bent coppers in London. I'm talking about serious crime and police involvement. DI Badcock wanted me to do a deal with him to stitch up my two co-defendants. He came into my cell with DS Bains just after I had been arrested. Do you have any idea how many people this lot have murdered?"

"Why didn't you deal with that at the time?"

"They would have shot me! These guys are hardcore criminals and I've got children to provide for. These coppers are setting up the jobs themselves. That's what they did to me. They set this whole thing up and they wanted me killed in this evil system. That's why they tried to 'A' cat me during my old style committal. They're evil!"

Mr Jones looked very bored:"I doubt it."

"Why don't you check it out? There were over 43 criminal gang murders in south east London in 1991 and they were looking to make me another statistic. I was sat in the bloody middle of it all. How dare they do this to me!"

Mr Jones whinged: "This isn't going to help you now."

I sat on the edge of my seat:"I've done everything the system has asked of me since I've been in prison. If your Probation Officer wants to drop around to my house to say "hello" I won't be rude to him. He can come in and have a chat, but I don't see why I should start reporting to his offices, like some bloody schoolboy!"

Mr Jones was trying to mediate with me. "Let's be reasonable about this, I've only just been given the case."

"Don't talk to me about being reasonable, Mr Jones. I know you are only doing your job. I also know that you are not here because you care about me. You're here to justify the system's existence."

"Well, tell me what you want me to tell the system then?"

"I have always remained firm in that the arresting officers stitched me up. When the time came for me to apply for parole I wrote across the form that I fully accepted that parole was not an option for me in this matter. I have explained this situation to my outside Parole Officer. I'm not prepared to report! I am quite happy to accept 1999 as my earliest date of release. My family and friends fully accept this situation, even though they would like us to be together earlier. I trust in the Lord completely in this matter and I am asking for nothing. So I don't really understand why you have come here today, Mr Jones. I think we're done here, don't you?"

The Chaplain added in his report, as did the other staff as follows:

"I have hardly touched on the most important fact in this man's life since he has been in prison. While at Exeter he made a deliberate decision to begin to live as a Christian. He had previously attended church from time to time, but this was something different. Many people make emotional choices under the stress of being in prison for the first time, but this is something, which has carried him through a whole range of very testing experiences at Exeter Prison, Maidstone and Channings Wood over a period of some four years.

"In my view he is an unusual case and merits very careful consideration. He has done everything required of him while serving his sentence to deserve early parole. It would be a strange commentary on our system of justice if he were refused, on the grounds of not facing up to his offence, if he is right that the offences were never committed.

"My view, based on very close knowledge of him over three years is that he should be released."

The result of this and other reports were as follows:

"Further to the parole review for this inmate which commenced on 12th October 1994, after careful consideration of the papers before it, including any representations made by or on behalf of the inmate following disclosure of his dossier, the Parole Board decided not to recommend release on licence for the following reason: He maintains his innocence of the offences and consequently has done no offence-focused work. Nor is he willing to do this under supervision, thus parole will not assist in reducing risk. The panel feel that a psychological and spiritual assessment would be helpful at his next review. The Home Secretary has therefore not authorised parole on this occasion."

After a spiritual and psychometric test and an examination by the prison psychiatrist, I was called to a meeting with Mrs Mary McDonald in the prison hospital. I had been told earlier by one of the lifers that both she and her husband were psychiatrists and I wondered what on earth they talked about when they got home. Did they analyse each other's behaviour?

I walked over to the reinforced steel fence that divided the main prison from the Vulnerable Prisoners' Unit and stood by the small gate, pressed the bell and waited for a screw to let me through. After a few minutes the gate opened and Mr Butcher, a tall, thin screw with a thick beard and a crop of coffee-coloured hair, opened the gate. I immediately thought: "Ah, the village idiot looking through a hedge". I smiled broadly. By his response, I began to wonder if he could read my mind. He was in a foul mood and snapped at me for no good reason: "You can't come in here! Piss off, Buller!"

Still smiling and trying to look positive, I said: "I've got an appointment with Mrs McDonald and I'm running late."

Mr Butcher appeared to be looking for confrontation and his powers of observation were meticulous: "You're not a lifer, so why does she want to see you?"

I really didn't feel that I needed to explain myself to Mr Butcher and I kept my response brief without being rude: "Because I've got an appointment with her, Mr Butcher. You can check if you like".

He was still unhappy. "You can't just wander around over here without being escorted." He pointed to the ground and said: "Stand there and wait for me, I'll have to take you through."

Quietly and politely "Thank you, Mr Butcher, you are very kind."

Mr Butcher led me through to Mrs McDonald's office and I knocked on her door and waited for a response. I heard a Scottish voice call out: "Come!" A strange response from someone who works in the VPU, I thought. I opened the door and walked into her office and waited for her to direct me to sit.

Mrs McDonald eventually looked up from her desk "Yes, yes, it's fine, you can sit down. I don't expect you to stand on ceremony in my office."

I nodded politely and sat myself down opposite her and waited. "I have scored your test."

Now I wasn't sure how to respond, "Oh, good, how did I get on?"

She looked puzzled "I am not sure. In fact I'm actually confused. Can I ask you a question?'

I had a strange feeling that I knew where this was going. "I was never confused. Of course you can, go ahead."

Mrs McDonald clicked her fingers "That's it, exactly! Are you homosexual?"

I wanted to say something amusing but quickly realised that she would be analyzing everything I did. "I have, during my time in custody, been approached and offered on a number of occasions a homosexual relationship. I have always said "Thank you for the compliment but I am not that way persuaded." I'm not homophobic, Mrs McDonald and I politely declined. I have also been the victim of an attempted rape in the showers at Maidstone Prison and I declined that rather more persuasive approach too. Unfortunately I had to use a bit more force that time to convince them of my sexual persuasion."

She leaned forward in her chair and her long brown curly hair fell forward and covered part of her face and she peered over the top of her bifocals. She was about 43, five foot six and looked dangerously sexy without her makeup on. She was obviously searching for a deeper understanding of this oddball sat in front of her. I could feel her eyes piercing mine, calling out and wanting to get to know more about this man who could understand and relate to her deeper feminine calling. Snapping back at me as she did was rather disappointing: "Then you must be a woman!"

Without a flicker of dented ego, I immediately responded by saying: "How do you feel about that?"

She was surprised that I had turned the conversation around to my advantage "Well, you have the complete profile of a women. A perfect profile!"

I smiled "If that's the case, can you recommend me for an

immediate transfer to Pucklechurch Prison, please?" She looked, briefly, a little uncomfortable and I thought about asking her some personal questions, like: "How do you get on with your husband, you nosey bitch?" and "Could you tell if your husband's cheating on you?" but she brought me back from my wandering thoughts again "I don't think so, and there's no need to be sarcastic. The test revealed something else, which is rather worrying."

"Oh, what's that then?"

"You have a behavioural problem."

"Oh, I see. Are you going to tell me what it is?" I asked and my mind was suddenly catapulted into overdrive. I wondered if she was my Mick's shrink. He was a lifer and I bet she had fun analyzing him, poor sod.

"Your scoring shows clearly that you are anti establishment to the point of paranoia."

"Thank God for that! I thought it was something serious."

"It is serious. It could mean that you are a risk to the public."

"Oh, like someone who's innocent and has been wrongfully imprisoned might be, you mean? I didn't think I hated the system, just a few policemen, that's all."

"You can go back to your cell now".

"Thank you."

After nearly four years and as many Christmases inside, Sarah had finally accepted that Michael and Luke could visit their dad in prison. I had written her a threatening letter the week before as I was still searching for answers, but I had no definite proof as to whether they had been involved in my predicament. I did say that when I got out I would let the children know the truth. So she agreed to drop the boys off outside the gates and I watched from inside the visits hall as Sarah and her new husband drove away.

Knowing Sarah the way I did, I knew she would not give them

any money to come in with. As a prisoner I was not allowed to approach the WRVS hatch to buy drinks, and I was not allowed to have money 'in possession' myself. So, thinking ahead, I had made an application to the Governor earlier in the week to arrange for a facility that allowed the children to buy drinks and for them to be deducted from my prison wages.

As Michael and Luke approached my table I was emotionally distraught. I fought to hold back the tears as I hugged them for the first time in over four years and my heart went out for them. I searched their faces for the little boys I had left behind and struggled to keep my composure, but as soon as the boys began to talk all their old characteristics flowed back.

"I brought the only photograph I have of you both" and held it up for them to see.

Michael remarked: "That's ancient, Dad. It's the one that was taken at Mum's wedding to Gordon!" Sarah had obviously chosen this photograph specially for me in order to rub salt into my wounds.

I managed a laugh "I wondered why you were wearing carnations!" I had already guessed Sarah's motive for including this photograph within one of her letters.

Again, thinking ahead, I had arranged to have two photographs of me taken at reception after having changed from prison uniform into my own clothing. The Governor had given special permission for them to be done and I had paid for them from my wages. I passed them over to them "Here you are boys, this is a little present from me."

They opened the envelopes together and huge smiles appeared over their faces. They got up to give me a hug and I embraced them both. "This hug is the best present you could have ever given me. Thank you. I love you both so very much and I miss you."

Michael whispered "I love you too, Dad. It's been so long since I last saw you."

Luke smiled broadly "Me too. I love and miss you all the time. When are they going to let you out, Dad?"

"That's a good question, son. I've no idea. At the moment it looks like the 17th April 1999."

"Luke looked very sad: "That's ages away."

They asked lots of questions about prison life and together they went over holidays and special times that we had spent together. I was amazed at how much they had remembered about me.

The visit ended so quickly and then they were gone, waving as they walked through the sliding doors and disappearing from sight. The screws could see that I had had a difficult visit and this time they let me walk through without a body search.

I walked up to the chapel, sat in the chair I used for my early morning prayers and began to weep. The tears were warm as they fell from my eyes and bounced down on to my blue prison sweat shirt, and I couldn't turn them off. I heard the Chaplain close and lock his office door and within a few moments I felt a reassuring arm around my shoulder, driving the last strength that I had from my body. I fell forward, resting on my elbows on the pew in front of me, weeping.

"Are you all right, Con?"

I couldn't speak and I couldn't think. I just leaned on the chair in front of me and the priest started to pray.

"Father of all, I give you thanks and praise that when Con was far away, you sent your Son into the world to set him free from the chains of evil. Strengthen him, your son, now and in his hour of need and thank you for bringing in his sons to see him today. Help restore him so that he can be with his children again. Amen."

As a man I was crushed, unable to talk, think or move. He held on to me tightly, giving me the reassurance I needed.

CHAPTER TWENTY THREE

■■■■■■■■

RELEASE

I was refused permission on several occasions to visit my father in hospital. Finally, when it became obvious that he was at death's door, they took me handcuffed to Heavitree and Wonford District Hospital to see him. My father had been placed in a private room. I asked if I could see him without the cuffs on: "No, you've only got ten minutes to say what you want to say and then we've got to take you back."

My father looked extremely weak. He whispered to the screw nearest to him: "Can I see my son as a free man before I go? Take his handcuffs off and leave us to be alone."

At his request, they released me. I walked to my father's side. "Hi, Dad, I got here in the end!"

He looked at me with tears in his eyes. "Where the hell have you been? I have been asking for you for ages."

"The screws have given me ten minutes, Dad."

His voice was croaky and weak. "Good. Shave me! I have got some things I want to tell you."

"OK Dad."

I shaved my father and cleaned him up so that he would be ready to meet his maker. "You're a good son and I love you. I did what I could for you. I thought I was doing the right thing, but as a father, sometimes nothing seems right. There is something I need to deal with, because it stands out in my mind as a time when I was harsh and unjust to you."

I could see him struggling to speak: "Dad, I know that you did what you could for all of us and yes there are scars, but nothing that can't be dealt with."

"You were young, about five years old, and we were living in Malta."

"I remember Malta, Dad. I remember them as happy years for me. Swimming every day after school and picnics in Busket Gardens among the orange and lemon trees."

"We lived in Army quarters then, a place called Coradino. I worked in the Military Police. Do you remember, Costa?"

"Yes Dad, I remember."

"As a Staff Sergeant I wielded a lot of power over the prisoners. They were young lads and my job was to break them and believe me I did just that, I broke them."

"I saw that, Dad. I saw what you did to them. I was only a child but I saw it with my own eyes. The men in my prison may not have been in the military but they are the same young men standing up against the cruel system that has incarcerated them."

"Yes, I can still see them; defiant, hurting inside, full of anger and hatred. Their faces haunt me, Costa." My father had been such a hard man and now he had been reduced to a weak old man.

"You need to give all that up to God and ask for His forgiveness, Dad. He will hear you and He will bless you. As for those young men, the same applies to them. Until they are able to understand where their anger comes from, they will not be able to deal with it."

My father's eyes welled up to overflowing. "Do you remember when you fell from the top of the cricket nets?"

I smiled: "It wasn't the cricket nets I fell from, it was the tree above the nets. I fell through the nets from the tree and it knocked me out cold!"

"You were in a coma for four months, Costa. I had given up on you, but your mother refused to let you go. She got a priest in to give you a blessing because we thought you were dying! Why did I give up on you so easily, Costa? Your mother refused to let you go."

"Don't worry about that now, Dad, It's not an issue now."

'Your mother was screaming, Costa. Wailing for you! Her cries went right through me and they still haunt me today."

"I know, Dad. I could see her."

"Could you?"

"Yes, I was floating around the room just below the ceiling, I was watching all of you! I saw her stick her fingers into my eye sockets and then I suddenly found myself back in my body. Just like that!"

"I just want to say I'm sorry for giving up on you so easily, Costa. You have been a good son to me."

"Thanks Dad, you have been the best dad in the world and I love you. Save me a place when you get up there, eh? You need to clean your heart before you go. Don't delay. Promise me you'll do that?"

"Yes, I will. Take this." He reached out with his right hand and put a roll of money into my hand: "I want you to take this and organise my funeral for me."

I was shocked and tried to pass it back to him. "I'm in prison, Dad. How can I organise your funeral? You should be asking Richard or John."

"I want you to organise it for me and I'm going to tell you the order of service and the hymns I want sung. There's one hundred and fifty pounds in cash to do it with. I'm depending on you son, so don't let me down."

I pushed the money down my trousers and into my underpants. "So what hymns do you want, Dad?"

"I want to be buried in the village and the Lord is my Shepherd to be sung. Here, I've made a list of the things I want done."

The time had passed quickly and I could see the screws coming to collect me. My dad sensed their arrival. "Go now and don't look back, son. I love you."

"I love you too, Dad. I'll see you on the other side."

I turned and started to walk towards the oncoming officers and they handcuffed me and I left the hospital in silence.

That evening I sat on my bed in my cell and prayed. Reaching out with my hands at midnight, palms upward, I saw my father and prayed: "'Lord, I commit my father to you." At this point my father appeared to be floating in front of me, in my mind's eye, above his hospital bed and I was watching his deified soul being taken. I felt an incredible peace, a waxing with him and the divine in complete inner silence and my father was collected with the same luminosity of glory of pure light, brighter than diamonds, which enveloped him and he drifted away.

The following morning, I was still awash in the Spirit when a screw approached me in quite a matter of fact way in the chapel. "Is the Chaplain around?"

As I looked into his eyes I could read what was on his mind and thought, he's come about my father.

"He isn't in yet. That's OK, you don't have to tell me, I know already. You've come to tell me that my father died at midnight last night. That's OK."

The officer looked genuinely shocked: "Yes. How did you find out about it?"

"God showed me."

The officer walked away with a rather confused look on his face and walked back down towards the wing.

In my next visit with my sister, Coralia, she told me: "The strangest thing happened when we were all stood at Dad's bedside at the moment when he died. At midnight he said: "No, not yet, I'm not ready to go! You're too early!"' As he spoke his last words a strange electricity radiated from around his eyes and then he was gone!"

"He didn't die, Coral, he just fell asleep."

The word was starting to get about on the wings. During morning prayer I said my more formal prayers and then cleared my mind of all thoughts and images. In my mind's eye I gently repeated the prayer "Lord Jesus Christ, Son of God, have mercy on me, a sinner" over and over again until my mind slowly descended into my heart. It was then that God came to me, initially, with feelings of inner groaning, as if I were a woman beginning labour.

When I returned to my normal state and returned to carry out my duties within the chapel, men began to seek me out. I saw one man called Darren, who was standing outside the main chapel doors looking very confused. I opened the door and asked "Are you all right, Darren?"

Darren was in a daze. He paused for a while longer "I felt guided to walk up to the chapel and I haven't got a clue why. I'm stuck here now not knowing what to do next!"

"That's OK, Darren, God's sent you up here. Come in and He will explain."

We walked to the right of the altar and sat down on the ledge to talk. "Tell me why you feel this deep guilt, Darren, particularly when you are with your wife?"

Darren looked shocked "How do you know about that?"

"I've no idea. Do you understand why you can't sit with her in the house, in the cool of the day?"

"No, I don't understand why! That's right! I can't be alone in the house with her and I've got to leave her alone and go up to the pub and find company. I just can't sit in the house and talk to her!"

I then told Darren the story of the boy and the golden ball and he began to cry, so much so that I had to go and get some tissues. At the same time I picked up a pencil and a piece of paper. Darren blew his nose and with tears rolling down his cheeks, "Would you like me to bring my empty bucket and help you clear the pond?"

Darren nodded "Would you? Would you do that for me? I don't know if I have the strength to do it on my own."

I drew a single line across the piece of paper "Of course, Darren. Let's begin." At the end of our talk I gave the piece of paper to Darren to hold "This is your burden. Keep filling it in until there is nothing left and then take it to the priest and he will pray on you and burn all of this on the altar".

About this time the number one Chaplain, Arthur, went on sick leave for a prolonged period of time and I was again asked if I would get the chapel opened and run morning prayer on my own in order to keep up the prayer vigil, which I felt privileged to be asked to do. Even though I was in prisoner's clothing, men would come in and truly believe I was the prison Chaplain. I explained that I was a prisoner the same as them, but they refused to believe that this was true and still confided in me completely.

There were also those who would come in with great inner pain to mock and verbally assault me for my faith and beliefs, saying "There is no God!" When these things happened I normally stood next to the book shelf in the lobby, which allowed me to pick up a bible to quote from when I needed to. These incidents normally happened after I had fasted for three days and managed, through the Jesus Prayer, to remain in a hesychastic unity with the divine. I was blessed to perceive and discern their inner thoughts and pain. Quite often this would either provoke them to anger or crumble them emotionally before me.

Prisoners are very streetwise and knew when someone was lying or putting on false graces. I never held myself up as someone of authority and constantly referred to myself as His servant and the greatest sinner of them all. I was trying to walk towards the goal of salvation, constantly fighting against my own ignorance, laziness and forgetfulness.

One afternoon I was alone in the chapel foyer and Father Anscar had been in deep prayer in his office until I took him a pot of coffee and some biscuits. I was stamping new books with the Chaplain's book stamp when a lifer called Gazza wandered into the foyer. The best way of describing Gazza would be to call him a walking corpse, because that's what he looked like. He was Tall, slender and undernourished with a bony face, which he insisted on covering in a smear of lard from the kitchen. He wore highly bulled Doc Marten boots and prison greys and striped shirt and had a Tommy Cooper laugh. Dresswise we could pass as two peas in a pod but in nature we were poles apart. Gazza planned to work for a funeral director when released because he liked being in the company of dead bodies. He was fascinated by them and they were all he ever talked about.

I was on my knees pulling books from the shelves when Gazza quickly grabbed the stamp and whacked it on to my forehead, leaving me with the impression "HMP Chaplaincy" in red, bang centre for all to see! He then turned on his heels and ran straight for the front door. I was stunned for a fraction of a second and then leapt to my feet and gave chase, sprinting across the foyer to catch him with my right foot between his legs, lifting him off his feet. He collapsed in a pile outside the chapel door, groaning. I quietly returned to my book stamping, feeling rather un-Christian and moody.

Gazza managed to climb back on to his feet and he wandered back into the Chapel to tell me: "Some fucking Christian you are, you bastard! That really hurt!"

I was trying to remain calm and spoke quietly back to him: "I am really trying to walk the walk, Gazza, but people keep frustrating me and calling back the old me. At the moment I am between the two, so don't push it!"

By this time Gazza had moved closer and was quick enough to catch hold of the stamp again but I was too quick this time to allow him to place another mark on my bald shiny head and I jumped to my feet again and started to chase him around the Chapel. He pulled everything he could behind him into my path in order to stop me retrieving the stamp. Gazza's screams brought Father Anscar out of his office: "What's going on!" he called.

"Father, I came in to see you and Buller attacked me for no reason!"

Father Anscar bowed slightly "You'd better come in. You will be safe in here with me." They both disappeared into his office and closed the door behind them and I went back to stamping books.

When Gazza finally emerged from Father Anscar's office, he laughed as he passed me uttering "Muppet!"

From nowhere, I was prompted to say "You shouldn't blame your twin brother for trying to kill you when you were born. You didn't need to return the favour."

Gazza went absolutely crazy "Who told you that? You've been reading my file, you bastard!"

"I haven't read your file, I was shown what happened."

Gazza then burst back into Father Anscar's office and reported me for reading his case papers, which was completely untrue, as Father Anscar knew.

The following Sunday Gazza turned up when the other prisoners were receiving Holy Communion with handful of stones and began to throw them over the inmates as they knelt before the altar. I had to ask him to desist and then I removed him from the building.

In the afternoon, I was overseeing a group of men in the chapel and the Quaker Minister arrived to take his 'silence' with one of the inmates. I had just made Arthur a cup of tea and placed it on his desk and I turned to the Quaker Minister "As you have twenty minutes before your silence, would you like me to make you a drink?"

"No thank you, Con. Why don't you join our meeting this afternoon, you'd be more than welcome?"

Without thinking, "I can't join your meeting because it's not Christian."

Arthur snapped back at me: "Of course it's Christian. Quakers are Christians and they do a lot of good work in the community!"

"They may do good work but they're not Christian."

The Quaker Minister was looking very angry "If Christian is what you call our work, then we are Christian."

Arthur was still suffering from shock "You shouldn't confront people like that, it's wrong."

"I'm sorry, but that means nothing to me and he's not a Christian. There's an easy way to sort this out, can I ask you a question?"

The Quaker Minister looked uneasy. "Yes, of course you can."

"OK, who is Jesus?"

The Quaker Minister had suddenly been struck dumb. I waited for a response, and waited and waited and then he replied "He's a very important man."

"Ah, yes He is, but who is He?"

He was now flustered "He's a very, very important man."

Arthur was now getting very angry with me and snapped: "Of course he's a Christian and you shouldn't be talking to him like this!"

"OK, let me ask you the same question, Arthur. Who is Jesus?"

Arthur replied instantly: "He's the Son of God!"

"This can only be said in the Holy Spirit. Good." I turned to the Quaker Minister and moved closer to see right into his eyes and raised my voice "I'll try again! Who is Jesus?"

The Quaker Minister was furious. He started to shake with rage and shouted "I've just told you! He's a very, very important man!" I growled in his face "You're not a Christian!"

Arthur raised his voice "I resent you insulting my guests, please leave my office now!" I turned and opened the door and left the room, closing it behind me.

When I walked through the double doors to join the group of inmates I had been holding a bible study meeting with, they were all on their feet and in a very excited state. Andrew, who was in his early twenties, squealed "Did you see it? Did you see it?"

"Did I see what?"

Andrew said "We all saw it and it came through that wall" and he pointed to the room I had just left. "You can't have missed it! It was a putrid, green monster. Like a ghost. It came from the office you were just in! You must have seen it? We all saw it! It came through the wall and it stank horribly and it went along that wall and out through that wall over there" and he pointed to the wall to the left of the altar.

Simon, who had been with them, looked at me. "Costa, honestly, we all saw it, exactly the same thing. If you were in that room you must have seen it!"

"Sorry, I didn't see anything but I did annoy the Quaker Minister, big time." and I explained what had happened while I was in the room.

I was eventually reduced to a 'D' category prisoner and this meant another move. The week I was due to move, I received word that my friend Gary, who had helped me in Exeter, had hanged himself in the Block in Dartmoor Prison. I'd been writing and receiving letters from Gary and I found this news inconsistent with the manner of his death.

Simon wandered into my cell as I was reading a letter and he was beaming. "They've paroled me! I'm out on Monday!" I dropped my letter on my desk and got up to give him a big hug. "I'm so pleased for you, Simon." His face radiated the sun and suddenly his joy turned sombre and he murmured "I'll keep in touch."

I was so pleased with his news and at the same time saddened at the thought of losing him as a companion and close friend. I raised both arms and hugged him and said: "Of course we will, Simon. You'll always be part of my family. Always. I'm really pleased for you."

Although he was not yet twenty five years old, Simon had the maturity and wisdom of a much older man. He thought for a moment: "There is a reason why we met in prison and I'm going to preach when I get out and tell everyone what happened in here."

"I believe you, Simon. God has got a very special plan for us both." I wanted to cry and hang on to my special friend and brother, but at the same time I knew our time together was coming to an end. It was so hard to disguise my feelings of loss, and I watched Simon's joy fade as the reality of our pending separation emerged. I could see that he was troubled.

"Is anyone going to believe what we found hidden behind these closed doors?" He reached over and gripped the cell door in his hand and moved it to and fro: "If the apostles didn't believe Mary Magdalene, how on earth are they going to believe us?"

"I've no idea, Simon, I have got so many questions and nobody is coming up with answers. I've asked all the chaplains, even Father Anscar, and the Abbot is denying all knowledge too. He reckons it's the activity of the brain that generates electricity. It doesn't make sense to me. There has to be someone who knows the truth out there."

"What was this guy's name again, Costa?

"Bernard Pyne Grenfell."

"He's got to know the answer. Can I have a copy?"

"Of course, Simon."

"Read it to me again."

I opened my study folder and flicked through the pages. "Here it is - "The Gospel of Mary was discovered in 1896 by Bernard Pyne Grenfell and his close friend and colleague, Arthur Surridge Hunt."

"Yeah, I know that. Read it to me again!"

"I've got to go over to the chapel, Simon. Later maybe."

"You've got time!"

"I'll get you a copy."

"No, I want you to read it now. Come on, Costa. It's not very long."

"OK, but then I'm off."

"Yeah, yeah, read it to me!"

"The Gospel According to Mary Magdalene is also referred to as The Gospel of Mary."

"I know all that! Get on with it, Costa!"

"Well, pages 1 to 6 of the manuscript, containing chapters 1 - 3, are lost and so the remaining text starts on page 7."

"I thought you were in a hurry?"

"Well chapter four starts: *"Will matter then be destroyed or not?"*" I read on:

"22) *The Saviour said, All nature, all formations, all creatures exist in and with one another, and they will be resolved again into their own roots.*

23) *For the nature of matter is resolved into the roots of its own nature alone.*

24) *He who has ears to hear, let him hear.*

25) *Peter said to him, Since you have explained everything to us, tell us this also: What is the sin of the world?*

26) *The Saviour said There is no sin, but it is you who make sin when you do the things that are like the nature of adultery, which is called sin.*

27) *That is why the Good came into your midst, to the essence of every nature in order to restore it to its root.*

28) *Then He continued and said, That is why you become sick and die, for you are deprived of the one who can heal you.*

29) *He who has a mind to understand, let him understand.*

30) *Matter gave birth to a passion that has no equal, which proceeded from something contrary to nature. Then there arises a disturbance in its whole body.*

31) *That is why I said to you, Be of good courage, and if you are discouraged be encouraged in the presence of the different forms of nature.*

32) *He who has ears to hear, let him hear.*

33) *When the Blessed One had said this, He greeted them all, saying, Peace be with you. Receive my peace unto yourselves.*

34) *Beware that no one lead you astray saying Lo here or lo there! For the Son of Man is within you.*

35) *Follow after Him!*

36) *Those who seek Him will find Him.*

37) *Go then and preach the gospel of the Kingdom.*

38) *Do not lay down any rules beyond what I appointed you, and do not give a law like the lawgiver lest you be constrained by it.*

39) *When He said this He departed.*

Chapter 5

1) *But they were grieved. They wept greatly, saying, How shall we go to the Gentiles and preach the gospel of the Kingdom of the Son of Man? If they did not spare Him, how will they spare us?*

2) *Then Mary stood up, greeted them all, and said to her brethren, Do not weep and do not grieve nor be irresolute, for His grace will be entirely with you and will protect you.*

3) *But rather, let us praise His greatness, for He has prepared us and made us into Men.*

4) *When Mary said this, she turned their hearts to the Good, and they began to discuss the words of the Saviour.*

5) *Peter said to Mary, Sister we know that the Saviour loved you more than the rest of woman.*

6) *Tell us the words of the Saviour which you remember which you know, but we do not, nor have we heard them.*

7) *Mary answered and said, What is hidden from you I will proclaim to you.*

8) *And she began to speak to them these words: I, she said, I saw the Lord in a vision and I said to Him, Lord I saw you today in a vision. He answered and said to me,*

9) *Blessed are you that you did not waver at the sight of Me. For where the mind is there is the treasure.*

10) *I said to Him, Lord, how does he who sees the vision see it, through the soul or through the spirit?*

11) *The Saviour answered and said, He does not see through the soul nor through the spirit, but the mind that is between the two that is what sees the vision and it is [...]"*

I told Simon "Pages 11-14 are missing from the manuscript and it then goes on to Chapter 8".

"Yes! That's it! That's what happened to you in the cell! You've not wavered since you had your vision and anyone that doesn't know you thinks you're mad. You saw actually Him, Costa! You actually saw God!"

"I saw it."

"God's not an 'It' you plonker! Don't disrespect Him by calling Him 'It'. I don't like it."

"Calm down. The 'It' that I'm referring to is from the Gospel of Mary, Simon."

"Oh, right. Go on then."

I read on:

10) *And desire said, I did not see you descending, but now I see you ascending. Why do you lie since you belong to me?*

11) *The soul answered and said, I saw you. You did not see me nor recognize me. I served you as a garment and you did not know me.*

12) *When it said this, it (the soul) went away rejoicing greatly.*

13)   *Again it came to the third power, which is called ignorance.*

14)   *The power questioned the soul, saying, Where are you going? In wickedness are you bound. But you are bound; do not judge!*

15)   *And the soul said, Why do you judge me, although I have not judged?*

16)   *I was bound, though I have not bound.*

17)   *I was not recognized. But I have recognized that the All is being dissolved, both the earthly things and the heavenly.*

18)   *When the soul had overcome the third power, it went upwards and saw the fourth power, which took seven forms.*

19)   *The first form is darkness, the second desire, the third ignorance, the fourth is the excitement of death, the fifth is the kingdom of the flesh, the sixth is the foolish wisdom of flesh, the seventh is the wrathful wisdom. These are the seven powers of wrath.*

20)   *They asked the soul, Whence do you come slayer of men, or where are you going, conqueror of space?*

21)   *The soul answered and said, What binds me has been slain, and what turns me about has been overcome,*

22)   *and my desire has been ended, and ignorance has died.*

23)   *In a aeon I was released from a world, and in a Type from a type, and from the fetter of oblivion which is transient.*

24)   *From this time on will I attain to the rest of the time, of the season, of the aeon, in silence.*

Chapter 9

1)   *When Mary had said this, she fell silent, since it was to this point that the Saviour had spoken with her.*

2)   *But Andrew answered and said to the brethren, Say what you wish*

to say about what she has said. I at least do not believe that the Saviour said this. For certainly these teachings are strange ideas.

3) *Peter answered and spoke concerning these same things.*

4) *He questioned them about the Saviour: Did He really speak privately with a woman and not openly to us? Are we to turn about and all listen to her? Did He prefer her to us?*

5) *Then Mary wept and said to Peter, My brother Peter, what do you think? Do you think that I have thought this up myself in my heart, or that I am lying about the Saviour?*

6) *Levi answered and said to Peter, Peter you have always been hot tempered.*

7) *Now I see you contending against the woman like the adversaries.*

8) *But if the Saviour made her worthy, who are you indeed to reject her? Surely the Saviour knows her very well.*

9) *That is why He loved her more than us. Rather let us be ashamed and put on the perfect Man, and separate as He commanded us and preach the gospel, not laying down any other rule or other law beyond what the Saviour said.*

10) *And when they heard this they began to go forth to proclaim and to preach".*"

"We're on to something here, Costa! These two friends found something really mind blowing and they've hidden it for a reason."

"I know, Simon and I'm not going to stop until I find the truth."

"Mary Magdalene was first at the tomb and she was really close to Jesus. He really loved her, you can tell, and he told her something really important. Mind bending! So much so that the apostles couldn't believe what they were hearing!"

"I know, Simon."

"But they reckon that Mary had a baby with Jesus."

"I know, Simon. Some people would rather believe a lie. What could be better than sending everyone in the wrong direction."

"I'm off. Find the missing link, Costa and prove it and let me know when you do. When I get out of this place I'm going to tell everyone!"

"They won't believe you, Simon. They've done a really good job brainwashing everyone."

"They're controlling everyone and they haven't got a clue."

"I'll see you later, Simon. I took you there, so you know it's true."

"I know."

I kept cutting the prisoners' hair and my work in the chapel continued until I was moved to an open prison; Leyhill Prison, near Bristol.

They were still unsure about my level of security, so I was refused permission to use public transport to make my way there and was taken by secure van instead. As I stepped out of the rear of the van, I walked into the car park outside the reception area and was amazed at the amount of open space around the prison buildings. Of course, there were no longer any fences around the perimeter.

I was given a job in the Wood Shop, which I found difficult to adjust to as there were so many dangerous machines to operate, after being locked up for so long and not having had any past experience of using them. The two civilian members of staff were most unhelpful. There were huge suction feeds above each machine to remove all the sawdust and they all fed into a network of pipes which ran into the rear of the building. It was the job of the 'bagman' to tie the bags of sawdust and stack them ready for collection to be sold as bedding to pet shops and the like.

The wood shop was massive. At one end tree trunks were dragged in by machine and hooked on to a thick chain which dragged them on to a conveyor belt. They were then sawn into thick planks. The wood then went through different machines until they came out at the other end as sash windows or prison doors, while the excess wood was stored in the rooms below.

I was shown a massive wood thicknesser machine and my supervisor, Mr Turner, pointed to four pallets stacked tall with high density seasoned red mirante wood panels.

Mr Turner looked sternly at me "I know you don't want to work in here but this job is really easy. You can use a ruler, can't you?"

I smiled knowingly. "Yes, of course I can. Anyone can use a ruler!"

"Well, today we're making new prison gates for Dartmoor Prison and these are the panels for them. Each panel needs to be run through the thicknesser to get them to fit into the frame. Here are the measurements and if you need help just ask."

"Shouldn't I have protective footwear to do this job?"

Mr Turner looked agitated "I thought you went to the stores to get protective boots?"

"I went to the stores like you told me to, but they didn't have any size twelve boots in stock. They're going to order some in and that might take a couple of weeks. I've been offered a job in the Officer's Mess as a cleaner and cleaners don't need protective boots. They want me to go over there right away. Can I leave and take that job instead?"

"No! You were allocated to the machine shop and that's where you'll stay for the next six months. You're staying here! Don't worry about the boots for now, just be careful."

Mr Turner then left me on my own to operate this massive

machine, which I had not been trained on. He went into his office to sit down with the other supervisor. I started by pressing a few of the buttons on the machine and the bed went up and down. It all seemed quite easy.

I had met Leo on the wing when I arrived; he was about 46 years old. He loved music and was a conductor, and he had been a sergeant in the SAS. He came across as a lovely man, six foot one with a huge handlebar moustache. The first thing I gave Leo was a proper haircut and he was really grateful.

It was Leo's turn to help me out. He left the conveyor belt at the point where he had a huge tree trunk on a chain that he had pulled about halfway on to the belt. He stopped his machine and came over to show me how to operate the thicknesser properly. After his demonstration he left me to carry on working on my own. I noticed that the two supervisors had left the building together.

I set my machine to what I thought was the correct width and passed the first panel through it. It chomped on to the panel and made such a horrendous grinding noise, I jumped back in surprise - I could hear all the sawdust roaring into the extractor above the machine. I turned around and everyone else was working away quite happily; the supervisors were still out of the building. So I started to send through all the panels, one after the other, catching them and stacking them on a pallet as they came out of the other end of the machine.

It wasn't long before the bagman appeared through the door at the back of the workshop. He looked as if he had just walked through a wood chip snowstorm. I couldn't really tell you what he looked like but he wasn't a happy man. He screamed at the top of his voice: "What the hell is going on in here? I can't bag it quick enough! It's going everywhere! Stop! Stop! Stop the bloody machines for a minute!" I did so.

After about ten minutes he returned in the same state, wiped his brow on his sleeve and said "OK, you can carry on now." He was clearly looking for help. "Where are the Supervisors?" he asked. I just shrugged my shoulders and everyone else carried on working.

I smiled to myself and said "OK, Father Christmas, this is for Gary and for not visiting me for the last five years. Enjoy your clean beds, bunny wunnies!" I pressed the button to turn on my machine and started firing the panels through again, and before I knew it they were all done. I did not go and check on the bagman, as he must have been truly buried in sawdust. I felt great. I was enjoying the thicknesser machine after all.

Mr Turner resurfaced about an hour later. He walked up to me, nodded politely and he lifted one of the hardwood panels to check the width. The side of his lip quivered. "You've taken too much off!"

I looked surprised: "Oh. Have I?"

"It's thirty millimetres too thin! For God's sake, don't do any more!"

He then walked up to examine the other panels which now only occupied three pallets. "I've finished." He turned to take a closer look at the stacks and by now his whole body was shaking with anger.

"You've done them all!"

"That's right, Mr Turner, like you said."

"Are you stupid?"

"No."

"If you weren't sure about what you were doing, you should have checked with me first. Why didn't you check?"

Keeping calm and polite, "You'd left the wood shop and I couldn't find a member of staff."

Knowing that I had been left unsupervised with the other inmates in the wood shop, which was strictly against Health and Safety, Mr Turner hadn't got a leg to stand on.

"You're fired!" he shouted. "Get out!"

After being sacked from the wood shop, I immediately started work in the Officers mess. My new job involved cleaning up the vomit after the screws' various parties. It was mostly the screws' wives who had thrown up in the toilets. So I cleaned, vacuumed and polished floors, emptied ashtrays and humped furniture around, which played havoc with my back. However, the work got me outside the main gate, which compensated in some way for the pain.

I kept up my hairdressing and became quite a popular figure. I was much sought after by the inmates and staff.

I asked the Chaplain if I could see an Orthodox priest. Fr Yves Dubois from the Orthodox Parish of Saint John of Kronstadt in Bath came in to see me in the visits hall. I thought this was a good opportunity to ask him the same questions I had asked all of the other ministers at Channings Wood.

My first question to him was "Do you believe we can fly?" He just smiled knowingly and said "I've got a little book called Orthodox Spirituality, I'll send it in for you." Father Yves didn't answer the question himself, but he stayed to listen intently to what I had to say and then he prayed with me. The book duly arrived and I read it through in one go. Everything I had been asking about was there. All of my questions were dealt with, and I was truly amazed.

Early one morning I was cutting the Principal Officer's hair in the gym when a female screw came in. She looked serious "Can you cut my hair before you go home tomorrow?" I was in the middle of explaining the benefit of doing an AVC to the Principal Officer's pension and looked up quickly to acknowledge her: "Yeah, sure."

I assumed she was worried about letting me cut her long

brown hair and shortening her fringe, because she hung on. Then she asked: "Are you sure you'll be able to do my hair before you leave tomorrow?"

I stopped cutting and gave her a reassuring look. "Yes, don't worry, I'll do your hair for you"

She stood erect with a big smile on her face, waiting for me to realise what she had just said. I was daydreaming and miles away in my own thoughts. I looked up again and then realised she had said something odd.

"Go home? What do you mean, go home?"

"Your parole has come through and you're leaving tomorrow!"

"Tomorrow, like Monday, the 20th May?"

"Yes!"

I was speechless. My thoughts drifted back to all the men's hair I had cut over the last four years and the odd female screw and the most memorable one of them all that stuck in my mind was Mario's. He was like a naughty little kid of about twenty three, short, slim and of mixed race with a 'brummy' accent and probably from English and Italian origin. He was so in love with himself but he couldn't get around to it. If he could, I'm sure he would! He had sewn dreadlocks into his own hair and when he walked around they flicked around his shoulders. I can remember his first words to me: "Hey pig! I'm going to kill all your family while you're in here!" I completely ignored him, which seemed to agitate him but he kept on: "Can you hear me, pig?"

"What sort of white Rasta are you then?"

Mario kept circling me and trying to get me to 'kick off' but his efforts were futile. "I'm not a white Rasta! Don't call me a fucking white Rasta!"

"OK, listen to me. One day you are going to come over to me

and beg me to cut all that shit out of your hair. You look pathetic!"

He had been hoping to gain some 'cred' by hounding me but now everyone was laughing at him on the wing. "I'm going to go around to your house and murder all your family and rape your wife. How'd you like that, pig? You couldn't do anything about it, 'cos you'll be doing a twelve! I'm going to fuck with your head!" He then started laughing aloud in a fiendish way.

"Grow up silly boy. So what happened to you, got caught nicking sweets from the corner shop?"

"I'm a drug Baron, you moron. I got caught with 10 k's of coke."

"Yeah, right."

I left him in Exeter thinking that I would never see him again and guess what, he was now hounding me at Channings Wood and still making the same threats. Just my luck. I'd found out from Simon that he had been caught by an undercover unit of the drug squad and I couldn't resist taunting him about it.

"Hey, Mario, big drug Baron, eh?"

"Yeah, so what? I'll be out before you. Everyone will be out before you!" He laughed sarcastically.

"Word has it that the guy who nicked you was wearing dreads as well?"

"Who told you that!"

"The word's on the street."

"Yeah, it was a massive case." Mario looked a bit uncomfortable.

"I heard he pulled his dreads off along with his woolly hat when he nicked you." I couldn't help laughing.

Well Mario did come back to me just before his release and, true to my word I made him beg me to cut all the dreads out. It was a pig of a job.

I finished cutting the Principal Officer's hair and wandered down to the Wood Shop, where I apologised to Mr Turner for being stupid, then wandered on down to the wing. It was true. All of this was finally coming to an end. I went to my cell and fell on to my knees and wept huge tears of joy. I let the tears cascade on to my bedcovers and they seemed to flow endlessly, bringing me indescribable comfort.

As I paraded the following day the reception officer said:

"You have to see your probation officer the day after tomorrow. He will tell you what to do from then on."

"Can I have a rail pass to Tiverton, please?"

The reception officer was carefully going through my papers. "The bus will take you to the railway station."

"I want to walk away from the prison myself. I don't want to be driven out. Can the driver pick me up as he goes past?"

"No problem. I can understand that. Here's your £46 and please, bring a friend next time you visit."

"That won't happen."

He laughed. "They all say that."

"I can assure you, I won't be back."

I popped my gear into the bus and started to walk away from the prison. Suddenly a tune came into my mind from my youth and I was unable to stop singing it. It was 'Tie a yellow ribbon round the old oak tree' by Tim Orlando. I laughed at this absurdity and shook my head from side to side to try to deflect it, but it was useless. It kept tripping off my tongue and I was relieved that, at this point, I wasn't actually on the bus!

I'm comin' home, I've done my time
Now I've got to know what is and isn't mine
If you received my letter telling you I'd soon be free

Then you'll know just what to do
If you still want me
If you still want me

Whoa, tie a yellow ribbon 'round the old oak tree
It's been five long years
Do ya still want me?
If I don't see a ribbon round the old oak tree
I'll stay on the bus
Forget about us
Put the blame on me
If I don't see a yellow ribbon round the old oak tree.

The prison bus pulled up alongside me, I climbed aboard and we made our way to Bristol railway station. The door opened and I stepped out into the warm sun, a free man.

Within a month of my release I was cutting hair as a barber in Bideford. I took on an old lease for a shop from the Bridge Trust, previously a funeral director's office. I painted the shop out and borrowed the money to purchase the equipment I needed. The business was slow to start with but soon began to escalate. I was making money but my back was killing me.

I was eventually forced to sell the shop and give up hairdressing for two reasons, first because of back pain. Second, because of certain things that began to happen to me.

I had been warned that I would be approached with a view to getting me 'stitched up' again to get me back in prison. With this in mind, I became very suspicious of a car that pulled up outside my shop one afternoon. I noticed two men talking furtively in the front of the car and then the passenger got out. He walked into the shop with a briefcase in his hand. He was wearing a light blue suit, matching blue and white floral shirt and tie and black shoes. He opened his case and took out a solid gold watch. "Here, hold this."

I went to take the watch but I then became suspicious and let it fall to the floor by my feet. "Hey! That's a gold watch. We've just finished a convention and we want to sell all these gold watches. Do you want one?"

I really wasn't interested. "No thank you."

He wasn't going to leave it there. "Just have a look at them. They're solid gold and you can have the lot. Just make me a stupid offer."

"I don't want your watches, now please leave!"

"Say any figure and they're yours. You can have the lot for stupid money."

I was getting angry with this man now. His driver got out of the car and joined him in my shop and I raised my voice. "If you don't get out of my shop now I will throw you both out!"

He put the watch back in his briefcase and they left.

I tried to explain my situation to my probation officer, Alan Wright, when he came in to the shop. "I suppose you'd call it unforgiveness if I were a criminal."

"I don't understand, please explain what you mean?"

"Let's say I was guilty of the offences I was incarcerated for. I served my time and some more and now I am trying to rebuild my life."

Alan was interested to know more. "Yes, go on."

"How can I rebuild it?"

"You're doing really well and making money."

"What about all the stick I have to take though?"

"What sort of stick?"

"The graffiti I have to clean off the windows and the posters I have to pull down. The banners dutifully warning people "This man has been to prison! Keep your children away from this shop!" The notes that are thrown through my letter box every other day. The comments people make as they walk past the door."

"I think you can tolerate that?"

"My point is, why should I have to?"

"You have to try and look ahead and move forward."

"Is that right? So why do the police feel they have to search my property two or three times a week with a warrant and disturb me when I'm working? How is that fair? How can I move forward with that happening all the time?"

"You'll be fine."

"No, I have to find another form of work, and quickly."

My probation officer knew I had a problem and that I was surrounded by bigoted people. But he refused to give me permission to visit my mother's grave in Greece as I was still on licence. He said I would have to wait until my licence expired in April 1999 before I could do that.

It was beginning to feel as if prison would never let go of me.

CHAPTER TWENTY FOUR

A FAIRYTALE

"So, there you have it" I told Marion. "I'm now knocking on doors and you have a convicted criminal sitting in your front room. You're probably wondering what the hell you have done."

Marion looked mystified. "Do you realise the time, Costa? It is 4.00 in the morning! I can't believe the British Justice System let you down like that. What's the matter with them? This is so wrong. I can't get my head around it all. You're going to have to let me think about everything you have told me. I believe what you have said, it's all just so overwhelming. I'm so sorry and I thought my life was a pain. It seems we have both suffered at the hands of other people. I did read somewhere that there is an independent public body that was set up to look into this sort of thing. I think it's called the CCRC. It's late now or rather early in the morning, we will have to discuss things further. Is that OK?"

"I understand, I really do. Don't worry about it but before I go, can I tell you a fairy story?"

"Are you going to tell me that everything you have told me is a fairy story?"

"No, not at all. It won't take long. It's a thank you for listening to me and this story is especially for you."

We sat on the sofa together and I held her silky smooth hand in mine.

"Just sit back and relax and let me tell you the story."

Once upon a time a long, long time ago, in a land far, far away, there was a Kingdom. This was a very happy and peaceful place where the sun seemed to shine all the time. The birds sang sweetly in the trees, the flowers smelled sweeter, the grass seemed greener and the air was just so much fresher. All in all, it was a loving, happy place, where everything seemed brighter.

Near the edge of the Kingdom was a small hamlet. In the centre of the hamlet was a tiny church. At one end of the church was a sharply-pointed steeple. The main roof was made up of black slate and in each corner were the ugly faces of trolls to fend away all the evil spirits. This seemed to work, because everyone was so happy. As I said earlier, it was a very happy and peaceful place indeed.

Behind the church was a very tiny school. It was so small that it could only hold about twelve children. It had a lovely thatched roof and the walls were made of chunky red bricks.

Behind the school was the tiniest little cottage anyone had ever seen. It had a thatched roof with the windows set into the thatch. The thatch snuggled over the frames like eyebrows. The cottage had a tiny door at the front that was split in the middle.

This little house was the house of the loneliest and saddest little girl in the entire world. She was only six years old and she had beautiful dark shiny hair. She lived in the house with her mummy and daddy. She really loved her mummy so much and her mummy loved her, but things were not always as simple as they might seem. Her mummy was very hard on the little girl. The little girl would do anything that she could to make her mummy happy, she really did!

The little girl's friends from school would call around to play, but her mummy would chase them away and she grew more and more lonely. Ah!

So the little girl was buried in work and she used to get so tired. She would sit on the doorstep and listen to the sound of the other children playing. She really wished that she could be with them and having a good time, but at the same time she really wanted her mummy to love her more. She really was so lonely.

The little girl would sit on the step and dream that she was a princess and her life was full of fun. She would dream that one day a prince would come along and find her. They would fall in love and then go off and marry and live happily ever after. She would dream of the palace that she would live in and the pretty garden and flowers she would look after. Oh how lonely she really was.

Her mother would look at her little girl and be so jealous because she was so pretty. Her mummy found it difficult to understand why she had these feelings towards her. The little girl would dream and dream her time away and her fingers were always sore from all the hard work she had to do.

The little girl's mummy would do everything for her! She knew this because her mummy kept telling her and she felt so inadequate. All she wanted to do was to make her love, for her mummy, perfect; like the love she showed to her! Oh how sad it made her. Ah!

As the little girl grew older her mummy became more and more spiteful to her. She would tell her that she wasn't a princess and that she really didn't look beautiful. She never told her directly, she just said things like "Oh, straighten your frock!" or "Tidy your hair, it looks awful!" or "Tidy your room, it's in a terrible state!"

So the little girl was convinced that she was ugly and nothing that she ever did seemed to match the perfect love that her mummy showed to her.

Slowly the little girl grew older and older and grew more and more lonely. She truly was the loneliest little girl in the whole wide world. She so desperately wanted a friend, you know, a real friend.

She kept dreaming of her prince, but she was certain that she was not a princess. She had watched her mother closely and knew there was something that she hadn't told her. Her mummy's love to her was perfect, but at the same time it was not complete!

So the little girl decided to make a plan and look for the loneliest little boy in the whole wide world. He was sure to want a friend! If she could find him, she would be able to love him and make her life complete. It was a plan, that she felt, was sure to work.

So the little girl looked and looked and looked. Then, one day she saw him! She knew well what it was like to be lonely and this little boy was definitely the one! He was so lonely that he couldn't even look up from the ground. It was definitely him. But how could she get him to look up?

The little girl tried as hard as she could, until one day the little boy looked up! He looked into the eyes of the most beautiful princess that he had ever seen in all his life! He had never seen a princess before but as sure as eggs is eggs this girl was one. The little boy never thought for one minute that the princess was looking at him, so the little boy looked down at the floor again. Ah!

The little girl was now in despair. She thought she was truly ugly and that no one would ever want her as a friend. She wasn't going to give up though, because she was so convinced that she had found the loneliest little boy in the entire world, so she kept trying and trying and trying to get his attention.

Eventually the little boy looked up again. This time the princess made sure that she showed her liking for the little boy. She smiled at him and he couldn't believe that the Princess was actually looking at him! He felt so stupid and so lonely that he found it so difficult to talk to her. What a silly billy!

So the little girl thought that she was the loneliest little girl in the entire world and certainly was not a princess. The little boy thought he was a 'little pratt' and often acted like one, because he was lost and lonely as well. Oh dearie, dearie me!

So the little boy and the little girl had a very odd and strange friendship. Little did they know what the future was to hold.

ACKNOWLEDGEMENTS

To my Mother for rebuking me for my ignorance and heretical beliefs.

To my Father for settling our grievances before he died.

To Marion Yolanda Clark for quietly listening to me, loving me, believing in me and standing by me through all the troubles life as an ex-con can bring, whether you are guilty, innocent or a victim of the crime.

THOMAS MERTON'S DEATH

■ ■ ■ ■ ■ ■ ■ ■

"John Russell: Merton died in circumstances that many still see as mysterious. John Howard Griffin, journalist and author of the award-winning Black Like Me and Merton's close friend and designated official biographer, described the circumstances.

John Howard Griffin: When he got to Bangkok, he gave his talk on the morning of the 10th, the anniversary of his entry into the monastery. And he was very tired, the heat was oppressive and he hadn't had a nap the day before so since he was going to have to answer the questions in the evening, he went to his cabin and took a shower and he was never a very practical man about things, he put on a pair of either shorts or short pyjamas, and barefoot and still damp, walked across the terrazzo floor and they had these very tall fans, and he reached for the fan to turn it on to the palette where he was going to take his nap on the floor.

It was DC current and it went into him and he was staying in a cabin with three other people, but it wasn't until about an hour later that they went, and the door was locked from the inside, it was a double kind of door, and there was a little curtain in the upper part and they saw him lying on the floor on his back with this big fan crosswise across his body. The blades had stopped rotating but the current was still alive and it was still burning. He was very deeply burnt, in that angle across the body.

There was a Benedictine nun superior from Korea at that meeting who was, before she became a religious, she was an

Austrian physician and a specialist in internal medicine, and a very, very fine one. The word spread immediately, something happened in my research, and she came immediately, thinking that she might be of some help. He was already dead, but she gave him an immediate examination, and she determined that he died from the effects of electric shock".

Transcript of an interview with John Russell on the CBC, 1980.

The Gospel According to Mary Magdalene
Mary asked: "Will matter then be destroyed or not?"

APPENDIX I

■■■■■■■■

ACRONYMS

ABH   Actual Bodily Harm

BCCI   Bank of Credit and Commerce International

CCRC   Criminal Cases Review Commission
           (set up in 1997)

CIB 1/2   Complaints Investigation Bureau

CIB3   Complaints Investigation Bureau 3 aka The
           Untouchables.

CID   Criminal Intelligence Department

CPS   Crown Prosecution Service

DCS   Detective Chief Superintendent

DI   Detective Inspector

DPP   Director of Public Prosecutions

DS   Detective Sergeant

D/Supt   Detective Superintendent

GBH   Grievous Bodily Harm

IPCC   Independent Police Complaints Commission
           (formerly the PCA)

PACE   Police & Criminal Evidence Act 1984

PCA	Police Complaints Authority (formerly the PCB)
PCB	Police Complaints Board
PNC	Police National Computer
SIS	Special Intelligence Section (part of SO11)
SO	Special Operations (Scotland Yard)
SO10	Undercover Unit
UC	Undercover officer from SO10
VAT'	Vodka and Tonic
WDC	Woman Detective Constable
VPU	Vulnerable Prisoner Unit
WPU	Witness Protection Unit

APPENDIX II

■ ■ ■ ■ ■ ■ ■ ■

APOSTOLIC SUCCESSION OF THE GREAT CHURCH OF CHRIST ANCIENT ORTHODOX CHURCH

Andrew the Apostle	
Stachys the Apostle	38-54
Onesimus	54-68
Polycarp I	71-89
Plutarch	89-105
Sedekion	105-114
Diogenes	114-129
Eleutherius	129-136
Felix	136-141
Polycarp II	141-144
Athenodorus (Athenogenes)	144-148
Efzois	148-154
Laurence	154-166
Alympius (Olympius)	166-169
Pertinax	169-187
Olympian	187-198
Mark I	198-211

Philadelphus	211-217
Cyriacus I	214-230
Castinus	230-237
Eugenius I	240-265
Titus	242-272
Dometius	—
Rufinus I	284-293
Probus	303-315
Metrophanes I	306-314
Alexander	314-337
Paul I	337-339, 341-342, 346-351
Eusebius of Nicomedia	339-342
Macedonius I	342-346, 351-360
Eudoxius (of Antioch)	360-370
Evagrius	370
Demophilus	370-380
Gregory I of Nazianzen	379-381
Maximus the Cynic	380
Nectarius	381-397
John I Chrysostom	398-404
Arsacius	404-405
Atticus	406-425
Sisinius	426-427
Nestorius	428-431
Maximian	431-434
Proclus	434-446

Flavian	446-449
Anatolius	449-458
Gennadios I	458-471
Acacius	472-489
Fravitas	489
Euphemius	489-495
Macedonius II	495-511
Timothy I	511-518
John II	518-520
Epiphanius	520-535
Anthimos I	535-536
Menas	536-552
Eutychius	552-565, 577-582
John III the Scholastic	565-577
John IV the Fasting	585-595
Cyriacus (Cyril)	595-606
Thomas I	607-610
Sergius I	610-638
Pyrrhos	638-641, 654
Paul II	641-653
Peter	654-666
Thomas II	667-669
John V	669-675
Costantine I	675-677
Theodore I	677-679, 686,687
George I	679-686

Paul III	687-693
Callinicus I	693-705
Cyrus	706-711
John VI	712-714
Germanos I	715-730
Anastasius	730-754
Constantine II	754-766
Nikitas I	766-780
Paul IV	780-784
Tarasios	784-806
Nikiohoros I	806- 815
Theodotos I Kassiteras	815-821
Antonius I Kassimatis	821-836
John VII Grammatikos	836-842
Methodius I	842-846
Ignatius I	846-858, 867-877
Photios I	858-867, 877-886
Stephanos I	886-893
Antonios II Kauleas	893-901
Nicholas I Mysticos	901-907, 912-925
Euthymios I	907-912
Stephanos II	925-928
Tryphon	928-931
Theophylaktos	931-956
Polyeuktos	956-970
Basil I Skamandrinos	970-974

Antonios III the Studite	974-980
Nicholas II Chrysovergis	984-995
Sisinius II	996-999
Sergius II	999-1019
Efstathius	1020-1025
Alexius Stoudite	1025-1043
Michael I Kiroularios	1043-1059
Constantine III Leichoudis	1059-1063
John VIII Xifilinos	1063-1075
Kosmas I of Jerusalem	1075-1081
Efstratius Garidas	1081-1084
Nicholas III the Kyrdiniates	1084-1111
John IX Ieromnemon	1111-1134
Leo Styppis	1134-1143
Michael II the Kourkouas	1143-1146
Kosmas II the Attic	1146-1147
Nicholas IV Mouzalon	1147-1151
Theodotos I	1151-1153
Neophytos I	1153
Constantine IV Chliarinos	1154-1156
Luke Chrysovergis	1156-1169
Michael III	1170-1177
Chariton Eugeniotis	1177-1178
Theodosius II Vorradiotis	1178-1183
Basil II Camateros	1183-1186
Nikitas II Mountanis	1187-1189

Leontius Theotokitis	1189-1190
Theodosius III or Disitheus	1190-1191
George II Xifilinos	1191-1198
John X Camateros	1198-1206
Michael IV Autoreianos	1207-1213
Theodore II the Peaceful	1213-1215
Maximos II	1215
Manuel I Charitopoulos	1215-1222
Germanos II	1222-1240
Methodius II	1240
Manuel II	1240-1255
Arsenios Autoreianos	1255-1260, 1261-1267
Victorious II	1260-1261
Germanos III	1267
Joseph I	1267-1275, 1282-1283
John XI Vekkos	1275-1282
Gregory II	1283-1289
Athanasius I	1289-1293, 1304-1310
John XII	1294-1304
Nifon I	1311-1315
John XIII Sweet	1316-1320
Gerasimos I	1320-1321
Isaias	1323-1334
John XIV Kaletas	1334-1347
Isidore I	1347-1349
Kallistos I	1350-1354, 1355-1363

Philotheos Kokkinos	1354-1355, 1364-1376
Makarios	1376-1379, 1390-1391
Neilos	1380-1388
Antonius IV	1389-1390, 1391-1397
Kallistos II Xanthopoulos	1397
Matthew I	1397-1410
Euthymios II	1410-1416
Joseph II	1416-1439
Metrophanes II	1440-1443
Gregory III Mammas	1443-1450
Athanasius II	1450-1453
Gennadios II the Scholar (1st time)	1454-1456
Isidore II	1456-1462
Gennadios II (2nd time)	1462
Sophronios I	1463-1464
Gennadios II (3rd time)	1464
Joasaph I	1465-1466
Mark II	1466
Symeon I (1st time)	1466
Dionysios I	1467-1471
Symeon I (2nd time)	1471-1475
Raphael I	1475-1476
Maximos III	1476-1481
Symeon I (3rd time)	1482-1486
Nifon II (1st time)	1486-1488
Dionysios I (2nd time)	1488-1490

Maximos IV	1491-1497
Nifon II (2nd time)	1497-1498
Joachim I (1st time)	1498-1502
Nifon II (3rd time)	1502
Pachomios I (1st time)	1503-1504
Joachim I (2nd time)	1504
Pachomios I (2nd time)	1504-1513
Theoliptos I	1513-1522
Jeremias I	1522-1545
Joannicios I	1526
Dionysios II	1546-1556
Joasaph II	1556-1565
Metrophanes III (1st time)	1565-1572
Jeremias II (1st time)	1572-1579
Metrophanes III (2nd time)	1579-1580
Jeremias II (2nd time)	1580-1584
Pachomius II	1584-1585
Theoliptos II	1585-1586
Jeremias II (3rd time)	1587-1595
Matthew II (1st time)	1596
Gabriel I	1596
Meletius I Pigas (overseer)	1597-1598
Matthew II (2nd time)	1598-1602
Neophytos II (1st time)	1602-1603
Matthew II (3rd time)	1603
Raphael II	1603-1607

Neophytos II (2nd time)	1607-1612
Cyril I Lucaris (overseer)	1612
Timothy II	1613-1620
Cyril I (2nd time)	1620-1623
Gregorios IV	1623
Anthimos II	1623
Cyril I (3rd time)	1623-1633
Cyril II (1st time)	1633
Cyril I (4th time)	1633-1634
Athanasius III (1st time)	1634
Cyril I (5th time)	1634-1635
Cyril II (2nd time)	1635-1366
Neophytos III	1636-1637
Cyril I (6th time)	1637-1638
Cyril II (3rd time)	1638-1639
Parthenius I	1639-1644
Parthenius II (1st time)	1644-1646
Joannicius II (1st time)	1646-1648
Parthenius II (2nd time)	1648-1651
Joannicius II (2nd time)	1651-1652
Cyril III (1st time)	1652
Athanasius III (2nd time)	1652
Paisios I (1st time)	1652-1653
Joannicius II (3rd time)	1653-1654
Cyril III (2nd time)	1654
Paisios I (2nd time)	1654-1655

Joannicius II (4th time)	1655-1656
Parthenius III [24 Mar.]	1656-1657
Gabriel II	1657
Parthenius IV (1st time)	1657-1662
Dionysios III	1662-1665
Parthenius IV (2nd time)	1665-1667
Clement	1667
Methodius III	1668-1671
Parthenios IV (3rd time)	1671-1673
Dionysios IV (1st time)	1671-1673
Gerasimos II	1673-1674
Parthenius IV (4th time)	1675-1676
Dionysios IV (2nd time)	1676-1679
Athanasius IV	1679
James (1st time)	1679-1682
Dionysios IV (3rd time)	1682-1684
Parthenius IV (5th time)	1684-1685
James (2nd time)	1685-1686
Dionysios IV (4th time)	1686-1687
James (3rd time)	1687-1688
Callinicus II (1st time)	1688
Neophytos IV	1688-1689
Callinicus II (2nd time)	1689-1693
Dionysios IV (5th time)	1693-1694
Callinicus II (3rd time)	1694-1702
Gabriel III	1702-1707

Neophytos V	1707
Cyprian I (1st time)	1707-1709
Athanasius V	1709-1711
Cyril IV	1711-1713
Cyprian I (2nd time)	1713-1714
Kosmas III	1714-1716
Jeremias III (1st time)	1716-1726
Paisios II (1st time)	1726-1732
Jeremias III (2nd time)	1732-1733
Seraphim I	1733-1734
Neophytos VI (1st time)	1734-1740
Paisios II (2nd time)	1740-1743
Neophytos VI (2nd time)	1743-1744
Paisios II (3rd time)	1744-1748
Cyril V (1st time)	1748-1751
Paisios II (4th time)	1751-1752
Cyril V (2nd time)	1752-1757
Callinicus III	1757
Seraphim II	1757-1761
Joannicios III	1761-1763
Samuel I (1st time)	1763-1768
Meletius II	1768-1769
Theodosios II	1769-1773
Samuel I (2nd time)	1773-1774
Sophronios II	1774-1780
Gabriel IV	1780-1785

Prokopios	1785-1789
Neophytos VII (1st time)	1789-1794
Gerasimos III	1794-1797
Gregory V (1st time)	1797-1798
Neophytos VII (2nd time)	1798-1801
Callinicus IV (1st time)	1801-1806
Gregory V (2nd time) [10 Apr.]	1806-1808
Callinicus IV (2nd time)	1808-1809
Jeremias IV	1809-1813
Cyril VI	1813-1818
Gregory V (3rd time) [10 Apr.]	1818-1821
Eugenius II	1821-1822
Anthimos III	1822-1824
Chrysanthos	1824-1826
Agathangelos	1826-1830
Constantios I	1830-1834
Constantios II	1834-1835
Gregory VI (1st time)	1835-1840
Anthimos IV (1st time)	1840-1841
Anthimos V	1841-1842
Germanos IV (1st time)	1842-1845
Meletius III	1845
Anthimos VI (1st time)	1845-1848
Anthimos IV (2nd time)	1848-1852
Germanos IV (2nd time)	1852-1853
Anthimos VI (2nd time)	1853-1855

Cyril VII	1855-1860
Joachim II (1st time)	1860-1863
Sophronios III	1863-1866
Gregory VI (2nd time)	1867-1871
Anthimos VI (3rd time)	1871-1873
Joachim II (2nd time)	1873-1878
Joachim III (1st time)	1878-1884
Joachim IV	1884-1886
Dionysios V	1887-1891
Neophytos VIII	1891-1894
Anthimos VII	1895-1897
Constantine V	1897-1901
Joachim III (2nd time)	1901-1912
Germanos V	1913-1918
Meletius IV	1921-1923
Gregory VII	1923-1924
Constantine VI	1924-1925
Basil III	1925-1929
Photios II	1929-1935
Benjamin	1936-1946
Maximos V	1946-1948
Athenagoras	1948-1972
Dimitrios	1972-1991
Bartholomew	22.10.1991

APPENDIX III

■ ■ ■ ■ ■ ■ ■ ■

THE OTTOMAN DYNASTY

During the period when the Georgiades family started their work as chefs, the Ottoman Turks had begun to absorb the other Turkish states and during the reign of Fatih Mehmed II (Muhammad II) had ended all other local Turkish dynasties between 1451 and 1481. It was the early period of Ottoman expansion that took place under Osman I, Orkhan, Murad I, and Beyazid I, contributing to the loss of the Byzantine Empire, Bulgaria and Serbia. Bursa fell in 1326 and Adrianople (the modern Edirne) in 1361; each in turn became the capital of the empire. The great Ottoman victories of Kosovo in 1389 and Nikopol in 1396 placed large parts of the Balkan Peninsula under Ottoman rule and awakened Europe to the Ottoman danger. The Ottoman siege of Constantinople was lifted at the appearance of Timur, who defeated and captured Beyazid in 1402. The Ottomans, however, soon rallied.

The empire, reunited by Mehmed I (Muhammad I), expanded victoriously under Mehmed's successors Murad II and Fatih Mehmed II (Muhammad II). The victory in 1444 at Varna over a crusading army led by Ladislaus III of Poland was followed in 1453 by the capture of Constantinople. Within a century the Ottomans had changed from a nomadic horde to the heirs of the most ancient surviving empire of Europe. Their success was due partly to the weakness and disunity of their adversaries and also partly due to their excellent and far superior military organization. Their army comprised of numerous Christians, not only conscripts, who were organized as the corps of Janissaries, but also volunteers. Turkish expansion reached its peak in the 16th century under Selim I and Sulayman I (Sulayman the Magnificent).

The Hungarian defeat in 1526 at Mohács prepared the way for the capture in 1541 of Buda and the absorption of the major part of Hungary by the Ottoman Empire; Transylvania became a tributary principality, as did Walachia and Moldavia. The Asian borders of the empire were pushed deep into Persia and Arabia. Selim I defeated the Mamluks of Egypt and Syria, took Cairo in 1517, and assumed the succession to the caliphate. Algiers was taken in 1518 and Mediterranean commerce was threatened by corsairs such as Barbarossa, who sailed under Turkish auspices. Most of the Venetian and other Latin possessions in Greece also fell to the sultans.

During the reign of Sulayman I (from 1535) the traditional friendship between France and Turkey was directed against Hapsburg, Austria and Spain. Sulayman reorganized the Turkish judicial system and his reign saw the flowering of Turkish literature, art and architecture. In practice the prerogatives of the sultan were limited by the spirit of Muslim canonical law (sharia), and he usually shared his authority with the chief preserver (sheyhülislam) of the sharia and with the grand vizier (chief executive officer).

In the progressive decay that followed Sulayman's death, the clergy (ulema) and the Janissaries gained power and exercised a profound, corrupting influence. The first serious blow by Europe to the empire was the naval defeat of Lepanto (1571; inflicted on the fleet of Selim II by the Spanish and Venetians under John of Austria. However, Murad IV in the 17th cent. temporarily restored Turkish military prestige by his victory (1638) over Persia. Crete was conquered from Venice, and in 1683 a huge Turkish army under Grand Vizier Kara Mustafa surrounded Vienna. The relief of Vienna by John III of Poland and the subsequent campaigns of Charles V of Lorraine, Louis of Baden, and Eugene of Savoy ended in negotiations in 1699 which cost Turkey Hungary and other territories.

The breakup of the state gained impetus with the Russo-Turkish Wars in the 18th century. Egypt was only temporarily lost to Napoleon's army, but the Greek War of Independence and its sequels, the Russo-Turkish War of 1828–29 and the war with Muhammad Ali of Egypt resulted in the loss of Greece and Egypt, the protectorate of Russia over Moldavia and Walachia, and the semi-independence of Serbia. Drastic reforms were introduced in the late 18th and early 19th century by Selim III and Mahmud II, but they came too late. By the 19th century Turkey was known as the Sick Man of Europe.

Through a series of treaties of capitulation from the 16th to the 18th century the Ottoman Empire gradually lost its economic independence. Although Turkey was theoretically among the victors in the Crimean War, it emerged from the war economically exhausted. The Congress of Paris in 1856 recognized the independence and integrity of the Ottoman Empire, but this event marked the confirmation of the empire's dependency rather than of its rights as a European power.

The rebellion in 1875 of Bosnia and Herzegovina precipitated the Russo-Turkish War of 1877–78, in which Turkey was defeated despite its surprisingly vigorous stand. Romania (i.e., Walachia and Moldavia), Serbia, and Montenegro were declared fully independent, and Bosnia and Herzegovina passed under Austrian administration. Bulgaria, made a virtually independent principality, annexed in 1885 Eastern Rumelia with impunity.

Sultan Abd al-Majid, who in 1839 issued a decree containing an important body of civil reforms, was followed (1861) by Abd al-Aziz, whose reign witnessed the rise of the liberal party. Its leader, Midhat Pasha, succeeded in deposing (1876) Abd al-Aziz. Abd al-Hamid II acceded (1876) after the brief reign of Murad V. A liberal constitution was framed by Midhat and the first Turkish parliament opened in 1877, but the sultan soon dismissed it and began a rule of personal despotism. The Armenian massacres of the late 19th cent. turned world public opinion against Turkey. Abd al-Hamid was victorious in the Greco-Turkish war of 1897, but Crete, which had been the issue, was ultimately gained by Greece.

In 1908 the Young Turk movement, a reformist and strongly nationalist group, with many adherents in the army, forced the restoration of the constitution of 1876, and in 1909 the parliament deposed the sultan and put Muhammad V on the throne. In the two successive Balkan Wars (1912–13), Turkey lost nearly its entire territory in Europe to Bulgaria, Serbia, Greece, and newly independent Albania. The nationalism of the Young Turks, whose leader Enver Pasha gained virtual dictatorial power by a coup in 1913, antagonized the remaining minorities in the empire.

APPENDIX IV

■ ■ ■ ■ ■ ■ ■ ■

PRISON COLLOQUIALISMS

A Cat. Category 'A' Prisoner - Closed prison - Those whose escape would be highly dangerous to the public or national security. Offences that may result in consideration for Category A or Restricted Status include murder, attempted murder, manslaughter, wounding with intent, rape, indecent assault, robbery or conspiracy to rob (with firearms), firearms offences, importing or supplying a Class A controlled drug, possessing or supplying explosives, offences connected with terrorism and offences under the Official Secrets Act.

A four - a four-year sentence

A twelve - a twelve-year sentence

A two - a two-year sentence

An eight - an eight-year sentence

Animal - a paedophile

Apps - Applications, such as applying to make a visits, phone calls, Probation, Governor etc.

Bacon, bacon head - a paedophile, (rhyming slang, bonce (head) or nonce)

Bang weights - to work out in the gym

Bang out, banging out - to beat up

Bang up, banging up - to lock in a cell

Bare - Plenty, lots of, as in 'I have bare cigarettes'.

Bash - to masturbate

Basic, put on basic - confined to cell with privileges (television, books, etc) removed

B Cat - Category 'B' Prisoner - closed prison - Those who do not require maximum security, but for whom escape needs to be made very difficult.

Beast - A paedophile

Bend Up, bending up - To restrain a prisoner in his cell, prior to moving him.

Bin - A prison

Bird - time in prison (rhyming slang, birdlime)

Bird, doing bird - To spend time in prison

Blag, blagging - to rob

Block - the punishment block

Bomb squad - Prisoners set to clean an area into which excrement has been thrown from the windows of the prison.

Boob - a prison

Boss - a prison officer

Box - cell within a cell

Brew - alcohol

Burn - tobacco

Burn cat - tobacco addict

Cage - cell within a cell

Carpet - a sentence of three years

C Cat - Category 'C' Prisoner, closed prison - those who cannot be trusted in open conditions but who are unlikely to try to escape.

Con - convict

D Cat - Category 'D' prisoner, open prison - Those who can be reasonably trusted not to try to escape, and are given the privilege of an open prison. Prisoners at 'D Cat' (as it is commonly known) prisons, are, subject to approval, given ROTL (Release On Temporary Licence) to work in the community or to go on 'home leave' once they have passed their FLED (Full Licence Eligibility Dates), which is usually a quarter of the way through the sentence.

Down the block - segregated, put in segregation.

Drum - house

Drum, Drumming - to burgle

Echo - an exercise yard

E-Man - Escapee required to wear distinctive, brightly coloured clothing when being moved both inside and outside of the prison and are handcuffed.

EPP - Extended (sentence) for Public Protection

Ghost, ghosting - To move a prisoner from one prison to another without warning

Ghost, to be ghosted - to go to the visitor centre and find that your visitor has not turned up

Gov - a prison officer

Grass - an informer

Hench - big, well-built

IPP - Indefinite sentence for Public Protection

Jam (Jam Roll) - parole

Jammer - A knife, usually a homemade one

Kanga - Prison officer (rhyming slang from Kangaroo to rhyme with screw)

Kite - a cheque

Kite, Kiting - to pass dud cheques

Knock out, knocking one out - to masturbate

Lock-down, locking down - to lock cells

Marga - small, skinny (a Jamaican word)

Meds - application to see a medical officer

Nicker - a Chaplain (rhyming slang, vicar)

Nonce - a paedophile

Nosh - a blow job

Nosh - food

Peter - a cell

Pig - policeman/ex-policeman

Plunge - stab with a knife

Raze up, razing up - to cut with a razor, as in 'I'll raze you up'

Ride, riding my bang - to spend time in prison

Roast, roasting - hanging about expecting something to happen

Rub down, rubbing down - to search a cell

Rush In, rushing in - to restrain a prisoner in his cell, prior to moving him

Salmon - tobacco

Screw - prison officer

Shank - a knife, usually a homemade one

Shipped out, shipping out - to be transferred from one prison to another without warning

Shiv - a knife, usually a homemade one

Skins - cigarette papers

Slop out - empty toilet buckets

Snitch - an informer

Snout - tobacco

Spin, spinning - to search a cell

Sweeper - someone who collects cigarette butts.

Swing, swinging a line - cell to cell communication, often by meanings of swinging a piece of string from one cell to another

Swooper - someone who bends down quickly to pick up cigarette butts without being seen

Tear up, tearing up - to beat up

Vanilla - a judge (rhyming slang, vanilla fudge)

Vera - cigarette paper (rhyming slang, Vera Lynn = a skin)

Visit, visiting - to leave the prison, as in: 'I'm going visiting'.

Wet-up, wetting-up - to cut up

Whack up, whacking up - to beat up

Winda warrior - someone who shouts out of windows.

Wood - an erection

Wrap up, wrapping up - to restrain a prisoner in his cell, prior to moving him

Wrong un - a paedophile

ND - #0059 - 270225 - C0 - 229/152/24 - PB - 9781909304956 - Matt Lamination